The International Politics of the
Armenian-Azerbaijani Conflict

Svante E. Cornell
Editor

The International Politics of the Armenian-Azerbaijani Conflict

The Original "Frozen Conflict" and European Security

palgrave
macmillan

Editor
Svante E. Cornell
Central Asia-Caucasus Institute & Silk
Road Studies Program Johns Hopkins
University-SAIS / Institute for Security
and Development Policy
Washington DC, USA / Stockholm,
Sweden

ISBN 978-1-137-60004-2 (hardback)   ISBN 978-1-137-60005-9 (paperback)
ISBN 978-1-137-60006-6   (eBook)
DOI 10.1057/978-1-137-60006-6

Library of Congress Control Number: 2016960299

Cover design by Jenny Vong

Printed on acid-free paper

This Palgrave Macmillan imprint is published by Springer Nature
The registered company is Nature America Inc.
The registered company address is: 1 New York Plaza, New York, NY 10004, U.S.A.

In Memoriam
Johanna Popjanevski
1980–2016

ACKNOWLEDGEMENTS

This book would not have been possible without the contribution of several colleagues at the Central Asia-Caucasus Institute & Silk Road Studies Program. Alec Forss, as always, provided excellent editing of both substance and language for the entire manuscript. Maria Hellborg and Ipek Velioğlu contributed to the editing and formatting of the text, as well as to the preparation of the index. Boris Ajeganov provided excellent research assistance, in particular concerning the EU's approach to unresolved conflicts in general and the Armenia–Azerbaijan conflict, in particular.

This book is dedicated to the memory of Johanna Popjanevski, who tragically passed away shortly after completing her contribution to this volume. Her love for the Caucasus was matched only by her commitment to justice.

CONTENTS

Notes on Contributors

Pavel K. Baev is Research Director and Professor at the Peace Research Institute Oslo (PRIO). He is also a Senior Non-Resident Fellow at the Brookings Institution, Washington, D.C., and a Senior Associate Fellow at the Institut Français des Relations Internationales (IFRI), Paris.

Stephen Blank is a Senior Fellow with the American Foreign Policy Council in Washington, DC. He previously served as Professor of Russian National Security Studies at the Strategic Studies Institute of the U.S. Army War College in Pennsylvania. In 1998–2001, he was Douglas MacArthur Professor of Research at the War College.

Nina Caspersen holds a PhD in Government from the London School of Economics and Political Science. She is Professor of Politics at the University of York. Before joining the Department as Senior Lecturer in Politics in 2012, she was Lecturer at Lancaster University.

Svante E. Cornell is Director of the Central Asia-Caucasus Institute & Silk Road Studies Program Joint Center. He is a co-founder and director of the Institute for Security and Development Policy in Stockholm, and an Associate Research Professor at the Johns Hopkins University's Paul H. Nitze School of Advanced International Studies.

Johanna Popjanevski was Deputy Director at the Silk Road Program and Research Fellow at the Institute for Security and Development Policy (ISDP) in Stockholm. She held an LL.M. degree from Lund University in cooperation with the Raoul Wallenberg Institute of Human Rights and Humanitarian Law.

Brenda Shaffer is a Nonresident Senior Fellow at the Atlantic Council's Global Energy Center. She is also a Visiting Researcher and Adjunct Professor at Georgetown University's Center for Eurasian, Russian, and Eastern European Studies (CERES).

James Sherr is an Associate Fellow of the Russia and Eurasia Programme of Chatham House, having been Head of the Programme between 2008 and 2011. He is also a Senior Associate Fellow of the Institute of Statecraft and a Visiting Fellow of the Razumkov Centre in Kyiv. Between 1993 and 2012, he was a member of the Social Studies Faculty of the University of Oxford. From 1995 to 2008, he was a Fellow of the Conflict Studies Research Centre of the UK Defence Academy.

LIST OF TABLE

CHAPTER 1

The Armenian-Azerbaijani Conflict and European Security

Svante E. Cornell

INTRODUCTION

The conflict between Armenia and Azerbaijan is the original "frozen" conflict of Eurasia. Beginning in late 1987, four years before the collapse of the Soviet Union, the conflict gradually intensified, escalating rapidly when Armenia and Azerbaijan became independent states in early 1992. The conflict not only spread from the territory of Nagorno-Karabakh to its surrounding regions, but in fact also engulfed much of the territory of the two states, which saw large-scale ethnic cleansing. After nearly 30,000 dead, a 1994 cease-fire left Armenia in control of Nagorno-Karabakh, as well as much larger lands in Azerbaijan that had been emptied of their predominantly Azerbaijani population.[1] That cease-fire signified a stalemate, but not a solution. And in the 22 years that have passed, the conflict has not moved any closer to a political resolution. Meanwhile, the economic and political balance between the two countries has shifted considerably. Armenia, the victor in the war, has seen a dwindling of its population and relative international standing; while the development of Azerbaijan's oil and gas resources has meant that its economy is now over six times larger than Armenia's, and for several years, its official defense budget grew larger than Armenia's entire state budget.

In this context, it should come as no surprise that the conflict has been on a path toward escalation in the past several years. The spring of 2016 saw the most significant violation of the cease-fire since its inception, with a sudden burst of violence over several days that killed 20 soldiers, followed by the Azerbaijani downing of an Armenian helicopter. In parallel, the rhetoric of the belligerents has escalated apace.

S.E. Cornell (✉)
Nacka, Sweden

© The Author(s) 2017
S.E. Cornell (ed.), *The International Politics of the Armenian-Azerbaijani Conflict*, DOI 10.1057/978-1-137-60006-6_1

This conflict is by no means a parochial squabble in a Eurasian backwater. The South Caucasus may have been peripheral to international politics when it first emerged out of the Soviet Union in 1992, but in the quarter century since, it has grown into a significant international hotspot. Indeed, in terms of both energy deliveries and military logistics, the region has become a key corridor linking Europe with the Caspian Sea and Central Asia. The prospect of a land corridor for trade between Europe and Asia is slowly being realized, and China has come to see the South Caucasus as a logistical hub at the doorstep of Europe. In security terms, the Russian invasion of Georgia in 2008—itself a precursor to its aggression directed at Ukraine five years later—indicated that the South Caucasus was a flashpoint in European security with an impact extending considerably beyond its borders.

This is the case at a time of considerable regional and international uncertainty. The South Caucasus lies sandwiched between the two arguably most acute security issues confronting the world today: Russia's aggression against Ukraine, and the dissolution of the post-World War One order in the Middle East. In the region itself, the relative stability of South Caucasus geopolitics that prevailed for more than a decade has dissolved following the 2008 war in Georgia, giving way to a much more fluid and unpredictable situation.

This is the context of the evolution of the Armenian-Azerbaijani conflict. And indeed, the dramatic changes that have taken place in the South Caucasus in the past 20 years have altered the dynamics of the conflict to a considerable degree, thus belying the notion of a "frozen" conflict. The conflict is certainly unresolved; but the concept of frozenness falsely connotes a lack of dynamism, as if the politics of the conflict are frozen in time and space. It also implies complacency, suggesting that there is no cost to maintaining the conflict's unresolved character.

As this book will illustrate, such notions are erroneous. The Armenian-Azerbaijani conflict is far from frozen: it has in fact evolved considerably in the past 20 years, to the point that it has transcended the local, inter-communal conflict it initially was. And far from existing in isolation, the conflict arguably forms the cornerstone of the geopolitics of the broader region, featuring prominently in the policies of great powers surrounding the South Caucasus, while affecting their mutual relations. Indeed, the conflict has both influenced, and been influenced by, subsequent regional controversies, be they in Kosovo, Georgia or Ukraine. Most importantly, the conflict appears to become more dangerous with every passing year it remains unresolved.

This, in turn, would suggest that Western policy-makers accord the conflict a considerable degree of attention, and give it a prominent role in their strategy toward the broader region—to the extent that such a strategy exists. Yet, this is not the case. Quite to the contrary, international instruments to address the conflict remain locked in the logic of the mid-1990s, when the Organization for Security and Co-operation in Europe (OSCE) Minsk Group was tasked to resolve the conflict, and grew into its present form. But since this arrangement was devised, the nature of the conflict has shifted, with its geopolitical component becoming at least as prominent as its inter-communal nature. Yet the peace process, and perceptions of the conflict in the West, do not reflect these realities. The process continues to be assigned to mid-career diplomats, which represents a woefully inadequate approach. And while the peace process has obviously stagnated, its mediators on occasion appear interested mostly in preserving the current format of the process rather than to achieve solutions. The OSCE as an organization has failed to live up to the lofty expectations of the 1990s; indeed, it has become an increasingly moribund institution. Furthermore, the notion of Russia as a mediator—questionable to begin with—has now become preposterous, given its behavior in the region more broadly as well as specifically toward Armenia and Azerbaijan. Notably, the conflict is also the only unresolved conflict in Eurasia where the EU does not have a seat at the table—yet another reflection of the world of the mid-1990s rather than the present.

This volume aspires to investigate the international politics of the Armenian-Azerbaijani conflict. As such, its focus is not on the conflict itself, and especially not on its intricate details, the claims and counter-claims of its protagonists, or its long and contentious history. The focus of the volume is rather on how the conflict interrelates with international politics and security affairs, and particularly its role in European security.

This conflict has numerous names—the most common being the "Nagorno-Karabakh conflict" and the "Armenian-Azerbaijani conflict"—and a note on terminology is in order. To illustrate, the nearby war between Russia and Georgia in 2008 is often termed the "South Ossetia conflict," although it went far beyond the territory of South Ossetia. That is a term the Russian side will prefer, since it would not appear to be involved. Georgian sources refer to it as the Russian-Georgian conflict or the Russian invasion of Georgia. Similarly in the case of Armenia and Azerbaijan, the Armenian side terms the conflict the "Artsakh liberation war," using the Armenian term for Nagorno-Karabakh. By contrast, Azerbaijani sources typically use the term "Armenian aggression against Azerbaijan." Thus, Armenia naturally focuses on the Nagorno-Karabakh element of the conflict, while Azerbaijan tends to stress the inter-state aspect.

Accordingly, this is a conflict that exists at several levels simultaneously. It is, on the one hand, an intra-state conflict, between the Armenian population of Nagorno-Karabakh and the government of Azerbaijan. While the main apple of discord in the conflict is indeed over the disputed territory of Nagorno-Karabakh, the conflict was never only over this territory, and most of the protagonists as well as victims of the conflict were not residents of Mountainous Karabakh. Indeed, terming it as such is somewhat reductionist, because it suggests the conflict is akin to a localized, almost tribal squabble over land. As will be seen, this is a conflict between two nations, the Armenians and the Azerbaijanis, which has come to also involve significant powerhouses of Eurasia and beyond. The conflict arose in the early twentieth century in parallel with the development of nation-states in the South Caucasus, and from 1992 onward, it for all practical purposes became a conflict between two independent states—in turn the reason why the conflict has come to play the crucial geopolitical role that it does.

Thus, the conflict is demonstrably *also* an inter-state conflict between Armenia and Azerbaijan—hence the divergence of terminology used to describe it. The most correct term would be the "Armenian-Azerbaijani conflict over Nagorno-Karabakh," a term that is nevertheless too long and unpractical to be used across this book, which will primarily refer to the conflict as the "Armenian-Azerbaijani conflict."

The remainder of this chapter aspires to set the scene for the subject of this volume, the international politics of the Armenian-Azerbaijani conflict. In so doing, it will provide a brief, and certainly imperfect, historical overview of the conflict.[2] It will then examine the impact of the conflict on the foreign policies and foreign relations of Armenia and Azerbaijan, in order to illustrate how the conflict contributed to forming the main geopolitical dividing line in the South Caucasus. Following this, the chapter discusses the evolution of South Caucasus geopolitics from 1992 until the present, showing how the nature of the conflict has increasingly come to be determined by factors beyond the control of either protagonist. Finally, it will move to an analysis of the role of unresolved conflicts in general, and the Armenian-Azerbaijani conflict in particular, on European security.

The remainder of the book delves into considerable detail on a number of aspects of this conflict. Chapter two, by Johanna Popjanevski, focuses on the international legal aspects of the conflict, particularly its central issue of discord: the status of the territory of Nagorno-Karabakh. In Chapter three, James Sherr situates the conflict in the increasingly contentious international politics of Eastern Europe. Chapters four through eight cover the role of external actors in the conflict. These begin, logically, with Pavel Baev's scrutiny of Russia's role. That is followed by this editor's treatment of Turkey's policies toward the conflict. Then, Brenda Shaffer studies the much-ignored and paradoxical role of Iran in the conflict, following which Stephen Blank examines that of the United States. Finally, this editor handles the evolution of Europe's relationship to the conflict. After these overviews of the roles of foreign powers, Nina Caspersen studies the history of international efforts to mediate the conflict. The volume ends with a brief overview of the prospects of this conflict, and a discussion of possible international efforts to ameliorate it.

BACKGROUND TO THE CONFLICT

At its most basic, the conflict between Armenia and Azerbaijan has its roots in the incompatibility of the concept of a nation-state with the demographic realities of the South Caucasus a century ago. The lands stretching from eastern Anatolia to the central regions of present-day Azerbaijan were not homogenously populated by ethnic groups that could neatly be divided by national boundaries. The countryside was settled by ethnically defined villages—primarily Armenian, Azerbaijani/Turkish or Kurdish—interspersed in a complex mosaic. Larger towns were more multi-ethnic, but divided into Christian and Muslim quarters. In the Ottoman Empire, Christians were second-class citizens and discriminated by the ruling Muslims; in the Russian Empire, these roles were reversed. Yet because these were empires and not nation-states, the urge toward ethnic and religious homogeneity was not yet a driving political force. That changed with the rise of nationalism, imported from Europe, in the second half of the nineteenth century. The urge to build cohesive nation-states effectively destroyed this mosaic over the 100-year period from 1894 to 1994—beginning roughly with the Hamidian massacres of Armenians in Sasun, and ending—for now—with the ethnic cleansing of Azerbaijanis from the provinces surrounding Karabakh.

As is well known, the largest concentrations of ethnic Armenians were in present-day eastern Turkey, areas from which they were obliterated in the massacres from 1890 to 1915 that Armenians call *Medz Yeghern*, the "Great Crime," and that most historians today term the "Armenian Genocide." In the Caucasus, demographic realities were different. The most homogeneously Armenian area was the Russian *Guberniia* of Yerevan, which overlaps largely with present-day Armenia's boundaries. But the *Guberniia* had had a Muslim majority in the 1826 Russian census, which was reversed by 1832 as a result of the Russian Empire's mass settlements of Armenians from Iran and Turkey. But the largest concentrations of Armenians were elsewhere: during the entire nineteenth century, Armenians were the largest ethnic group in Tbilisi, currently the capital of Georgia, and on the eve of the First World War, there were as many Armenians as Azerbaijanis in Baku. Thus, the urge to create nation-states left the Armenians at a profound disadvantage. Simply put, there was a clear Georgian homeland and a clear Azerbaijani homeland, but there was no similarly easily discernible territory that would unify the Armenian population.

Developments in the late nineteenth century rapidly exacerbated the tensions between the two groups. Obviously, the violence in eastern Anatolia affected the situation in the Caucasus. To many Armenians, the Azerbaijanis were simply "Turks," even though they had no involvement in the massacres and deportations in Anatolia. Meanwhile, in Tsarist Russia, competition over resources in the aftermath of the Baku oil boom of the 1870s took on increasingly ethnic tones, with resentment growing in the Azerbaijani community of benefits accorded to Armenians. Tsarist policies, in Audrey Altstadt's words, manipulated historical differences "to incite jealousy, perhaps violence, as a means of control."[3]

Over the ensuing century, and starting in 1905, a pattern of violence would repeat itself: the weakening of Russian central power ushered in intercommunal violence that pitted well-organized Armenian groups against less disciplined and more spontaneously formed Azerbaijani counterparts. In parallel, Russian policies tended to be criminally negligent: aside from long-standing ethnic manipulation, in a remarkable number of incidents Russian soldiers were ordered not to intervene in the killing and rampage that was taking place. This was the case during the first Russian Revolution of 1905, and again in 1988–90.

The 1905 clashes led to over 10,000 deaths, and brought relations between the two nations to a freezing point. Only just over a decade later, the Russian Revolution of 1917 led to a sudden Russian withdrawal from the Caucasus, and in the anarchy that ensued, the formation of a Transcaucasian state—an impossible union of Armenians, Azerbaijanis, and Georgians—was doomed to fail. The First World War was still raging, and all three groups had different orientations, especially toward Ottoman Turkey. Azerbaijanis welcomed the Ottoman advance into the Caucasus, whereas Armenians vehemently opposed it and Georgians sought German support to avoid its repercussions. The state fell apart within two months, ushering in three national republics that would not survive more than two years. The Caucasus had now irrevocably fractured along ethnic lines, and the process of carving out Armenian and Azerbaijani nation-states now began in earnest. Both republics laid claim to the southwestern corner of the South Caucasus, encompassing the ethnically mixed regions of Nakhichevan, Zangezur and Mountainous Karabakh. In practice, Karabakh formed part of the Azerbaijan Democratic Republic. Deadly clashes ensued in Baku in 1918, with Armenians massacring Azerbaijanis in March, and an Ottoman-Azerbaijani joint force massacring Armenians in September. Bloody struggles over Karabakh and Nakhichevan took place in the fall of 1919 and the spring of 1920, ending only with the imposition of Soviet rule over Azerbaijan in April, and Armenia in November of 1920.

Soviet rule paused the conflict, but did not end it. Through processes that remain opaque, the Soviet leadership settled on a complicated and in many ways illogical territorial settlement. Soviet nationality policy did provide for asymmetric ethnic-based federalism, in other words, the division of the Union into ethnic-based national homelands with different levels of self-rule ranging including full Union Republics, Autonomous Republics and Autonomous Regions. But in principle, it allowed only for one national homeland per ethnic group. Thus, national minorities such as Russians in Kazakhstan or Tajiks in Uzbekistan, who numbered in the millions, did not possess any particular status. Exceptions to this were made only in the Caucasus, where the small Ossetian people, for example, were divided into autonomous entities in Russia and Georgia. Concerning Armenia and Azerbaijan, the solution was even more complex. Armenia and Azerbaijan were made into Union Republics; Zangezur was handed to Armenia without any form of autonomy; and Nagorno-Karabakh was made an autonomous region under Azerbaijani jurisdiction, without any common border with Armenia. There were, in other words, two Armenian homelands in the Soviet Union. Even more perplexing, there were two Azerbaijani homelands as well, the second being the Nakhichevan Autonomous Republic, also under Azerbaijani jurisdiction. The logic behind these decisions remains untraceable; the process involved little or no consultation with local leaders, and therefore, the legitimacy of the delimitation was always subject to question. What was not subject to question, however, was that it left Armenia the loser of the Soviet delimitation, as it handed two of the three prized contentious territories to Azerbaijan.

At various points in the seven decades of Soviet rule that ensued, successive Armenian leaders would try and fail to contest this delimitation. In the final decades of Soviet rule, however, such attempts were quite futile. The leader of Soviet Azerbaijan, Heydar Aliyev, had become one of the closest protégés of Soviet leaders Leonid Brezhnev and, particularly, Yuri Andropov, who made him a First Deputy Chairman of the Soviet Union's Council of Ministers. Aliyev valiantly defended his republic's interests in Moscow, and rendered any Armenian attempts to change the status quo moot. But Aliyev was part of the old guard, and soon fell from favor when Mikhail Gorbachev became Soviet leader in 1985. It is no coincidence that the Armenian drive to benefit from the new openness under Gorbachev began at the exact time that Aliyev was demoted in 1987—while the Armenian Abel Aganbeyan rose to become one of Gorbachev's main advisors. In the fall of that year, the first Azerbaijanis were made to leave Armenia. By February 1988, the petition drive in Armenia and Nagorno-Karabakh had escalated to huge demonstrations in Yerevan, and on February 20, the parliament of Nagorno-Karabakh officially demanded to be transferred to Armenia. Six days later, resettled Azerbaijanis from Armenia went on a rampage against Armenians in the Azerbaijani coastal city of Sumgait—with Soviet interior troops three miles away electing not to interfere, an indication of Soviet instigation of these events. Following Sumgait, inter-ethnic violence intensified and militia groups on both sides worked to ethnically cleanse their respective republics, a process that was completed by late 1990.

The Armenian and Azerbaijani elites at this point made fateful choices. Armenia found that while Gorbachev was sympathetic to their demands, he had decided to maintain the status quo in fear of the potential domino effect of allowing a change of internal boundaries. Therefore, Armenia grew increasingly anti-Soviet, and the Armenian National Movement ended up taking control of the republic in the elections held in fall 1990. By contrast, Azerbaijan was the status quo power, and decided to rely on the Soviet central powers to maintain its rule over Nagorno-Karabakh. This seemed a fine bet at first, as Soviet interior troops worked with Azerbaijani authorities to suppress Armenian irregular formations in and around Nagorno-Karabakh in 1990–91, uprooting a number of Armenian villages in the process. But it also meant that Armenia developed its own governing institutions while Azerbaijan did not, and that Yerevan moved to assert control over the various irregular armed formations that had emerged—while Baku was in no position to build any army of its own. This meant that once the August coup of 1991 in Moscow had failed and Soviet power collapsed, Armenia was now the party prepared to take advantage, while Azerbaijan proved essentially helpless. Led by a determined nationalist leadership, Armenia moved on the offensive in early 1992, while Azerbaijan was led by an inept Communist leadership that did not create a national army until March that year. Without Soviet forces to prevent the belligerents, the conflict escalated to full-scale war in the spring of 1992.

The Armenian side benefited greatly from the domestic preoccupations of the Azerbaijani elite. The Popular Front only managed to remove the Communist government in May 1992. But by then, Armenians had taken the citadel city of Shusha and the Lachin region, forming a corridor linking Armenia to Nagorno-Karabakh. Moreover, the single largest atrocity of this episode of the conflict had occurred—the February 1992 massacre of 600 civilian Azerbaijanis in the town of Khojaly. While the new nationalist leadership in Azerbaijan mounted a counter-offensive in the summer of 1992, internal infighting in Azerbaijan led to large troop units defecting from the front. In early 1993, Armenia conquered the province of Kelbajar sandwiched between Armenia and Nagorno-Karabakh, and began moving in territories to the southeast of the region. In June, a renegade Azerbaijani commander fielded a military coup against the nationalist government, prompting its downfall. The Armenian side did not miss the opportunity to benefit from the power vacuum in Azerbaijan, and moved to conquer and ethnically cleanse the southern Azerbaijani provinces of Fizuli, Jebrail, Qubatli and Zangilan, as well as parts of Agdam province to the east of Nagorno-Karabakh. From exile in his native Nakhichevan, Heydar Aliyev emerged to take the reins of power in Baku, and managed in short order to stabilize the government of the country. But the damage had been done, and Azerbaijan had lost Nagorno-Karabakh as well as (in whole or in part) seven provinces surrounding it. The CSCE Minsk Group and Russian officials both worked on ending the conflict, and while the Minsk Group co-chairs conducted most of the negotiations, it was Moscow that reaped the benefits by announcing a cease-fire in May 1994.

Since then, the conflict has been purportedly "frozen." Indeed, the cease-fire has largely held in the 22 years that have passed, while no solution to the conflict has been found. This is where the conflicts in the former Soviet Union differ from those in the former Yugoslavia. The conflicts in Bosnia-Herzegovina and Kosovo all came to a form of closure, which has proven more or less irrevocable. But in Nagorno-Karabakh, Abkhazia, South Ossetia and Transnistria, conflicts were "ended" by cease-fire regimes that left them in legal and political limbo. The key difference, of course, is that international involvement in the former Yugoslav conflicts was much more decisive, whereas this did not take place in the former Soviet conflicts. Indeed, nothing akin to the NATO-led Implementation Force (IFOR) or Kosovo Force (KFOR) was deployed in Nagorno-Karabakh. It is relatively unique in being a major unresolved conflict where two armies are eyeball to eyeball across a cease-fire line and not separated by a peacekeeping force—comparable perhaps only to the Demilitarized Zone separating North and South Korea.

But on another level, the notion of a frozen conflict is erroneous, because the status quo is untenable. Armenia has proven entirely unwilling to negotiate away the fruits of a military conquest that many Armenians consider their first victory in many centuries; and it continues to hold the occupied territories as a bargaining chip to achieve the recognition of their control over Nagorno-Karabakh. But precisely because the Azerbaijani defeat was so total and so decisive, there is no prospect of Azerbaijan simply accepting its defeat and moving on. While Armenia initially enjoyed considerable international sympathy, its ethnic cleansing of three-quarter of a million Azerbaijanis from territories that were never disputed helped turn world opinion against it. Even if the world might have closed its eyes to Armenia's conquest of Nagorno-Karabakh, the occupation of the seven surrounding provinces was, in effect, biting off more than it could chew. It ensured that Azerbaijan would see itself as the aggrieved party, the victim of aggression, and thus never come to terms with the outcome of the 1988–94 conflict. In fact, it all but guaranteed a new bout of fighting at some point in the future unless a negotiated solution could be found.

This was all the more the case because of the fundamental economic and strategic disparity between the two nations, and the exceptional situation that allowed Armenia to claim victory in 1994. Armenia won the war largely because Azerbaijan had collapsed into a failed state. But Armenia's pre-war population was roughly three million, which has shrunk as a result of emigration to a permanent population of roughly two-and-a-half million today. Azerbaijan's population, by contrast, stands at nine million presently, over triple that of Armenia's. And while Azerbaijan's GDP was only double that of Armenia in 1995, oil and gas have currently made it six times larger. What is more, the conflict has resulted in the strategic isolation of Armenia from the large infrastructural projects of the region, in accordance with Azerbaijani and Turkish preferences. The reason is obvious: in pure geostrategic terms, the value of the South Caucasus is its role as a conduit between Europe and Central Asia. In such terms, Armenia can be circumvented by transiting through Georgia, but Azerbaijan—bordering both Russia and Iran—is the only irreplaceable country in the corridor. In sum, in the past two decades, the balance of power between Armenia and Azerbaijan has shifted dramatically, to the favor of the latter.

Revanchist sentiments in Azerbaijan are growing stronger by the year; and while outside military experts might disagree, the preponderance of Azerbaijanis now believe that their military is capable of taking the lost territories back if they were assured that Russia would not intervene on Armenia's behalf. In parallel, the incidence of violence along the cease-fire line has grown in an almost linear fashion since 2010. War, of course, can start for any number of reasons: whether by intent or by mistake; or whether for strategic or domestic political reasons. But the growing imbalance between the parties, and the volatile nature of regional politics, indicates that no one should be surprised when a new episode of the Armenian-Azerbaijani conflict erupts.

The Conflict and Foreign Policy-Making in Armenia and Azerbaijan

As the dust settled on the front lines in 1994, the importance of the Armenian-Azerbaijani conflict did not diminish. Quite to the contrary, it helped determine the foreign policy orientations of both countries, and in turn, became a chief dividing line in the geopolitics of the region. The conflict had an inverse effect on the two countries' geopolitical choices: it led Armenia to return to the Russian fold, pushed Azerbaijan toward the West, and contributed to the alignment of Georgia and Azerbaijan.

Whereas Armenia had been the anti-Soviet republic seeking to unravel the status quo, this rapidly changed in 1992. Part of the Soviet Union, Armenia had not needed to consider external threats. But with the USSR gone, independent Armenia became highly vulnerable. It faced a new situation whereby the potential of Turkish intervention in the conflict on Azerbaijan's side appeared very real, especially as Armenia's conquest of territory expanded. The new reality led Armenia's leaders to a historically familiar conclusion: to present themselves as Moscow's chief partner, indeed its anchor, in the South Caucasus—a notion that appealed to Moscow because both Azerbaijan and Georgia sought to escape the Russian shadow. It is unclear to what degree the *quid pro quo* was explicit, but the logic was straightforward: Armenia would align with Russia in regional affairs, and in exchange receive Russian sanction and protection for its control of Nagorno-Karabakh. This has been the main operating principle of the bilateral relationship ever since. It was illustrated most vividly and recently in 2013, when Armenia, citing national security reasons, made a drastic U-turn to jettison an Association Agreement with the European Union (EU) in favor of joining the Eurasian Economic Union.

Azerbaijan, by contrast, had initially aligned with Moscow in the late 1980s, gambling that the central power would safeguard its control over Nagorno-Karabakh. But the bloody Soviet military intervention in Baku on January 20, 1990, changed matters. It was justified as an attempt to quell ethnic rioting earlier that month, but it was launched *after* riots had ended, and mainly targeted the Azerbaijani Popular Front movement. And as the conflict with Armenia escalated, Azerbaijanis became convinced that Russia had become not only Armenia's main sponsor but also a direct participant in the conflict. Evidence suggests that Russian forces took part in the Khojaly massacre in February 1992.[4] The Armenian offensive in Shusha and Lachin began on May 17, 1992—the very day after Armenia signed a mutual defense treaty with Russia. Azerbaijan's nationalist government, which came to power the next month, moved rapidly out of Moscow's orbit, and began to orient the country toward Turkey and the West. With considerable evidence to make their case, Azerbaijanis blame Russia for instigating the coup that brought down the Popular Front government in June 1993, and which precipitated Azerbaijan's military defeat. When Heydar Aliyev came to power, in effect thwarting a Russian-inspired coup, he adopted a more diplomatic approach to Moscow than his predecessor. But ever since, Azerbaijan has remained at the greatest distance possible from all Russian efforts to reintegrate the former Soviet states. Banking on the power of its energy resources, Baku turned westwards, seeking a strategic relationship with Turkey and the United States to bolster its sovereignty and independence—and to build a position of strength that would compel Armenia to an agreeable negotiated solution.

For Armenia, having won the war, safeguarding its military victory was the highest priority, and to this end, Yerevan proved willing to depend on Russia for its security with the result of compromising its national independence. Azerbaijan, which lost the war, made the opposite decision: its leadership has made the maintenance of independence its highest political priority, trumping the return of the occupied territories. Azerbaijan has had little reason to trust the periodic (and intensifying) Russian entreaties suggesting that the conflict could be "solved" if Baku reoriented its foreign policy. Instead, Azerbaijan began to cultivate forces willing to counterbalance Russia. Given close historical and linguistic ties, Turkey was an obvious partner, but it put considerably more emphasis on building ties with the West, primarily the United States. In the process, this also led to a close partnership between Azerbaijan and Georgia. The two had been subjected to similar humiliations and loss of territory, and viewed Russia as the main culprit. They both sought a Western orientation built on the strategic east-west energy corridor, in which Georgia became the key transit route for Azerbaijani oil and gas resources to the West.

Further afield, the conflict also helped clarify the intentions of regional powers. The conflict gave form to Turkey's policy toward the Caucasus, based on an alignment with Azerbaijan, the containment of Armenia through the closure of the border between the countries, and a strategic partnership with Georgia and Azerbaijan in building the energy and transportation corridor to the Caspian Sea. Georgia and Azerbaijan also constitute Turkey's land conduit to Central Asia. This policy has largely held since 1993, with the sole exception of the abortive attempt to normalize Turkish-Armenian relations in 2008–09, and remains in force today. As for Iran, the Armenian-Azerbaijani conflict brought a surprising twist: the Islamic republic effectively supported Christian Armenia's territorial conquest of one-sixth of the territory of one of the world's four Shia-majority states. The reason was straightforward: given the presence of an ethnic Azerbaijani population double the size of that in Azerbaijan itself, Tehran at all cost sought to prevent the emergence of a wealthy, secular and Western-aligned state on its northern border, even if that meant supporting Armenia.

For the West, the conflict has mainly been an impediment to the realization of both its strategic and normative goals in the region. The conflict, as well as those in Georgia, delays or hampers the building of a functioning and stable South Caucasus corridor, in particular because it makes Armenia and Azerbaijan incapable of cooperation, and therefore essentially prevents the South Caucasus from functioning as a region. Moreover, it facilitated the return of more authoritarian tendencies in both Azerbaijan and Armenia, and provided a useful instrument of manipulation for those external forces that sought to prevent the West from gaining a foothold in the region.

Thus, by the middle of the 1990s, the Armenian-Azerbaijani conflict had become the main dividing line in a budding geostrategic alignment in and around the Caucasus. On one side was a north-south axis linking Armenia, Russia and Iran; on the other, an east-west axis of Azerbaijan, Georgia and Turkey, supported in many ways by the United States.

This alignment generated a balance of power or, more accurately perhaps, stalemate (and indeed a remarkably stable one given the volatility of the region) that lasted until 2008. Since then, as will be seen below, a series of events have "shaken up" the Caucasus, and made the politics surrounding the conflict much more unpredictable. These have not changed the fact that the Armenian-Azerbaijani conflict is the basic dividing line preventing the development of a stable and Western-oriented South Caucasus. They have, however, made the region more volatile, and increased the risks of its non-resolution. Before turning to the role of unresolved conflicts in European security, a close look at the geopolitics of the South Caucasus is in order.

Geopolitics of the South Caucasus

When the Soviet Union collapsed, the geopolitical importance of the South Caucasus was not immediately obvious to Western powers. Expertise on the region was weak; it appeared a hopeless quagmire of warring ethnic groups, and there was a strong tendency to consider the region a part of Russia's backyard. Moreover, the conflicts in the Caucasus took place at a time when much more pressing issues were on the Western agenda. These included the Gulf War, the wars in the Balkans much closer to the heart of Europe, and the managing of the Russian transition, not least the fate of Russia's nuclear arsenal.

But already in the early 1990s, it was clear that Russia's leadership—particularly the defense and security services—paid an inordinate amount of attention to reasserting Russian power in the South Caucasus, including through the manipulation of ethnic conflicts. This effort had no parallel even in other parts of the former Soviet Union, indicating that Russian leaders saw the region as exceptionally important. Moreover, it took place at a time when Russia itself was not only weak, but also dealing with serious internal problems. Between 1991 and 1994, Chechnya and Tatarstan had both declared independence, and it would have seemed natural for Russia's leadership to focus on putting its own house in order before attempting to secure its influence in the South Caucasus. But instead, Russia's leadership spent scarce resources on subduing the newly independent states of the South Caucasus. As already noted, Russia quickly secured its influence over Armenia, and deployed subversive efforts to topple the nationalist government of Azerbaijan. But nowhere were Russia's intentions more obvious than in Georgia, where Russia both trained North Caucasian volunteers and deployed its air force and other assets in the conflicts on the side of South Ossetian and Abkhaz rebels, thus helping to create unresolved conflicts from 1991 to 1993. Moscow also worked hard to subdue the independent-minded leadership of Eduard Shevardnadze through various subversive efforts, which succeeded in forcing Georgia to join the Commonwealth of Independent States (CIS) as well as accepting Russian control over its border with Turkey and the deployment of four Russian military bases on its territory.

This was no coincidence: it reflects the long-standing geopolitical importance Russia has attached to the Caucasus, which it identified in the late eighteenth century as its buffer to the Middle East. Indeed, the key importance of the Caucasus lies in its crucial geographical location at the crossing point of both east-west and north-south corridors of transport and trade. For millennia, the Caucasus has been a link—or buffer—between the Black and Caspian Sea, and thus between Europe and Asia as well as between Russia and the Middle East. In contemporary international affairs, its key value lies in its location at the mouth of the east-west corridor connecting Europe with Central Asia and beyond; and simultaneously, at the intersection of powers playing key roles in international politics, most prominently Russia, Iran and Turkey. As a result, the Caucasus is a key factor shaping the intersection of Europe and the Middle East.

From 1828 to 1991—with a brief interlude in 1918–21—the South Caucasus was absorbed into the Russian Empire, and cut off from its historical neighbors to the south and west. But since the mid-1990s, the South Caucasus has once again begun to emerge as an important east-west corridor. This has taken place in three related areas: in the realms of energy resources, military logistics and civilian trade.

The development of the Caspian Sea basin's energy resources began in earnest in the mid-1990s. The successful projects, involving Western multinational companies, to develop the oil and gas resources of Azerbaijan, Kazakhstan and Turkmenistan have proven crucial to the economic and political independence of the states of the Caucasus and Central Asia. Indeed, they were the only independent income stream that enabled these countries to consolidate their sovereignty. Specifically, the creation of the pipeline system connecting Azerbaijan's energy resources via Georgia to Turkey and beyond provided an opportunity to develop these resources while avoiding the control of the former colonial overlord. While this primarily benefited Azerbaijan resources, it held great importance for Central Asian states as well. This infrastructure broke the Russian monopoly over the transportation of energy resources, and only after this was accomplished was China able to further shatter that monopoly through inroads into Central Asia, particularly through the Turkmenistan-China gas pipeline. The bulk of Kazakhstan's oil and Turkmenistan's gas resources have yet to come online, but the further potential of the South Caucasus to serve as a key corridor for these energy resources is enormous.

Secondly, the role of the South Caucasus for international security was proven in the aftermath of the terrorist attacks of September 11, 2001. Waging a war in the heart of the Eurasian continent, thousands of miles from the closest US military bases, posed enormous logistical challenges to the United States. The rapid American response, which led to the crippling of the Taliban and Al Qaeda in Afghanistan, was possible only through the introduction of US military power into Afghanistan via the Caucasus and Central Asia. Because Iran was not an option and Russia provided highly restricted terms for the use of its airspace, the overwhelming majority of the overflights that supplied the US forces in Central Asia transited the air corridor of Georgia and Azerbaijan. A decade later, when the USA expanded its troop levels in Afghanistan, the Caucasus corridor ensured that America was not solely dependent upon Northern Distribution Network (NDN) routes across Russia. At least 30 percent of the transit was conducted through the territories of Georgia and Azerbaijan. And following the deterioration of US–Russian relations since 2014, the Caucasus corridor will certainly be crucial to any future Western presence in Afghanistan or Central Asia.

Thirdly, the Caucasus has also emerged as a crucial artery and the most efficient component of an emerging system of continental trade by land. Most east-west trade between China, India and Europe at present is by sea and air. But land routes across Eurasia provide a third option, which is far cheaper than air travel and much faster than sea routes. As in the case of the NDN, the Caucasus is far from the only route, but it is the best means of assuring that neither Russia nor Iran has a monopoly on these emerging transportation corridors. Considerable investments have already been made in port facilities in Georgia, Azerbaijan and Turkmenistan as well as railroads across the region. In the longer term, the stability of the South Caucasus will be a concern not just for major Western oil and gas firms, but also for Chinese and Indian interests in uninterrupted trade between Asia and Europe.

Looking at the South Caucasus differently, the region is sandwiched between the two most salient challenges to the transatlantic alliance today that are fundamentally reshaping the security environment to Europe's east and south: Russia's aggressive expansionism and the Islamic radicalism emanating from the Middle East. And far from just comprising "flyover" countries, the South Caucasus (together with Central Asia) is an important pressure point in both directions. On the one hand, the task of countering Putin's Russian imperialism goes beyond Ukraine, and requires a firm strategy of bolstering the states on Russia's southern periphery. On the other hand, the Caucasus and Central Asia contain half of all the secular Muslim-majority states in the world. These states may have far to go in terms of democratic development but, importantly, their governments and populations are committed to the separation of state and religion and to secular laws. Thus, the Caucasus and Central Asia are potential bulwarks against both Moscow and the Islamic radicalism of the Middle East, the latter encompassing the threat of Sunni radicalism as well as the Iranian theocracy that continues to assertively expand its regional influence from Syria to Yemen.

In sum, therefore, the Caucasus has come to figure with increasing prominence in international politics. But while this trend could be seen already in the late 1990s, the relative stability of the region has deteriorated since around 2007, when Vladimir Putin delivered his infamous speech in Munich in which he warned against America's "global supremacy."[5] There have been at least three factors behind this deterioration.

The first factor was the Russian invasion of Georgia in August 2008, which immediately changed everyone's calculations of Russia's intentions and level of determination. In a sense, Azerbaijan and Georgia had placed their bets on an implicit Western deterrence of Russia—based on the notion that wars no longer happen in Europe. But when Russia called that bluff, it exposed the unwillingness of the West to challenge its primacy in the post-Soviet space with anything beyond words. European sanctions lasted only a few months, and the incoming Obama administration rewarded Russia with the ill-fated "Reset" policy. This was, in turn, a result primarily of the second key factor: the Western financial crisis, which rocked the foundations of the world economy and made both the United States and Europe look increasingly inward—leading to a growing disengagement from the security affairs of the Caucasus.

Third, the USA and Europe did not grasp that after failing to stop the escalation to war in Georgia, it was now imperative to turn their attention to the more serious unresolved conflict, that between Armenia and Azerbaijan. Instead, they pushed for the Turkish-Armenian reconciliation process—a futile attempt in the prevailing conditions, as discussed in Chap. 5 and one whose only lasting consequences have been to weaken Armenia's leadership internally, damage Azerbaijan's ties with Turkey, and in practice end its strategic relationship with America. Indeed, this myopia regarding the relevance of the unresolved conflicts directly influenced Russia's decision, in early 2014, to employ that very instrument to mortally wound post-Euromaidan Ukraine through the annexation of Crimea and the manufacture of unresolved conflict in the Donbass.

These factors, and several others including uncertainty stemming from the Iranian nuclear deal and the Syrian civil war, have rendered the regional situation much more unpredictable than at any time in the past two decades. Only a few hundred miles southwest from the Caucasus as a Russian cruise missile flies, the three major powers surrounding the South Caucasus are now involved on different sides in the Syrian civil war.

Thus, there is a profound strategic uncertainty in the Caucasus today. Old patterns of alignment no longer apply; but no new order seems to be on the horizon either. Armenia is safely ensconced in the Russian embrace, its current leadership finding that its options had been severely limited by choices made to safeguard Karabakh in the 1990s. As for Azerbaijan, seeing no prospect for a Western strategic presence, it has sought to avoid moving into Moscow's arms by pursuing instead a foreign policy that mostly resembles non-alignment.

Both countries' leaderships are visibly frustrated, with their economies reeling from collateral damage from the mutual sanctions between the West and Russia, and in Azerbaijan's case, the collapse of oil prices. And one of the areas where they have proved able to vent their frustration is by raising the stakes in Nagorno-Karabakh.

In sum, the growing geopolitical relevance of the South Caucasus has altered the nature of the region's unresolved conflicts. While the Armenia-Azerbaijan conflict began as a local, inter-communal conflict, over time it acquired a second and parallel identity with geopolitics playing an increasingly important role in the conflict. Indeed, the conflict became a major pressure point in the international rivalry in the region, involving a growing array of great powers. Most directly, the conflict became an instrument for those forces—primarily Russia but also Iran—who sought to prevent the West from gaining ground in the Caucasus and developing the east-west artery through the region. Because the conflict dictated the foreign policy orientations of Armenia and Azerbaijan, it also helped determine the fault lines of the geopolitical alignments in the broader region. The obvious implication of this is that while Armenia and Azerbaijan are the main protagonists in the conflict, the international politics of the conflict are no longer mainly, or even perhaps primarily, about them. It involves the major powers with interests in the region, all of which have considerable instruments to torpedo a resolution to the conflict that is not in their interest.

THE SOUTH CAUCASUS AND "FROZEN CONFLICTS" IN EUROPEAN SECURITY

If the Armenian-Azerbaijani conflict is indeed a key fault line in the geopolitics of the South Caucasus, or even of the intersection of the Middle East and the post-Soviet space, what are the implications for European security? As will be seen, the answer is that over the past two decades the South Caucasus has been increasingly tightly integrated into European security structures—and that a flare-up of violence would immediately require a response by European institutions, primarily the EU. To back up this assertion, an overview of the region's relationship with European institutions is in order.

The post-communist order in Eastern Europe relies primarily on four interlinked European organizations: from the most to least inclusive, these are the OSCE, the Council of Europe, the North Atlantic Treaty Organization (NATO) and the EU. Upon the dissolution of the USSR, the erstwhile Conference for Security and Cooperation in Europe, created by the 1975 Helsinki Final Act, was rapidly upgraded to the status of Organization and tasked with being the umbrella organization for security in Europe and political development across the continent. As a result, all former Soviet states including those in Central Asia became members of this organization. While members of the OSCE pledged to develop toward liberal democracies, no particular standards were required for membership. The Council of Europe was more exclusive, in two ways. First, the organization requires certain basic criteria concerning human rights and rule of law for membership; and second, it drew a geographic line at the Caspian Sea, leaving Central Asian states out of consideration. By the end of the first decade of independence, the Council had expanded to include the South Caucasus: Georgia became a member in 1999, and Armenia and Azerbaijan two years later.

The most restricted organizations, of course, are NATO and the EU. By their more exclusive nature, these organizations moved east more diligently, with a major enlargement in 2005–07 that saw most of the Central and Eastern European countries becoming members of both organizations. Importantly, this brought both organizations to the shores of the Black Sea—making the EU a direct neighbor of the South Caucasus, while NATO already was on account of Turkey's membership. In parallel, the "color revolutions" in Georgia and Ukraine in 2003–04 led to a strong urge by the new leaderships of both countries to join NATO as well as the EU, forcing both organizations to respond. NATO soon experienced deep internal divisions over the question of Georgian and Ukrainian membership, with the US and East European members tending to support, and continental European members tending to oppose, such steps. At the Bucharest NATO Summit in 2008, a curious compromise was reached: Georgia and Ukraine were *not* given Membership Action Plans, but were simultaneously promised that at an undetermined future point, they *would* become members of NATO. For their part, neither Armenia nor Azerbaijan have sought membership, although both (Azerbaijan more so than Armenia) have developed cooperative structures with NATO under the Partnership for Peace program.

The EU has long groped with the question of dealing with its neighborhood. In the 1990s, the main instrument was Partnership and Cooperation Agreements (PCAs), similar to those the EU negotiates with countries worldwide. In 2003, the EU appointed a Special Representative for the South Caucasus; the same year, it unveiled the European Neighborhood Policy (ENP) targeted at its East European and Mediterranean neighbors. The countries of the South Caucasus were initially not included in the policy, under the justification that they were not "direct" neighbors to the EU. This led to the almost absurd implication that Libya and Syria were included, while three members of the Council of Europe were left out. Nevertheless, this mistake was reversed in 2004 and the three countries were made full members of the ENP. In 2008, the EU launched a new instrument for the Eastern neighborhood: the Eastern Partnership, which from the outset comprised the three South Caucasian states, as well as Ukraine, Moldova and Belarus. Through the Eastern Partnership, the EU offered the six countries the opportunity to negotiate Association Agreements with the EU, which included Deep and Comprehensive Free Trade Agreements (DCFTA). This was the major innovation of the Eastern Partnership, and it allowed the EU to square the contentious circle of the membership issue by simply ignoring it. The implementation of DCFTAs would lead signatory countries to fulfill up to 80 percent or more of the *Acquis Communautaire*, the body of EU laws and regulations. As a result, they would for all practical purposes be integrated into the EU economically, while being ready for rapid inclusion if and when a political consensus among EU states materialized. Since 2008, while all South Caucasian countries have joined the Eastern Partnership, each has related differently to it. Azerbaijan never aspired to a DCFTA, seeking instead a "strategic partnership" with the EU. Armenia finalized negotiations for the DCFTA but at the last minute jettisoned it for membership in the Eurasian Economic Union. Georgia, which aspires to EU membership, has signed a DCFTA and is in the process of implementing it.

In hindsight, it is remarkable to what extent both the EU's thinking on the South Caucasus and its practical instruments evolved from 2003 to 2008. From having initially denied that the region was part of its neighborhood, in the space of five years the EU had generated instruments that in practice would allow the regional states to come very close to membership of it. Underlying this evolution is a paradox: it was driven to a large extent by the growing European realization of the importance of the security affairs of the region; but simultaneously, the EU has not evolved into a strong force in the field of security and defense.

Indeed, closer study of European involvement in the region reveals a stubborn aversion to involvement in the security issues in the South Caucasus, and particularly the unresolved conflicts. This began in 1992–94, when the OSCE Minsk Group was created to seek a peaceful resolution to the Armenian-Azerbaijani conflict. The format originally allowed for a single chairman; but faced with the reality that the May 1994 cease-fire had been reached through Russia's parallel and unilateral mediation, the OSCE resolved to make Russia a permanent co-chair of the Group in December 1994. (It subsequently made France and the United States co-chairs in 1997.) At the same summit, the OSCE expressed its intention to deploy an OSCE peacekeeping force in the conflict zone. Yet for a combination of reasons, such a force never materialized. OSCE member states were swamped with their obligations in the Balkans and elsewhere, and moreover, member states were highly reluctant to insert forces in a zone perceived to be under Russian influence, where Moscow made clear it did not desire a foreign presence.

Thus, the conflict stands out by the lack of any peacekeeping function. Yet, the situation in Georgia was considerably worse: in Abkhazia, a Russian peacekeeping force under a nominal CIS mandate was deployed, monitored by a 120-strong unarmed United Nations (UN) mission. No international conflict resolution mechanism whatsoever was introduced, although the UN created an informal body known as the "Group of Friends of the Secretary-General," which in any case never convened direct talks. In South Ossetia, a tripartite Russian-led peacekeeping mission that included Russia's republic of North Ossetia and Georgia was created; while the only format for dialogue was the Joint Control Commission, which included Russia, South Ossetia, North Ossetia and Georgia, with the OSCE merely an observer. Thus, until the 2008 war, Georgia endured a situation where conflict resolution and peacekeeping were entirely dominated by Russia, itself for all practical purposes a party to the conflicts. In this light, the absence of a peacekeeping force separating Armenia and Azerbaijan could be seen as a benefit rather than liability; and the Minsk Group came to include two major Western powers as co-chairs.

On a regional level, however, the instruments that were created in the 1990s were never altered to adapt to the evolving circumstances from 2000 to 2008—including the growing Russian involvement in the conflicts, and the growing profile of the region following Georgia's Rose Revolution and the completion of the Baku–Ceyhan pipeline. In fact, they remained hopelessly mired in the realities of the early 1990s, when the South Caucasus was an after-thought in international politics. This was most egregious in Georgia, where Russia—while a peacekeeper and mediator in the conflicts—began to exert direct control over Abkhazia and South Ossetia, including the distribution of Russian passports to the populations and the appointment of Russian military and security personnel to key positions in the self-proclaimed governments of these territories. While this made a mockery of Russia's obligations as an hon-est broker, Western powers went along with the charade up until the Russian invasion of Georgia in 2008.

In the case of Armenia and Azerbaijan, the Russian role was less blatant, but nonetheless incongruent with its role as a mediator. First, Russia's military trea-ties with Armenia signed from 1995 to 1997—and its deployment of a large military base at Gyumri—made it partial to one of the sides in the conflict. Second, Russia has actively stoked the arms race between the two countries, providing advanced weaponry at heavily discounted prices to Armenia, and for international prices to Azerbaijan. In 2010, Russia even deepened its defense obligations with Armenia, extending and upgrading a mutual defense treaty dating to 1995 and strengthening its commitment to Armenia's security. By 2015, Armenia was a party to the Russian-led Eurasian Union and Collective Security Treaty Organization (CSTO), while Azerbaijan was not.

Yet Western leaders, and particularly US and French officials, have continued to play along with the notion that Russia takes its role in the Minsk Group seri-ously, and treat Moscow as an honest broker in the conflict. Most egregiously, Western leaders did not object to then Russian President Dmitry Medvedev's initiative to take the lead in the resolution of the conflict, announced in October 2008—barely a month after Russia had invaded their common neigh-bor, Georgia. This was a transparent effort to indicate to all countries of the region and beyond that Moscow alone would henceforth be the arbiter of war and peace in the Caucasus. But far from objecting to this blatant usurpation, the Western powers gratefully went along with it, and continued to support the Russian-led talks down to their collapse at a summit in Kazan in June 2011.

Thus, while their interests in the South Caucasus have increased exponen-tially since the early 1990s, Western leaders have never challenged the growing

Russian manipulation of the unresolved conflicts, its effective takeover of secessionist territories, or its efforts to dominate processes of conflict resolution and peacekeeping in the region. Yet what the war in Georgia made clear is that when war breaks out in the South Caucasus, it by default lands in Europe's lap. On that occasion, the Bush administration was happy to hand the issue to the EU, arguing that it would be less divisive and controversial than a direct American role. The same rationale excluded a NATO role. With the OSCE practically emasculated as an organization, the EU became the only force capable of inserting itself to stop the conflict. The cease-fire of August 12, 2008, was negotiated by the French EU presidency, and since then, an EU Monitoring Mission has been deployed in the conflict zone. There is no reason to think that the EU, or European institutions more broadly, could remain on the sidelines if a war flares up between Armenia and Azerbaijan. Similarly, the events of 2015 have made clear which way any refugee flows would be directed.

Yet a closer look at the EU's role in conflict resolution processes in Eastern Europe reveals an anomaly: the Armenian-Azerbaijani conflict is the only one in which the EU is not represented. In Transnistria, the EU is part of the 5+2 mechanism for discussions surrounding the conflict. Following the 2008 war, the EU is one of the co-chairs of the "Geneva International Discussions" on Abkhazia and South Ossetia, together with the UN and OSCE. And of course, the EU is part of the Minsk Agreements on Ukraine. It is only in the Minsk *Group* that the EU does *not* have a role, although it is indirectly represented by France.

CONCLUSIONS

Over the past two decades, the South Caucasus has inexorably become more closely integrated into the European security architecture. But the lack of functioning security mechanisms for countries of Eastern Europe makes it the most volatile part of this architecture. Indeed, four countries in Eastern Europe are part of no collective security mechanism whatsoever: Azerbaijan, Georgia, Moldova and Ukraine. It is no coincidence that following recent events in Ukraine, unresolved conflicts exist on the territories of all four.

But as Georgia and Ukraine have shown, this state of affairs is far from stable, and breaches of peace and stability in Eastern Europe inevitably affect the security of Europe more broadly as well as involve the EU in efforts to mitigate the damage. Over the past half-decade, the conflict between Armenia and Azerbaijan has shown clear signs of escalation—yet European policy-makers have little influence on a process that they are bound to be seriously affected by. Hence, the rationale for this book: not only is the Armenian-Azerbaijani conflict a key and underestimated issue in European security, but also comprehending its politics is key to understanding the nature of security politics in Eastern Europe.

NOTES

1. The standard work on the conflict is Thomas de Waal, *Black Garden: Armenia and Azerbaijan through Peace and War* (New York: New York University Press, 2013). Earlier treatments include Michael P. Croissant, *The Armenia-Azerbaijan Conflict: Causes and Implications* (Westport: Praeger, 1998) and Svante E. Cornell, *The Nagorno-*Karabakh Conflict (Uppsala: Department of East European Studies, Report no. 46, 1999).
2. Much more detailed historical overviews are available in de Waal, *Black Garden;* Croissant, *The Armenia-Azerbaijan Conflict;* and Svante E. Cornell, *Small Nations and Great Powers: A Study of Ethnopolitical Conflict in the Caucasus* (London and New York: Taylor & Francis, 2000).
3. Audrey Altstadt, *The Azerbaijani Turks: Power and Identity Under Russian Rule* (Stanford: Hoover Institution Press, 1992), 43.
4. de Waal, *Black Garden,* 172–73.
5. Oliver Rolofs, "A Breeze of Cold War," Munich Security Conference, 2007, https://www.securityconference.de/en/about/munich-moments/a-breeze-of-cold-war/

CHAPTER 2

International Law and the Nagorno-Karabakh Conflict

Johanna Popjanevski

Out of the separatist conflicts that emerged upon the dissolution of the Soviet Union, the conflict over Nagorno-Karabakh has claimed the highest number of victims, amounting up to 30,000 casualties and more than a million Internally Displaced Persons (IDPs). Since the outbreak of armed warfare between Azerbaijan and Armenia over the territory in 1992, Armenia has occupied an area of 12,000 km² originally within Soviet Azerbaijani borders, including Nagorno-Karabakh and seven surrounding districts, amounting in total to ca. 15 percent of Azerbaijani territory. The international community at large has repeatedly called on Yerevan to withdraw its troops from the region, halt political and financial assistance to the separatist authorities, and allow for the return of the expelled Azerbaijani IDPs. While Nagorno-Karabakh has proclaimed itself an independent state, it is not recognized as such by any state. Notably, that includes Armenia, which nevertheless supports Nagorno-Karabakh's right to secede from Azerbaijan. As a result, elections held in the region are not internationally recognized. The Organization for Security and Co-operation in Europe (OSCE)-led Minsk Group has failed to achieve a mediated solution between the parties.

J. Popjanevski (✉)
Washington, DC, USA

© The Author(s) 2017
S.E. Cornell (ed.), *The International Politics of the Armenian-Azerbaijani Conflict*, DOI 10.1057/978-1-137-60006-6_2

This chapter seeks to map out the key legal issues connected to the conflict and its evolution and analyze these from the viewpoint of international law and practice, focusing on the issue of the disputed region's status. Central to the analysis is the right to self-determination (as claimed by the post-war population of the region), and how it relates to secession, versus the principle of territorial integrity and the right for Azerbaijan to maintain the borders it inherited from the Soviet Union. The chapter will assess the legality behind the region's de facto secession from Azerbaijan and its implications for the future status of the region, especially in light of the use of force and humanitarian crimes committed in the region since the early 1990s. It will also draw comparisons to other separatist conflicts, especially in Eurasia, and discuss the role and application of international law in previous similar cases. The chapter also addresses the role of geopolitical interests in the interpretation by international actors of international principles in their policy formulations and rhetoric in relation to the conflict.

NAGORNO-KARABAKH'S RIGHT TO SELF-DETERMINATION?

The separatist authorities of Nagorno-Karabakh largely base their claims for secession on the right to self-determination in international law. Indeed, this right[1] is laid down in several international documents, including the Charter of the United Nations,[2] the International Covenant of Civil and Political Rights (ICCPR), and the United Nations Friendly Relations Declaration (FRD).[3] The latter document states that "all peoples have the right freely to determine, without external interference, their political status and to pursue their economic, social and cultural development, and every State has the duty to respect this right in accordance with the provisions of the Charter." As such, the principle constitutes a core principle of international law and is widely quoted in relation to the protection of national and ethnic minorities.

However, the nature of the principle of self-determination is frequently subject to mistaken assumptions, especially when referred to as a basis for the right to secession. In fact, the vast majority of legal scholars will dismiss the notion that the principle provides a right for minority-populated regions to decide on their existence as a state.[4] Nonetheless, the post-war population of Nagorno-Karabakh, just like those of Abkhazia and South Ossetia in Georgia, has continuously attempted to invoke the principle as a legal basis for independence. Following Russia's recognition of Georgia's secessionist territories in August 2008, even Moscow voiced support for self-determination as a basis for secession. Then, Russian President Dmitry Medvedev linked Moscow's recognition of Abkhazia and South Ossetia to "the freely expressed will of the Ossetian and Abkhaz peoples and being guided by the provisions of the UN Charter, the 1970 Declaration on the Principles of International Law Governing Friendly Relations Between States, the CSCE Helsinki Final Act of 1975 and other fundamental international instruments."[5] Notably, however, Yerevan—while openly supporting Nagorno-Karabakh's right to secession from Azerbaijan—has refrained from making references to the region's right to self-determination, instead basing the region's right to secession on Soviet national legislation. This will be discussed in more detail below.

What, then, makes the principle of self-determination inapplicable to the case of Nagorno-Karabakh, and what is its true nature? While, indeed, the principle originally emerged as a means of protecting the rights of peoples within certain territories, the principle was intended for residents of territories under colonized rule, not those of sovereign states.[6] Its aim was to provide a right for oppressed populations subject to colonization to determine their own political fate. In the post-colonization era, especially as representatives of ethnic minority groups increasingly started voicing self-determination claims, legal scholars began making references to two separate principles, the right to *internal* and *external* self-determination.[7]

Internal self-determination is relevant to all peoples and refers to the right of a population or group to a certain form of political and cultural autonomy within the state in which they reside. *External* self-determination, meanwhile, is more complex and widely debated as it may entail the right for a protected group to secede from the parent state. However, it is important to note that self-determination does not automatically provide a right for a people to form a new state.[8] The principle of external self-determination, due to its stark contrast to the prevailing principle of territorial integrity (or *uti possidetis*: border inviolability),[9] has been applied restrictively in state practice. Scholars will argue that in order for the external self-determination principle to be invoked, it has to be preceded by severe and systematic oppression, large-scale human rights violations or significant restrictions by a government of fundamental rights under international law.[10]

If the presence of these conditions is necessary for external self-determination to apply (in this case, to provide the right for Nagorno-Karabakh to secede from Azerbaijan), a key question would be if the population of the region can be regarded as having been exposed to exploitation, or deprived of their fundamental rights, by either Baku or an authority or group in the territory in which they reside.

Indeed, the Nagorno-Karabakh conflict has been marked by serious human rights violations, large numbers of civilian casualties and mass ethnic expulsions. However, these humanitarian crimes have neither been one sided nor have they taken place exclusively in the territory of Nagorno-Karabakh; and nor did they occur primarily *before* the territory sought to secede. As noted previously, the conflict has resulted in over one million IDPs and refugees, of which the vast majority consist of ethnic Azerbaijanis that were evicted from the territories presently occupied by Armenian forces.[11] The refugee flows started already in late 1987, when Armenians began expelling ethnic Azerbaijanis from Armenia. These refugees settled predominantly in the industrial Baku suburb of Sumgait. Hostilities in the Nagorno-Karabakh region broke out in late February 1988, when two Azerbaijanis were killed in the village of Askeran on the Azerbaijani side in the vicinity of the administrative border line. What followed was a series of revenge actions in Sumgait, with mainly Azerbaijani groups attacking ethnic Armenians, leaving at least 32 (26 Armenians and 6 Azerbaijani) dead with homes looted and burnt. In the following months, violence spread to Armenia where Azerbaijanis were exposed to harassment and mass expulsions in several villages, including Ararat and Manis close to the Turkish border. After a period of relative calm over the summer of 1988, continuous disagreements over the status of Nagorno-Karabakh at the political level generated a new wave of refugee flows. By the end of November, unofficial sources stated that up to 180,000 Armenians had fled Azerbaijan and 160,000 Azeris had left Armenia.[12] By 1989, Soviet sources reported that 87 people had died and 1,500 had been wounded in clashes between Armenians and Azerbaijanis.[13] In spite of attempts by the central Soviet authorities in Moscow to take control of the region, seemingly to ease tensions, serious violence erupted in the region in 1989 with regular shootouts between armed rebel groups.

However, during 1990–1991 most of the deadly clashes did not take place in Nagorno-Karabakh itself, but in the districts of Khanlar and Goranboy/Shahumian. In January 1990, villages in these regions were almost entirely cleansed of ethnic Armenians. Meanwhile, hostilities broke out also in Baku in connection with anti-government rallies, resulting in the death of 500–1,000 people, and the eviction of most of the city's ethnic Armenian population.[14] As a result, tensions escalated in Nagorno-Karabakh with paramilitary groups forming on both sides. Armenia was particularly active in bringing in arms to the region, flown in from Lebanon and transported via the mainland from Yerevan to Nagorno-Karabakh.[15]

In response to the alleged resettlement of ethnic Armenians to Nagorno-Karabakh and the Khanlar and Goranboy/Shahumian regions (which was illegal under Soviet law), Azerbaijan, backed up by Soviet Interior troops, launched a forceful offensive in the region in the spring and summer of 1991, famously known as "Operation Ring." While the operation was officially aimed at carrying out identity controls, in reality it entailed searching out and eradicating Armenian paramilitary groups and confiscating weapons.[16] The operation ultimately involved operations in 22–24 Armenian villages north of Nagorno-Karabakh, and reportedly resulted in serious human rights violations and hundreds of casualties.[17]

Following the December 1991 referendum in Nagorno-Karabakh on its secession from Azerbaijan, tensions rose again and soon escalated into full-scale war. Finding itself in the midst of the dissolution of the Soviet Union, Baku, previously reliant on the assistance of Moscow, then found itself in a particularly vulnerable situation. With Soviet troops withdrawn from the region, Azerbaijan stood relatively unprepared to counter an attack from the Armenian side, which had invested far more into its defense than Azerbaijan. As a result, one of the bloodiest episodes of the conflict took place in February 1992, when an estimated 600 ethnic Azerbaijani civilians were killed in an Armenian-led attack against the village of Khojaly in Nagorno-Karabakh.[18] Armenian troops, allegedly supported by the 366th regiment of the Russian

Army, thereafter seized the ethnically Azerbaijani-populated citadel town of Shusha in Nagorno-Karabakh (which served as a firing base for Azerbaijani attacks against Stepanakert), as well as the Azerbaijani town of Lachin, located between Nagorno-Karabakh and Armenia, and thus the corridor separating Armenia from Karabakh. In total, thousands of ethnic Azerbaijanis were killed and deported, and serious human rights violations were reported. As a result of the conflict, there are virtually no ethnic Azerbaijanis left in Nagorno-Karabakh, including in towns and villages such as Shusha, where Azerbaijanis previously made up the majority.

In sum, the ethnic groups on both sides have been exposed to war crimes that are attributable to both parties to the conflict. As such, the current population of Nagorno-Karabakh can hardly be said to meet the threshold for being regarded as oppressed from the viewpoint of international law and standards. By comparison, Iraqi Kurdistan and Chechnya, where grave human rights crimes have taken place, have both failed to gain support for secession based on external self-determination by international organizations. Georgia's separatist regions of Abkhazia and South Ossetia are further examples where claims for external self-determination have been unsuccessful at the international level— witness Moscow's great disappointment at the low number of countries that followed its 2008 recognition of these territories. Whatever the motivation for this absence of recognition, it proves the high threshold set for any deviations from the principle of territorial integrity in international practice. One could retort that Kosovo constitutes an exception in this regard. But Kosovo ultimately did not gain recognition in the West based on a right to external self-determination. In fact, the attempt by Kosovo to invoke this principle was explicitly rejected by the UN Security Council in 1999.[19] The decision by the majority of Western states to recognize Kosovo was instead the result of political considerations. The implications of the Kosovo case will be examined in more detail later in this chapter.

Since Azerbaijan has lacked access to the region since the war in the early 1990s, it is difficult to argue that Baku has systematically violated the rights of its current population. For the same reason, and as there are virtually no Azerbaijanis left in the region, the population of Nagorno-Karabakh can hardly argue that they are exposed to repression or hardship on ethnic-based grounds. While the Karabakh Armenians allege systematic discrimination in the pre-independence period, there is no evidence of the type of suffering that would warrant a deviation from prevailing international norms. Azerbaijan, as the parent state, has also on several occasions offered wide autonomy to the region to allow for the exercise of a level of self-governance and the protection of cultural and political rights. An example of this was during the OSCE Lisbon Summit in December 1996, when the Minsk Group presented a draft statement offering Nagorno-Karabakh the highest level of self-governance within the borders of Azerbaijan. The statement was supported by Azerbaijan, but Armenia ultimately used its veto against the parts of the document that concerned the settlement of the conflict.[20] In light of the political rights offered to the region, the notion that its current population is subject to oppression by Baku does not hold up to closer scrutiny. Baku's frequent threats of military action to reassert control over the territory are often taken by the Armenian side as evidence that Nagorno-Karabakh cannot be a part of Azerbaijan; but again, the legal value of such claims is dubious, given that such threats, and their implementation, have not affected the legal standing of either Chechnya or the territory controlled by Tamil rebels before their recapture by Sri Lankan forces in 2009.

As a result, accepting the claims of the current Nagorno-Karabakh population to a right to secession based on external self-determination would bring with it serious legal and political implications, as it would risk legitimizing the ethnic cleansing of the Azerbaijani population of the region and its surrounding provinces. This stands in direct contrast to international human rights law, itself a more important component of the self-determination principle than any territorial claims that may flow from it. In this light, the right to self-determination cannot be seen as applicable as a basis for secession in relation to the Nagorno-Karabakh region.

The repeated international references to Azerbaijan's territorial integrity further testify to the supremacy of the principle of *uti possidetis* over any right to external self-determination in relation to Nagorno-Karabakh.[21] Further strengthening this argument is the fact that the region has never historically enjoyed independence. Throughout history, it has belonged to different empires including the Ottoman Empire, Iran and later Russia, before its administrative districts became part of the Republic of Azerbaijan. Nonetheless, both Stepanakert and Yerevan argue that the inviolability of borders does not apply in the case of Nagorno-Karabakh, as the region did not originally lie within the internationally recognized borders of the first Republic of Azerbaijan in 1918–1920. Yet Karabakh was *de facto* within the Azerbaijan Democratic Republic, and legal scholars will argue that the application of *uti possidetis* is dependent on the effectiveness of administrative borders since the development of modern international law. In that light, circumstances dating back to the era before 1920 (when Azerbaijan's independence was rejected by the League of Nations)[22] do not affect the status of contemporary Azerbaijani borders.[23] Following the invasion of Azerbaijan by the Red Army, and later Nagorno-Karabakh, the *Kavburo* (Caucasian Bureau of the Central Committee of the Russian Communist Party) declared in 1921 the region to be part of the Soviet Republic of Azerbaijan.[24] According to the *Kavburo*, the region would remain part of Soviet Azerbaijan but granted autonomous status.[25] This was reaffirmed in article 86 of the 1977 Soviet constitution.

THE RIGHT TO FORM A STATE

Having ruled out the applicability of the right of external self-determination in the case of Nagorno-Karabakh, the question arises on what other basis the region could argue a right to separation from Azerbaijani *de jure* control. One of these, albeit not explicitly argued by either Stepanakert or Yerevan, is the issue of whether the region measures up to the traditional requirements for independent statehood in international law.

These criteria are laid down principally in the Montevideo Convention of 1933,[26] which provides three main requirements to be fulfilled in order to achieve statehood: (i) a permanent population, (ii) a defined territory and (iii) an effective government.[27] While state practice has since had an effect on the interpretation of the provisions of the convention, they still play a strong guiding role in the determination of territories' right to establish independent states.

In the case of Nagorno-Karabakh, all three of these requirements pose obstacles for the establishment of a *de jure* state. As noted previously in this chapter, since the war in the early 1990s Armenia has exercised effective control not only of Nagorno-Karabakh itself, but also of seven surrounding administrative districts. This makes the existence of fixed borders or a defined territory highly questionable. As noted above, from 1921, the region was declared as a *de jure* part of Soviet Azerbaijan and remained so throughout the Soviet era. Indeed, on December 1, 1989, the Supreme Soviet of Armenia attempted to formally annex the region through proclaiming Nagorno-Karabakh a part of Armenia.[28] Its subsequent occupation of internationally recognized Azerbaijani territory further speaks against the existence of defined borders in the region.

The criterion of permanent population is equally problematic, given that virtually the entire ethnic Azerbaijani population has been expelled from the region. Indeed, while the question of whether the population in the meaning of the Convention needs to be of a certain size or composition remains open to interpretation, it is reasonable to assume the requirement of a level of consistency with regard to inhabitance of the territory. The mass expulsions from the region that took place in the early 1990s, which led up to 7 percent of Azerbaijan's population being displaced,[29] speaks strongly against any permanency in the region's demographic situation.

Most important of the three principles, perhaps, is the one of effective governance. Naturally, effective governance means that control over the territory needs, as far as possible, to be exercised independently from external actors.[30] A widely quoted basis for this interpretation is the approach by the League of Nations in 1920 in relation to the case of the Åland Islands between Sweden and Finland. The League's legal committee noted the difficulty in establishing when exactly the Republic of Finland had become a constituted sovereign state, due to its dependence on Russia's troop presence.[31] Another often quoted case where the criterion of effective control has been questioned is Palestine, whose de facto leadership is unable to effectively control its territory due to the Israeli occupation.[32] The same should be true of Abkhazia and South Ossetia in Georgia, Transnistria in Moldova and Northern Cyprus, where occupation by foreign states (Russia in the first three cases, and Turkey in the latter) prevents the leaderships from exercising independent control of the territories.

Thus, in the case of Nagorno-Karabakh, it is relevant to examine the level of interference of Armenia in the region, and its implications for effective control over the territory. Key questions in this regard are the role of Armenia in Nagorno-Karabakh's separation from Azerbaijan, and the extent to which Armenia continues to influence the secessionist authorities. Indeed, starting from 1986, ethnic Armenians actively demanded the integration of Nagorno-Karabakh with Soviet Armenia. This predominantly included spreading propaganda in the region, facilitated by the policy of glasnost under Gorbachev. Flyers were printed and transported into the region from Yerevan. From 1986, Armenia began also mobilizing itself militarily in the region through providing weapons to the separatist army.[33] Over the following years, Yerevan's role in Nagorno-Karabakh became all the more pronounced. Following self-proclaimed elections in 1989, a "National Movement" was formed in the region, which was recognized by Yerevan as the only legitimate representative of the Karabakh Armenians. As previously mentioned, the Supreme Soviet soon declared the unification of Nagorno-Karabakh with Armenia. In 1990–1991, Armenian paramilitary groups were brought into the region to support this quest, seemingly with Yerevan's blessing.[34] What followed was an escalation of violence, including the above-mentioned Operation Ring and the massacre in Khojaly. While it is difficult to determine the exact level of involvement of Yerevan in the violence carried out by the insurgents, Human Rights Watch concluded in 1995 that, from the beginning of the conflict, Armenia had provided aid, weapons and volunteers to the region—assistance that grew increasingly overt rather than covert following the Azerbaijani offensive in mid-1992.[35] The open warfare between Azerbaijan and Armenia that spilled beyond Nagorno-Karabakh itself further testified to Yerevan's interest in controlling the region, especially in light of its forceful offensive against the strategically important Kelbajar region that separates Nagorno-Karabakh from Armenia, an operation that was reportedly launched from Armenian territory in the west.[36]

Ever since the ceasefire agreement was signed in May 1994, Armenia has maintained a firm military and financial influence in the region, amounting to the existence of a loose federation between the two. The International Crisis Group reported in 2005 that Armenian nationals make up half of the region's defense force, and, as such, that the region continues to depend heavily on Armenia militarily. It also reported that Armenia may have provided up to 90 percent of the region's budget in the shape of interest-free loans, and continues to support the region's economy to the level of approximately 50 percent.[37] It is estimated that Armenia at present has up to 20,000 troops stationed on the territory to protect it from a potential Azerbaijani military attempt to reintegrate the region.[38] Yerevan is reportedly also pursuing a passportization policy in the region, similar to that of Russia in Georgia's separatist region, and seeking to synchronize the local currency with the Armenian *dram*.[39]

In assessing the significance of Yerevan's troop presence in the region, and how it effects the ability of the separatist authorities to exercise effective control over its territory, it is relevant to recall the conclusions drawn by the European Court of Human Rights (ECHR) in the case of *Ilascu and Others* in relation to Moldova's secessionist region of Transnistria. The Court stated, *inter alia*, that Russia's military and political support to the secessionist authorities amounted to effective control of the region.[40] Meanwhile, it should be noted that Russia's troop presence in Transnistria at the time (estimated at around 2,000) was significantly lower than Armenian presence in Nagorno-Karabakh. Indeed, an ECHR ruling in June 2015 confirms this interpretation. In the case of *Chiragov and Others vs. Armenia*, the Court concluded as follows:

> All of the above reveals that the Republic of Armenia, from the early days of the Nagorno-Karabakh conflict, has had a significant and decisive influence over the "NKR", that the two entities are highly integrated in virtually all important matters and that this situation persists to this day. In other words, the "NKR" and its administration survives by virtue of the military, political, financial and other support given to it by Armenia which, consequently, exercises effective control over Nagorno-Karabakh and the surrounding territories, including the district of Lachin.[41]

Thus, it has been established that the establishment of a separatist movement in Nagorno-Karabakh in 1986–1992 was significantly supported by Yerevan, and that the region continues to rely on Armenia both militarily and financially. The fact that the international community widely regards Nagorno-Karabakh and the surrounding regions as being occupied further supports this notion. The issue of occupation will be discussed in more detail below.

In addition to the influence exerted by Yerevan in the region, Russia too has played a part in the conflict and in providing support for the separatists. During the last years of the Soviet Union, Gorbachev actively sought to counteract secessionism to keep the Union from dissolving. Thus, starting from 1988, when the region's desire to separate from Azerbaijani control and join Armenia became increasingly pronounced, Moscow deemed it a violation of article 78 of the Soviet constitution and provided direct military support to Azerbaijan in fighting the separatists. However, from 1992 Moscow's position changed, and the newly independent Russian Federation began instead to openly support the Armenian side of the separatist region, apparently through the provision of military aid, including weapons and mercenaries.[42] It should be noted, however, that Russian weapons were also used and mercenaries fought on the Azerbaijani side, though to a much lesser degree. Since then, Armenia has emerged as a committed ally of Russia, and many expect Moscow to be ready to intervene on Yerevan's side if war with Azerbaijan over Nagorno-Karabakh were to erupt again. This is likely a key reason why Azerbaijan is showing restraint in relation to the conflict. Given that Baku's defense budget for several years exceeded the entire state budget of Armenia, Russia's role as protector of Armenian interests—including a large military presence in the country—appears to be the most influential factor hindering Azerbaijan from attempting to restore its territorial integrity and control over Nagorno-Karabakh and surrounding occupied regions. In light of the very close relationships and personnel exchanges between the Armenian and Nagorno-Karabakh leaderships, this raises the question of Moscow's indirect influence over the Nagorno-Karabakh secessionist authorities.

In sum, the de facto government in Stepanakert can hardly be said to exercise sufficient independent control over its territory to fulfill the requirement of effective governance as envisaged in international law and practice.

Finally, article 11 of the Montevideo Convention underlines the importance of the inviolability of borders and prohibits military occupation by another state. Importantly, the Convention also establishes an "obligation not to recognize territorial acquisitions or special advantages which have been obtained by force." This principle was first coined by Washington after Japan's unlawful invasion of Manchuria in China in 1931, and, as such, became known as the "Stimson Doctrine," after Henry L. Stimson, Secretary of State in the Hoover administration.[43] In essence, the principle prohibits statehood when based on unlawful acts, such as the use of force or other breaches of a state's sovereign rights.[44] This suggests that even where the requirements for statehood are fulfilled, the claim for such is void if the process of creating the state is based on illegal means.[45] The serious humanitarian crimes committed in Nagorno-Karabakh, including acts of ethnic cleansing, therefore add yet another obstacle to the region's separation from Azerbaijan. Since the majority of victims of ethnic cleansing were on the Azerbaijani side, this may even be argued to pose an obligation on the international community not to recognize the region's *de jure* secession from Azerbaijan. Here, again, the question of Armenia's role in the conflict becomes relevant. UN Charter article 4, paragraph 2, prohibits the use of force against the territorial integrity or political independence of states. While force is not defined in the Charter, it appears reasonable to argue that it includes military intervention by another state. The Friendly Relations Declaration, while not a binding document, elaborates on the meaning of the term "force" and stipulates that both occupation and acquisition of another state's territory are covered by the prohibition of use of force in the Charter. Thus, if Armenia provides military assistance to the separatist authorities in Stepanakert, amounting to occupation of the region, the Stimson Doctrine should apply and the international community is obliged to refrain from recognition of the region's independence.

THE CASE OF KOSOVO

When addressing the issue of the status of Nagorno-Karabakh, another issue to examine is the implication of Kosovo's declaration of independence and its recognition by the majority of Western states in 2008. Indeed, the establishment of new states in modern times, including, for instance, Timor-Leste and Montenegro, followed by Russia's recognition of Abkhazia and South Ossetia, has put into question the traditional approaches to statehood and secession: that is, has the international system become more accepting of the right to secession in the wake of these developments, and what is then the legal basis of this right? Could Kosovo be viewed as a legal precedent concerning secession, or simply an exception to traditional rules? Finally, what does it mean for the separation of Nagorno-Karabakh from Azerbaijan?

As in regard to most unrecognized territories, a question for the future of Nagorno-Karabakh is whether the Kosovo case has changed the fundaments of international law through lessening the Montevideo criteria, making the establishment of statehood more dependent on recognition by other states. Moscow, in particular, relied on the Kosovo case as a direct precedent for recognizing the Georgian separatist regions of Abkhazia and South Ossetia in August 2008, in spite of previously having been strongly opposed to the decision of the vast majority of Western countries to recognize Kosovo's independence.[46] Indeed, at the time of Kosovo's independence declaration in 2008, followed by its recognition by the West, Kosovo could not be viewed to fulfill either the traditional requirements for forming a state in accordance with the Montevideo Convention, nor the high threshold for external self-determination from the viewpoint of international law. Thus, at the international policy level, the decision to recognize Kosovo did not come without controversy. The USA in particular maintained the position that the recognition of the region should be viewed as an exception to international law, and that the situation left no other choice but recognition to end the raging conflict with the Serbs. A number of countries also openly objected to the recognition, warning that it could set a dangerous precedent for other regions.[47] Notably, this included Russia, which—seemingly concerned about secessionism in its southern regions—requested the UN Security Council to dismiss Kosovo's declaration of independence. Moscow openly warned the West about a potential domino effect with dangerous consequences for the world order.[48] Ironically, Moscow later followed up on its threats through rhetorically using the Kosovo example in defense of its recognition of Georgia's separatist regions of Abkhazia and South Ossetia.

However, the notion that Kosovo alone has set a precedent in international law as regards secessionism does not hold up to closer scrutiny, for several reasons. First, the international system continues to rely on state sovereignty as a core principle. As noted in relation to the restriction of the right to external self-determination, the principle of territorial integrity continues to prevail in international law and relations, leaving little room for exceptions. Legal scholars will predominantly agree that changes to the international legal system requires a certain consistency in state practice, as well as *opinio juris*, that is, an intention by states to establish a new international norm by undertaking a certain action. In this light, one or even a few exceptions to an established rule does challenge its prevalence. Secondly, even if one would argue that Kosovo has established a legal precedent for secession (either through external self-determination or recognition), there are fundamental contextual differences between Kosovo and Nagorno-Karabakh that rule out its applicability in this case. In 1999, the previously autonomous region of Serbia became subject to large-scale ethnic cleansing by the Milošević regime, resulting in the expulsion of up to 500,000 ethnic Albanians from the region. Discrimination against Albanians was systematic and had been actively pursued by the Serbian leadership for decades. The same cannot be argued in the case of Nagorno-Karabakh. While serious human rights crimes have taken place in the Armenian-Azerbaijani conflict as well, they are not attributable to one side alone. What is more, given that the declaration of independence of Nagorno-Karabakh predated the armed conflict and instances of ethnic cleansing, Azerbaijan as the parent state cannot be viewed as having lost its claims to the region the way Serbia had with Kosovo. Instead, in light of the events in the late 1980s and early 1990s, which included mass expulsions of ethnic Azerbaijanis, it is unquestionable that the Azerbaijani side suffered the most serious humanitarian consequences.

Following NATO's intervention in 1999 and Serbia's surrender, in 2007 UN Special Envoy Martti Ahtisaari stated in a report to the UN that attempts to come to a mutual agreement between Serbia and Kosovo regarding the status of the region had been exhausted and that "the only viable option for Kosovo is independence."[49] As a consequence of Serbia's systematic humanitarian violations in the region, reunification of Kosovo with Serbia appeared implausible. The Serbian leadership also consistently refused to engage in negotiations concerning Kosovo's future status. As noted previously, Baku, by contrast, has made repeated offers to Stepanakert of wide autonomy for the region but within the borders of Azerbaijan. Thus, arguing that independence for Nagorno-Karabakh would constitute an inevitable recourse for the international community would have little bearing.

It is also important to note that the Kosovar authorities, unlike the secessionist authorities in Nagorno-Karabakh, Abkhazia, Transnistria and Taiwan, never pointed at any legal principles as a basis for secession from Serbia. Seemingly aware that it had no grounds in international law for independence, Priština quoted in its independence declaration the international line that Kosovo constitutes "a special case arising from Yugoslavia's non-consensual breakup and is not a precedent for any other situation."[50]

In sum, the Kosovo case can hardly be viewed as a precedent for the secessionist regions in the post-Soviet space, including Nagorno-Karabakh. At the same time, Russia's recognition of Abkhazia and South Ossetia in August 2008 proved the implications that the Kosovo case has at the policy level, as it will inevitably serve as a reference point for secessionist claims elsewhere. However, as Western powers have been firm on the notion that Kosovo constituted an unavoidable exception to internationally recognized norms, it is unlikely to serve as a precedent for recognition of other secessionist regions.

COMPARING INTERNATIONAL LEGAL RHETORIC: THE CRIMEA CASE

In spite of the severe nature of the conflict between Armenia and Azerbaijan over Nagorno-Karabakh, and the glaring violations by Armenia of fundamental international norms concerning territorial integrity, the inviolability of borders, and humanitarian rights, the international response has been far less consistent with regard to Nagorno-Karabakh than to Moscow's actions in Georgia and more lately in Ukraine.

Already before Russia's formal annexation of Crimea in March 2014, the West adopted a comparatively firm stance against Russia on the issue of Ukraine's right to its territorial integrity. In a February 2014 White House press statement, President Obama sent a clear warning to President Putin on the issue of its troop presence in Eastern Ukraine, stating that: "any violation of Ukraine's sovereignty and territorial integrity would be deeply destabilizing, which is not in the interest of Ukraine, Russia, or Europe [...] It would be a clear violation of Russia's commitment to respect the independence and sovereignty and borders of Ukraine, and of international laws."[51] European capitals followed suit. At the Security Council's 7124th meeting on March 1, the United Kingdom and France joined the USA in condemning Russia's military movement into Ukraine, with repeated references to the escalating situation as a threat to Ukraine's territorial integrity and international law.[52] References to these threats were echoed by both the U.S. and European countries at the Council's subsequent meeting on March 3.[53]

As the situation worsened, Europe's and Washington's rhetoric with regard to violations of Ukraine's territorial integrity only sharpened.[54] This was accompanied by numerous statements by international organizations in favor of Ukraine's territorial integrity, including NATO, which stated in a March 2 press release that: "Military action against Ukraine by forces of the Russian Federation is a breach of international law and contravenes the principles of the NATO-Russia Council."[55] The Council of Europe's Parliamentary Assembly (PACE) on March 7 "strongly condemned the violation by the Russian Federation of the country's sovereignty and territorial integrity [...] in direct violation of international law."[56] The G7 group of countries also condemned Moscow's violation of Ukraine's sovereignty and territorial integrity, and in response suspended the June 2014 G8 summit that was to be held in Sochi.[57] Perhaps most significantly, following Russia's formal annexation of Crimea on March 18, the UN General Assembly adopted a resolution concerning the "Territorial integrity of Ukraine"[58] recalling the obligation of all states under article 2 in the UN Charter "to refrain in their international relations from the threat or use of force against the territorial integrity or political independence of any State." The resolution also affirmed Ukraine's "sovereignty, political independence, unity and territorial integrity of Ukraine within its internationally recognized borders." Notably, on February 17, 2015, the Security Council adopted Resolution 2202,[59] where it recalled "the purposes and principles enshrined in the Charter of the United Nations and reaffirming its full respect for the sovereignty, independence and territorial integrity of Ukraine."

The repeated rhetorical support for Ukraine's territorial integrity in the West, coupled with a regime of economic sanctions against Russia, stands in stark contrast to Western rhetoric in relation to the conflict over Nagorno-Karabakh. As has already been pointed out, divisions among the co-chairs and the influence of the Armenian diaspora in the USA and France has led to certain hesitation in stressing Azerbaijan's sovereignty. However, the lack of consistency with regard to legal narratives poses a twofold threat. First, it is a threat to stability in the region: indeed, it may be interpreted as the international community's negligence or inability to coordinate its policies in relation to the peace process, in turn leading the parties, especially Baku, to abandon their commitment to the non-use of force. Second, as the conflicts in the post-Soviet space bear close similarities, the adoption of different legal narratives in relation to the conflicts for political reasons risks undermining the international normative system in relation to state sovereignty and border inviolability.

THE QUESTION OF OCCUPATION

In spite of Armenia having no legal basis for its military presence in Nagorno-Karabakh, the international community has been somewhat divided on how decisive to be in its rhetoric, both regarding Armenian troop withdrawal and occupation. When in March 2008, the UN General Assembly passed a resolution[60] recognizing the region as an integral part of Azerbaijan and calling on Yerevan to withdraw its troops, 39 member states supported the document. Seven states, including Russia and notably also France and the United States, rejected the resolution (the latter two with reference to the resolution being unhelpful to the Minsk Process). The rest of the General Assembly members abstained from voting.

Two main reasons can be delineated in term of this split among foreign governments. First, international law does not provide for a clear and established definition of occupation. This makes it difficult to determine what exactly constitutes occupation, and what it implies. The Hague regulations stipulate that "a territory is considered 'occupied' when it is under the control or authority of the forces of the opposing State, without the consent of the government concerned."[61] International doctrine speaks of two main conditions for a territory to be considered occupied: first, that the occupied government is no longer capable of exercising its authority in the area in question and, second, that the occupying power is in a position to substitute its own authority for that of the former government.[62]

Thus, when a foreign power takes control of another state's territory through military intervention and prevents the state from exercising control over its territory, the question of whether an occupying power is exercising "authority" and "control" appears rather clear-cut. This is particularly true if the intervening force replaces the authority of the government territory in question without its consent, in which case there should be little doubt that the territory is under occupation by the foreign power. A more complex situation is when there is a de facto government in power in the territory in question, which claims to be exercising control over the territory under alleged occupation. Indeed, this is the case in Nagorno-Karabakh, as well as for instance in Georgia's separatist regions of Abkhazia and South Ossetia.

Not surprisingly, Armenia disputes that its presence in Nagorno-Karabakh and surrounding regions, and/or support to the separatist authorities, amounts to occupation. This position on the part of Yerevan is flawed for several reasons. International law on occupation is first and foremost concerned with the protection of the population residing on the occupied territory, rather than the status of the territory in question. As it is ultimately only states that can assure the protection of individuals, international law is less concerned with the division of responsibilities between the occupant and an unrecognized government than with that of the occupier and the occupied state. In this light, it is either Azerbaijan or Armenia that can be regarded as responsible for Nagorno-Karabakh and its surrounding regions. A key question, therefore, is not what level of influence Armenia exercises over the regional de facto authorities, but instead whether Yerevan exercises enough control in the region to replace Baku as the protector of human rights and humanitarian standards there. Considering Azerbaijan's lack of access to the region, international occupation law should apply in the case of Nagorno-Karabakh. International practice supports this notion, including the previously mentioned ECHR *Ilascu and Others* case. The ECHR presented the following evidence for Russia's responsibility in the region: "the military and political support" by Russia, "military, economic, financial and political support given by the Russian Federation," as well as "the participation of its military personnel in the fighting."[63] In commenting on Georgia's Law on Occupied Territories, the Council of Europe's Venice Commission concluded that Russia appeared to be exercising effective control in South Ossetia and Abkhazia.[64] Just like in the case of Transnistria, Russia's troop presence is significantly lower in Abkhazia and South Ossetia (more than 3,500 in each region) than Armenia's presence in Nagorno-Karabakh. In its 2009 assessment of the Georgia-Russia war, the EU's so-called Tagliavini Commission came to a similar conclusion, stating that:

> If [...] Russia's military intervention cannot be justified under international law, and if neither Abkhazia nor South Ossetia is a recognized independent state, IHL [International Humanitarian Law]—and in particular the rules concerning the protection of the civilian population [...] and occupation—was and may still be applicable.[65]

The commission also stated that the number of troops is not necessarily what determines whether its presence constitutes occupation in terms of international law.[66]

Secondly, the hesitation in the West to use the term occupation also appears to be linked to its politicized and stigmatized nature. At the policy level, utilizing the term occupation is seemingly interpreted as declaring the military presence of the occupying force or the events leading up to it as illegal. Thus, for states with a large Armenian diaspora and lobby, including France and the USA, using the term occupation has been particularly sensitive. In reality, this notion is a misinterpretation of the nature of the law on occupation.

The main purpose for declaring a territory occupied is to establish a legal regime during the phase of occupation, aimed mainly at protecting the rights of the individuals on the territory.[67] As such, the occupying force is subject to a number of obligations under international humanitarian law, such as protecting the individuals under occupation and refraining from annexation, exploiting resources, and property, as well altering the demographic situation of the territory.[68] The term occupation also suggests that the military presence is temporary, and thus, establishes the withdrawal of forces as the ultimate objective.

As such, recognizing that Nagorno-Karabakh is occupied by Armenia is important for several reasons. First, it prevents a silent acceptance of Armenia's continuous and large-scale military intervention into Azerbaijani territory, and Armenian further annexation thereof. Second, any failure to recognize Armenian occupation of Nagorno-Karabakh and its surrounding regions leaves the population in a normative vacuum where it is not clear who is responsible for its protection. As such, adopting a united international front on Armenia's occupation of Azerbaijani territory appears all the more urgent.

SOVIET LEGISLATION

Another argument put forward by Stepanakert and Yerevan is that the Nagorno-Karabakh region had a right to secession from Azerbaijan already under Soviet national legislation, particularly the Law of Secession (hereinafter LoS) that was introduced in 1990. They argue that the region fulfilled the requirements of the LoS through its declaration of independence in September 1991 and its subsequent referendum. Baku disputes this, arguing that Nagorno-Karabakh did not satisfy the procedural requirements of the law.[69]

In order to determine whether there is any basis for the argument advanced by Nagorno-Karabakh and Armenia, it is first necessary to look at the status of the region within the USSR. In accordance with the Soviet constitution of 1977, the territories of the Union were divided into different categories—the USSR being the supreme unit, followed by union republics, which in turn comprised territories with different levels of autonomous status: autonomous republics, autonomous regions and autonomous areas. Within this hierarchy, Nagorno-Karabakh held the status of an autonomous region,[70] essentially providing it with cultural and economic autonomy under the legislative control of Azerbaijan. As such, the region had no legal right to secession under the Soviet constitution, whose article 72 provided the right only for union states to freely secede from the USSR—importantly, not even for the autonomous republics, which were a notch higher on the echelon compared to Nagorno-Karabakh. Article 86 stipulated that autonomous regions, the category to which Nagorno-Karabakh belonged, were subordinated to the union states (in this case, Azerbaijan) and as such could not benefit from the right to secession awarded to their parent union state.

Moreover, article 78 of the constitution stated that the territory of a union state could not be altered without its consent. These constitutional principles regarding secession speak against any notion that additional legislation would have intended to provide the right for the autonomous regions of the USSR to secede from their parent states, especially not in the midst of the dissolution of the Soviet Union.

Indeed, the LoS of 1990 asserted, in article 3,[71] that an autonomous region of a union state (that in turn had the right to secession) had the right to choose if to stay with the seceding union state or with the USSR. But the applicability of this right in the case of Nagorno-Karabakh is debatable for several important reasons. First, the constitutionality of the provision was highly questionable, as the constitution clearly stated that any alteration to a union state's territory required its consent. Article 173 of the Constitution also required national laws to be in compliance with the Constitution. Moreover, as Kruger points out, the subtitle of the LoS—"Law Concerning the Procedure of Secession of a Soviet Republic from the Union of Soviet Socialist Republics"—clearly indicated that the law first and foremost dealt with the secession of union republics, not autonomous republics or regions.[72] Second, article 3 of the LoS provides the right for autonomous regions to secede only in the event that the (parent) union state followed certain secession procedures. As article 72 of the Constitution already granted union states the right to secede freely from the USSR, entailing no consequences to its territory, none of the union states ultimately claimed the LoS as a basis for their secession from the USSR, or followed its complex procedural rules. Instead they seceded on the basis of article 72 of the Constitution. This practice was approved by the Soviet Congress of People's Deputies, the highest legislative organ at the time.[73] Provided that the nature of article 3 of the LoS was based on the assumption that Azerbaijan itself followed its procedures, which it did not do, the LoS was arguably never valid for Nagorno-Karabakh. Azerbaijan already fulfilled the right for secession from the viewpoint of international law, and as such could not be accused of unlawful secession. As has been concluded above, the same was not true for the Nagorno-Karabakh autonomous region. In any case, excluded from this analysis is the fact that Nagorno-Karabakh itself did not fulfill the procedural requirements of the LoS.

So why, then, was the LoS introduced in the first place? Its adoption should be viewed in light of the political situation at the time, when Gorbachev was trying to keep the Soviet Union intact. It therefore appears reasonable to assume that the procedural rules of the law were designed in a way to make secession a complicated and lengthy endeavor, suggesting that it was in fact adopted to delay the dissolution of the Union. Through introducing very complex rules for seceding from the USSR, with the obvious risk for the union republics of losing their autonomous regions, the LoS may have constituted a political attempt by the Soviet leadership to keep the Union from breaking apart.

CONCLUSIONS

In light of the analysis above, it is possible to conclude that Nagorno-Karabakh does not fulfill the requirements for statehood in international law. While the de facto authorities in Stepanakert continue to argue the region's right to self-determination, this principle does not automatically entail a right for a protected group to separate from its parent state. While external self-determination may provide such a right (and this notion is debatable), its application needs to have been preceded by serious and systematic violations of the rights of the seceding population by the parent state, whereafter secession appears to be the only solution. This is not the case in regard to Nagorno-Karabakh. This also rules out the applicability of the right to external self-determination based on repression by another ethnic group. The principle of territorial integrity continues to prevail in international law, leaving little room for exception.

Equally, the analysis in this chapter suggests that there is no right for the Nagorno-Karabakh region to form a new state according to the traditional criteria for statehood in contemporary international law. Nagorno-Karabakh fails on all three of the requirements laid down in the 1933 Montevideo Convention, as it lacks fixed borders, a permanent population, and, most importantly, effective and independent governance. Stepanakert's heavy reliance on Armenia for financial and military support leads to the inescapable conclusion, recognized by the European Court of Human Rights, that it does not independently exercise enough control over its territory to live up to the requirement of effective governance. International practice, especially the Stimson Doctrine, moreover suggests that the formation of a state is unlawful if it is based on the use of force or other violations of international norms. The violence in the region in the early 1990s, the demographic changes that have taken place, and Armenia's continuous illegal troop presence all speak against Nagorno-Karabakh's right to independence in this regard.

The notion that Kosovo's independence in February 2008 constitutes a legal precedent for the independence of Nagorno-Karabakh has also proven invalid. The recognition of Kosovo in the West lacked an international legal basis; rather, it constituted a last resort to solve the conflict in the region. In order for a precedent to be set in international law, a certain conformity in state practice is required, as well as a willingness in the international community to establish new standards or principles. The repeated reference among Western states to Kosovo's independence as an exemption to recognized norms testify to the lack of such conformity or willingness.

It has also been argued in this chapter that Armenia's troop presence in Nagorno-Karabakh for all intents and purposes amounts to occupation of Azerbaijani territory. Concluding from international court practice, there is little doubt that Armenia's military presence in, and overall influence over, Nagorno-Karabakh amounts to effective control over the region. This, in turn, invokes the international law on occupation, which predominantly aims at protecting humanitarian standards in the territory.

Finally, the argument by Stepanakert and Yerevan that Soviet law provided a right to secession for Nagorno-Karabakh does not hold water. Neither the Soviet constitution, nor the LoS, could be interpreted as having supported the right for Nagorno-Karabakh to separate from Azerbaijan. While the LoS did provide a right for autonomous regions, such as Nagorno-Karabakh, to choose whether to stay with its parent union state or with the USSR, this right depended on the compliance of the union state to the procedural rules of the law in its own secession from the Soviet Union, which Azerbaijan did not do. Instead, Baku's independence declaration relied on the right to secede in the Soviet constitution, thus ruling out the possibility for Nagorno-Karabakh to secede based on the LoS—whose procedures it did not follow.

International mediation attempts in relation to the Nagorno-Karabakh conflict have failed to yield any results. The divisions in the Minsk Group, in particular the hesitance among the co-chairs to adopt a determined stance on the issue of Armenia's military presence, appear largely the result of political considerations. The significant Armenian diaspora in the USA and France has played a significant role in this regard. There is seemingly also uncertainty within the international community regarding the international legal aspects of the Nagorno-Karabakh conflict. This relates not only to the issue of the future status of the region, but also to the question of occupation and legality of Armenia's military presence and overall support to the secessionist authorities.

The current status quo in the region is not only unsustainable, but also problematic for several important reasons. First, it directly conflicts with Western interests in the region. Continued instability in the South Caucasus, or worse, the eruption of warfare, has detrimental implications for the West, as it hampers economic development and trade and risks bringing with it spillover effects in the shape of illegal refugee flows and a rise in organized crime. It also prevents the West from expanding its energy imports from the Caspian basin, and to further utilize the region's potential as a vital trade corridor to Central Asia and beyond. Second, Armenia's significant troop presence on Azerbaijani territory constitutes a clear violation of recognized international law and standards. If unchallenged, this risks setting dangerous precedents in international practice with implications beyond the region.

To fulfill the objective of restoring Azerbaijan's territorial integrity, it is crucial that the West adopts a united and firm stance on the issue of Armenia's occupation of Nagorno-Karabakh and its surrounding regions, on the importance of border inviolability, and establishes the reversal of the Armenian troop presence as a clearly articulated objective. This would serve not only to delegitimize Armenia's troop presence in the region, but also underline that the current situation in the region is of a temporary rather than permanent nature and that the ultimate goal is to reestablish Azerbaijan's territorial integrity and ensure the return of the expelled IDPs to the region. It would also clarify the level of humanitarian responsibility that Armenia has assumed through its presence as an occupying force in the territory. Finally, continuous lack of consistency with regard to legal narratives in connection with the region's conflicts, especially with regard to the issue of territorial integrity, not only undermines the international normative system but may also lead to erroneous interpretations of internationally recognized law and standards with dangerous consequences for security in the region and elsewhere.

NOTES

1. Concerning the role of self-determination in international law, see e.g. Malcolm N. Shaw, *International Law*, 6th edition (Cambridge University Press, 2008), and Rupert Emerson, "Self-Determination," *American Journal of International Law*, vol. 65, no. 3, July (1971): 459–75.
2. The Charter of the United Nations, signed on June 26, 1945, articles 1 (2) and 55.
3. The United Nation General Assembly Resolution 2625 (XXV) on "Declaration of Principles of International Law Concerning Friendly Relations and Co-operation Among States in Accordance with the Charter of the United Nations" of October 24, 1970.
4. See e.g. Shaw, *International Law*; Emerson, "Self-Determination"; and Heiko Kruger, *The Nagorno-Karabakh Conflict: A Legal Analysis* (Springer-Verlag Berlin Heidelberg, 2010).
5. Statement by Russian President Dmitry Medvedev on August 26, 2008, available at: http://archive.kremlin.ru/eng/speeches/2008/08/26/1543_type82912_205752.shtml
6. This was confirmed by the International Court of Justice in its advisory opinions on *Namibia* (ICJ Reports, 1971) and *Western Sahara* (ICJ Reports, 1975). Moreover, in 1998, the Canadian Supreme Court assessed the issue of self-determination and secession in relation to Quebec, and made a careful examination of the guiding principles on the matter. The Court noted that: "a right of secession exists "where 'a people' is governed as part of a colonial empire; where 'a people' is subject to alien subjugation, domination or exploitation; and possibly where 'a people' is denied any meaningful exercise of its right to self-determination within the state of which it forms a part." Reference re Secession of Quebec, [1998] 2 S.C.R. 217—In the matter of Section 53 of the *Supreme Court Act*, R.S.C., 1985, c. S-26, at http://scc.lexum.umontreal.ca/en/1998/1998scr2-217/1998scr2-217.pdf. Its findings have been guiding in several other cases on the right to self-determination and are widely quoted in international doctrine.
7. See e.g. Milena Sterio, "On the Right to Self-Determination: 'Selfistans', Secession and the Great Powers' Rule," *Minnesota Journal of International Law*, vol. 19, no. 1 (2010): 137–176.
8. For a detailed discussion on the role and limits of the right to self-determination, see e.g. Emerson, "Self-Determination."

9. Territorial integrity is a dominating principle in international law, allowing for few exceptions, protecting the sovereignty of a state and its borders. International documents that support this notion include *UN General Assembly Resolution* 1514, *CSCE Helsinki Final Act* of 1975, and *OSCE Charter of Paris* of 1990.

10. See e.g. Hurst Hannum, "The Specter of Secession: Responding to Claims for Ethnic Self-Determination," *Foreign Affairs*, vol. 77, 1998.

11. See e.g. Svante E. Cornell, "The Nagorno-Karabakh Conflict," Report no. 46 (Department of East European Studies, Uppsala University, 1999), available at: http://expert-translations.ro/uploads/Nagorno%20Karabah.pdf

12. Ibid.

13. See David Remnick, "Ethnic Clashes Have Killed 87, Soviets Say," in *The Washington Post*, February 8, 1989.

14. For more information about the Baku events, see Cornell, "The Nagorno-Karabakh Conflict."

15. See e.g. Human Rights Watch, "Azerbaijan: Seven Years of Conflict in Nagorno-Karabakh," December 1994, https://www.hrw.org/sites/default/files/reports/AZER%20Conflict%20in%20N-K%20Dec94.pdf

16. Ibid., and Human Rights Watch, "Bloodshed in the Caucasus—Escalation of the Conflict in Nagorno-Karabakh," September 1992, https://www.hrw.org/report/1992/09/01/bloodshed-caucasus/escalation-armed-conflict-nagorno-karabakh

17. Ibid.

18. According to Human Rights Watch, at least 161 civilians were killed in the incident, although Azerbaijan estimates the number of casualties to have been around 800. See Human Rights Watch report on "The Former Soviet Union—Human Rights Developments," 1993, https://www.hrw.org/reports/1993/WR93/Hsw-07.htm. The estimate of 600 civilians is generally accepted. See e.g. Michael Kambeck and Sargis Ghazaryan, "Timeline 1918–2011," in *Europe's Next Avoidable War: Nagorno-Karabakh*, eds. Kambeck and Ghazaryan (London: Palgrave Macmillan, 2013), 24–32.

19. The United Nations Security Council Resolution 1244 of June 10, 1999, reaffirmed the territorial integrity of the Federal Republic of Yugoslavia (http://daccess-dds-ny.un.org/doc/UNDOC/GEN/N99/172/89/PDF/N9917289.pdf?OpenElement). See also Kruger, *The Nagorno-Karabakh Conflict: A Legal Analysis*.

20. See Cornell, "The Nagorno-Karabakh Conflict."

21. Including e.g. PACE resolution 1416 of 2005, Security Council resolutions 853 and 884 of 1993, and OSCE Chairman statement at the Lisbon Summit on December 2–3, 1996.

22. League of Nations, "Admission of Azerbaijan to the League of Nation: Memorandum of the Secretary-General" of November 1920, 20/48/108.

23. Kruger, *The Nagorno-Karabakh Conflict: A Legal Analysis.*
24. Ibid.
25. Minutes of the Caucasian Bureau session of July 5, 1921, no. 12, point 2.
26. The "Montevideo Convention on the Rights and Duties of States," signed in Montevideo at the 7th International Conference of American States, December 26, 1933.
27. Its article 4 reads: The state as a person of international law should possess the following qualifications: (a) a permanent population; (b) a defined territory and (c) government. An additional fourth criterion provides a state to have (d) capacity to enter into relations with the other states, albeit this is naturally dependent on the acceptance by other states of the first three requirements.
28. Tim Potier, *Conflict in Nagorno-Karabakh, Abkhazia and South Ossetia: A Legal Appraisal* (The Hague: Kluwer Law, 2001), 103.
29. Azerbaijan has one of the highest per capita concentrations of IDPs in the world. The majority of IDPs—approximately 90 percent—originate from seven territories around Nagorno-Karabakh, which has been occupied by Armenia since open conflict erupted in the early 1990s. See UNHCR, "Azerbaijan: Analysis of Gaps in the Protection of Internally Displaced People (IDPs)," October 2009, at http://www.unhcr.org/4bd7edbd9.html
30. See e.g. Shaw, *International Law.*
31. The commission noted that: "…this certainly did not take place until a stable political organization had been created, and until the public authorities had become strong enough to assert themselves throughout the territories of the State without the assistance of foreign troops. It would appear that it was in May, 1918, that the civil war ended and that the foreign troops began to leave the country, so that from that time onwards it was possible to re-establish order and normal political and social life, little by little." See "Report of the International Committee of Jurists entrusted by the Council of the League of Nations with the task of giving an Advisory Opinion upon the Legal Aspects of the Aaland Islands question," *League of Nations—Official Journal* (1920), 3, at: http://www.ilsa.org/jessup/jessup10/basicmats/aaland1.pdf
32. See e.g. James Crawford, "The Creation of the State of Palestine: Too Much Too Soon?" in *European Journal of International Law*, vol. 1, no.1 (1990): 307–313; and Frederic L. Kirgis Jr., "Admission of 'Palestine' as a Member of a Specialized Agency and Withholding the Assessments of Payments in Response," *American Journal of International Law*, vol. 84 (1990): 218–230. The PLO's lack of control over Palestine Territory was also confirmed by the UNESCO Executive Board in its response to Palestine's application to become a member of the organization, see UNESCO Archives 131 EX/INF.7, Paris, May 26, 1989.

33. See e.g. Thomas de Waal, *Black Garden: Armenia and Azerbaijan Through Peace and War* (New York University Press, 2003).
34. Ibid.
35. Human Rights Watch, "Azerbaijan: Seven Years of Conflict in Nagorno-Karabakh."
36. Potier, *Conflict in Nagorno-Karabakh, Abkhazia and South Ossetia: A Legal Appraisal.*
37. International Crisis Group, "Nagorno-Karabakh: Viewing the Conflict from the Ground," *Europe Report* no. 166, September 14, 2005, http://www.crisisgroup.org/~/media/Files/europe/166_nagorno_karabakh_viewing_the_conflict_from_the_ground.pdf
38. Kruger, *The Nagorno-Karabakh Conflict: A Legal Analysis.*
39. Nicole Itano, "the Wannabe Nation of Nagorno-Karabakh", *Christian Science Monitor*, May 30, 2007; Mumin Shakirov, "Karabakh: The Agony of a Stagnant Peace", *Moscow Times*, February 5, 2002.
40. European Court of Human Rights, "Ilascu and Others v. Moldova and the Russian Federation" (App. No. 48787/99), judgment of July 8, 2004.
41. European Court of Human Rights, "Case of Chiragov and Others vs. Armenia", (App. no. 13216/05), Grand Chamber Judgment of June 16, 2015. (https://lovdata.no/static/EMDN/emd-2005-013216-2.pdf), p. 56.
42. de Waal, *Black Garden.*
43. See U.S. Department of State, "The Mukden Incident of 1931 and the Stimson Doctrine," available at https://history.state.gov/milestones/1921-1936/mukden-incident
44. The principle has later been laid down in several legal documents, including the UN General Assembly resolution on the "Definition of Aggression," of 1975; and the International Law Commission's "Draft Articles on State Responsibility for Internationally Wrongful Acts," of 2001.
45. See e.g. David Raič, *Statehood and the Law of Self-Determination* (The Hague: Kluwer Law International, 2002).
46. In total, 108 UN member states have recognized Kosovo's independence. Furthermore, Kosovo is a member of the IMF and the World Bank. Powers that have not recognized Kosovo include Russia, China, and Spain (along with four other EU member states).
47. E.g. China, Spain, Cyprus, Greece, Russia, Slovakia, and Romania.
48. See statement of the Russian Ministry of Foreign Affairs on Kosovo, Information and Press Department, February 17, 2008, http://www.mid.ru/brp_4.nsf/e78a48070f128a7b43256999005bcbb3/041c5af46913d38ac32573f30027b380?OpenDocument
49. Report of the Special Envoy of the Secretary-General on Kosovo's Future Status, S/2007/168, 2007, at http://www.unosek.org/docref/report-english.pdf

50. See Kosovo's Declaration of Independence of February 17, 2008, available at: http://www.assembly-kosova.org/?cid=2,128,1635.

51. See White House Statement by the President on Ukraine, February 28, 2014, available at https://www.whitehouse.gov/the-press-office/2014/02/28/statement-president-ukraine

52. UK representative Sir Lyall Grant expressed his deep concern over the situation, referring to the action as a "grave threat to the sovereignty, independence and territorial integrity of Ukraine." French representative Araud assured that France would work for a settlement of the conflict that "preserves the territorial integrity and sovereignty of the country". Report available at http://www.securitycouncilreport.org/atf/cf/%7B65BFCF9B-6D27-4E9C-8CD3-CF6E4FF96FF9%7D/s_pv_7124.pdf

53. The U.S. stated that the military action was a "violation of international law and of Ukraine's territorial integrity of Ukraine"; the UK referred to Russia's control over Crimea as a "clear violation of its sovereignty, independence and territorial integrity" and "a flagrant breach of international law" with no justification. Report available at http://www.securitycouncilreport.org/atf/cf/%7B65BFCF9B-6D27-4E9C-8CD3-CF6E4FF96FF9%7D/s_pv_7125.pdf

54. See e.g. the wordings of German Chancellor Angela Merkel on March 3 including "This clearly is a violation of the sovereignty, independence and territorial integrity of Ukraine," *The Guardian*, March 3, 2014, http://www.theguardian.com/world/2014/mar/03/ukraine-vladimir-putin-angela-merkel-russian; U.S. Secretary of State John Kerry: "It's an incredible act of aggression [...] Russia is in violation of the sovereignty of Ukraine. Russia is in violation of its international obligations," *Reuters*, March 2, 2014, http://www.reuters.com/article/us-ukraine-crisis-usa-kerry-idUSBREA210DG20140302; The White House: "Obama expressed deep concern over Russia's violation of Ukrainian sovereignty and territorial integrity...[and] breach of international law," *The Washington Post*, March 1, 2014, https://www.washingtonpost.com/world/national-security/us-and-allies-try-to--decide-on-response-to-ukraine-crisis/2014/03/01/463d1922-a174-11e3-b8d8-94577ff66b28_story.html; and EU High Representative Catherine Ashton: "The unity, sovereignty and territorial integrity of Ukraine must be respected at all times and by all sides. Any violation of these principles is unacceptable," European Union External Action Service, http://eeas.europa.eu/statements/docs/2014/140301_01_en.pdf

55. "North Atlantic Council statement on the situation in Ukraine," http://www.nato.int/cps/en/natolive/official_texts_107681.htm

56. "PACE strongly supports Ukraine's territorial integrity and national sovereignty," http://www.assembly.coe.int/nw/xml/News/News-View-EN.asp?newsid=4908&lang=2&cat=17

57. See "Ukraine crisis: Russia faces 'costs and consequences,' warns William Hague," *The Telegraph*, March 3, 2014, http://www.telegraph.co.uk/news/worldnews/europe/ukraine/10672977/Ukraine-crisis-Russia-faces-costs-and-consequences-warns-William-Hague.html.

58. Resolution adopted by the General Assembly, no. 68/262, of March 27, 2014, available at http://www.securitycouncilreport.org/atf/cf/%7B65BFCF9B-6D27-4E9C-8CD3-CF6E4FF96FF9%7D/a_res_68_262.pdf

59. See http://www.securitycouncilreport.org/atf/cf/%7B65BFCF9B-6D27-4E9C-8CD3-CF6E4FF96FF9%7D/s_res_2202.pdf

60. United Nations General Assembly Resolution 62/243 on "The Situation in the Occupied Territories of Azerbaijan," adopted on March 14, 2008, at its 62nd session.

61. Article 42 of the "Regulations concerning the Laws and Customs of War on Land" (The Hague Regulations), of October 18, 1907, available at: http://www.icrc.org/ihl.nsf/385ec082b509e76c41256739003e636d/1d1726425f6955aec125641e0038bfd6

62. See e.g. Shaw, *International Law.*

63. ECHR ruling, "Ilascu and Others," paras. 382 and 392.

64. European Commission for Democracy through Law (Venice Commission) opinion on the Law on Occupied Territories of Georgia, adopted by the Venice Commission at its 78th Plenary Session (Venice, March 13–14, 2009), para. 38.

65. Report by the Independent International Fact-Finding Mission on the Conflict in Georgia (Tagliavini Commission), Volume II, p. 311.

66. Ibid.

67. Art. 43 of the Hague Regulations reads: "The authority of the legitimate power having in fact passed into the hands of the occupant, the latter shall take all the measures in his power to restore, and ensure, as far as possible, public order and safety, while respecting, unless absolutely prevented, the laws in force in the country." As noted by Shaw (p. 1178), this is both a right and an obligation by the occupier.

68. See articles 46-56 of the Hague Regulations, and articles 47 and 49 of the *Convention (IV) Relative to the Protection of Civilian Persons in Time of War*, Geneva, August 12, 1949.

69. Kruger, *The Nagorno-Karabakh Conflict: A Legal Analysis.*

70. Constitution of the USSR of 1977, Art. 87, para 3.

71. Ibid., para 1, sentence 2.

72. Kruger, *The Nagorno-Karabakh Conflict: A Legal Analysis.*

73. Ibid.

CHAPTER 3

Nagorno-Karabakh Between Old and New Geopolitics

James Sherr

The world has changed three times since the outbreak of what we have come to call the Nagorno-Karabakh conflict. Yet the conflict's dynamics have proved remarkably impervious to geopolitical change. This is ironic because, in its dubiously "frozen" state, the conflict has stymied the development of a geopolitically critical region. As Thomas de Waal has summarized it:

> Communications are blocked in the whole area between the Black and Caspian Seas, the political evolution of two countries has been stunted, economic resources have been diverted from basic needs into weaponry ... The current situation visits continuing hardship on ordinary people all across the region.[1]

The irony is explained by the fact that for each of the players that count, economic development and human betterment are secondary to other more cardinal interests. To date, the core antagonists, Armenia and Azerbaijan, have been powerless to realize the maximalist objectives to which they are morally and politically committed; while the key external actors have repeatedly found that the baleful status quo refuses to submit to peaceful revision. They have also concluded, if for disparate and discordant reasons, that its forceful revision would be far more dangerous than its preservation. This and this alone explains why Washington and Moscow have managed to work in a constructive spirit over Nagorno-Karabakh despite a steadily worsening East-West relationship.

Yet, the latest geopolitical changes set in motion by the Ukraine conflict threaten to tip these awkward balances over fault lines and even precipices. Unlike the aftermath of the Russia-Georgia war, which saw East-West relations

J. Sherr (✉)
London, UK

© The Author(s) 2017

S.E. Cornell (ed.), *The International Politics of the Armenian-Azerbaijani Conflict*, DOI 10.1057/978-1-137-60006-6_3

recover their deceptive normality, Russia's annexation of Crimea and intervention in Donbas have rightly been seen as a direct assault on the legal framework that established the post-Cold War world and defined the parameters of competition within it. Russia's avowed desire to replace the principles of Helsinki with the principles of Yalta has fanned apprehension and antagonism far beyond Ukraine's borders. In the Near East, it has given a fresh and menacing twist to an already horrendous and destabilizing conflict. More than at any time in the recent past, the South Caucasus finds itself becoming a rear staging area for conflict elsewhere. Energy and defense are but two areas drawing Georgia, Armenia, and Azerbaijan into problems not of their own making, while dangerously exacerbating the problems they already have.

The aim of this chapter is to draw these threads together, assess their cumulative impact, and consider the dangers they pose. But these changes cannot be understood in the absence of the tensions that produced them. We therefore begin with a synoptic portrayal of the misleading consensus that underpinned the post-Cold War order, as well as the new complacencies that fell into place after the seven day Russia-Georgia war.

The Illusory Geopolitics of Partnership: 1991–99

The collapse of the USSR and with it, the Cold War system, produced a geopolitical revolution that promised at first sight to be as sweeping as that which followed the collapse of Nazi Germany in 1945. Within two years, the triumph of 1945 had given way to a new division of the continent. The triumphalists of 1991 forecast no new division but instead "the end of history" and a "Europe whole and free." For their part, Russia's own triumphalists, soon to be dubbed "romantics" by some of their compatriots and traitors by others, anticipated that the distinction between East and West would disappear. They also anticipated that the "special responsibility" of a democratic Russia in the former USSR would be welcomed by the West and accepted by former subjects that, in Moscow's view, lacked the means to give substance to their titular independence.

It took much of the ensuing decade to establish that these were not realistic assumptions. The analogy between Adenauer's Germany and Yeltsin's Russia was flawed from the start. The former emerged after military defeat, occupation, and de-Nazification under allied authorities. The USSR's defeat was ideological and geopolitical (and only in Afghanistan, military). Its disintegration (which the USA feared rather than fostered) was the product of economic dislocation, the erosion of "command" authority, a reawakening of national sentiment, and discreditation of the ideology that legitimized the multi-national state. The Russian Federation's formation was an internal affair, presided over by the Soviet establishment's most radical members rather than its most radical foes. The USSR's defense and security establishments were neither dismantled nor transformed; they became diminished, neglected, and resentful reincarnations of their former selves. Alongside other sovietized elites in the political and economic spheres, they ensured that Russia's "second revolution" would have a transient and schizophrenic character.

On two points the "romantics" were at one with their antagonists. First, their sense of entitlement in the newly designated "near abroad" was unequivocal. Even in the ostentatiously liberal Russian Ministry of Foreign Affairs, it was axiomatic as early as summer 1992 that Russia should remain the "leader of stability and military security on the entire territory of the former USSR."[2]

Second, they swiftly understood that the newly formed Commonwealth of Independent States (CIS) was threatened by conflict. Although the disintegration of the USSR was far less violent than many feared, it was not peaceful. The relationship between bottom-up and top-down dynamics was not only impulsive and discordant; it ruined any possibility of the successor states making a "fresh start." Outside the Slavic republics (where tensions did not turn to conflict), national aspirations and demands gave rise to outbreaks of violence well before the USSR formally dissolved in December 1991. The ostensible start of the (resuscitated) conflict that defines this volume dates from the appeal of the NKAO Soviet to the USSR Supreme Soviet in February 1988, but Armenian-Azerbaijani tensions had revealed their murderous potential months before the events in Stepanakert, not to say the Sumgait pogrom later that month. While dynamics in Moldova and Georgia were markedly different from those of Nagorno-Karabakh and from one another, conflict in these territories also predated collapse.[3] Gorbachev warned Karabakh Armenians that they risked igniting "several dozen potential conflicts" in the USSR, and this doubtless played a role in persuading him that their demands could not be met.

But the accolades that Gorbachev received in the West for declining to preserve the USSR by force are not fully warranted. His political and temperamental proclivity for moderation, conciliation, and "Party methods" receded whenever he sensed that the existence of the Union, and more directly the Communist Party, was at stake. The April 1989 "massacre of spades" in Tbilisi foreshadowed the brutal suppression of the Azerbaijan Popular Front several months later by MVD Interior Troops and the launch of "Operation Ring" against Armenia in spring 1991. In the South Caucasus, unlike Estonia and Lithuania, where violent suppression was swiftly aborted, the West had an itinerant interest or none, and Gorbachev had little difficulty spinning the truth for its consumption. Inside the region, where he had no hope of doing this, his turn to repression handed a poisoned chalice to his successors.

Those who took up the reins of the Russian state after 1991 had difficulty distinguishing cause and effect. The conflicts in Nagorno-Karabakh and elsewhere were not caused by "the breakdown of Soviet order." They merely followed it. The cause lay in the establishment and compulsive re-engineering of the Soviet power vertical and the modalities of "divide and rule," which upon "Russia's rebirth" resurfaced as "divide and influence."[4] The habits of horizontal communication between communities, not to say nations, had been largely extinguished after the 1920s. Other Soviet obsessions and ills—opacity, deception, distrust of "voluntarism"—fanned anxiety, fed conspiracies, and destroyed trust between communities. To leaders of the Karabakh Armenian movement, the local Azerbaijanis (25 percent of the region's population) were not an apprehensive minority, but "instruments of power, instruments of violence over us."[5] The "vertical" created pockets of ignorance from bottom to top. In Yerevan and Baku, it was widely and falsely rumored that Gorbachev was conspiring to betray their respective interests. Inside his own bubble, Gorbachev had a poor idea of what others made of his decisions or how they would influence events on the ground.

The Soviet collapse produced a multiplicity of power vacuums, not just one. If in the European metropolitan centers of Russia the departure of the state meant the arrival of oligarchic politics, on the Caucasus ridge, it cleared the path to banditry and anarchy. In spring 1992, the Institute of Geography of the Russian Academy of Sciences identified 76 "flashpoints" (*goryachie tochki*) out of a total of 180 actual and potential zones of conflict in the former USSR.[6] For "liberals" and "reasoned nationalists" alike, the risk was that these conflicts would be exported to Russia. The danger existed because the Russian Federation was a post-imperial formation of 100 nationalities rather than the "normal nation state" that Andrey Kozyrev and Anatoly Chubais portrayed to their Western colleagues. That 80 percent of Russia's citizens were now ethnic Russians (as opposed to fewer than 50 percent in the USSR) was undeniable, but this was not true everywhere, least of all in the north Caucasus. The old maxim, "he who wishes to control the north Caucasus must control the south" gradually reappeared.

So did other security dilemmas of the past. Russia was once again a country in which the frontiers between nation, state, and empire (*aka* "union," *aka* "commonwealth") were difficult to draw and maintain. In the past, this geopolitical indeterminacy had fostered a set of security "needs" out of kilter and scale with those of neighboring states and most rival powers. In the "new" Russia, the traditional preoccupation with security perimeters slowly re-emerged, as did traditional solutions: buffer zones and client states. To these constructs, two new ones were added: peacekeeping (i.e., "peace-making") and "frozen conflicts." As early as May 1992, military doctrines resurrected Imperial Russia's preoccupation with control of "space." From that point forward, threat and danger have been defined by the "presence" of foreign military forces "in the vicinity of Russia's borders" rather than their purpose. Retention of Soviet borders as the baseline of "vicinity" enlarged the threat perceived (e.g. in 1999 when Russia warned NATO that Yugoslavia was a country "in the vicinity of Russia's borders.")

With 600,000 troops deployed in the former Union Republics, the Russian Armed Forces (so re-designated in May 1992) were, alongside the former KGB, the best placed to uphold such orthodoxies. The foreign ministry, which lacked expertise in what only recently were domestic matters, was not. Not surprisingly, the armed forces were neither willing nor able to employ the "civilized methods" that Moscow's reformers wished to uphold. In conditions of disintegration and perceived threat, the central tenet of Gorbachev's "new thinking"—that is, "the impermissibility of using force to solve political problems"—fell to the ground. According to the commander responsible for the newly established practice of peacekeeping, literally peace-*making'* (*mirot-vorcheskiye operatsii*), "[h]ere in Russia, everything is the other way around. First we use overwhelming force, *then* we bring the parties to the negotiating table."[7]

The West was conspicuously truant in coming to grips with these realities, not to say the real direction of Russia's "transition." Like Moscow, Washington maintained a top-down perspective of the USSR until it became preposterous to do so, and it harbored a Gorbachevian abhorrence of "national factionalism" until the "factions" turned into internationally recognized states. The belated appointment in 1990 of Paul Goble as Special Adviser to the US State Department testified to this, as did his resignation after President Bush's so-called "Chicken Kyiv" speech, which entirely ignored his advice. It took much hard work by Eduard Shevardnadze and Leonid Kravchuk (Ukraine's first president) to alter this mono-focal preoccupation with Russia and Yeltsin. Were it not for Ukraine's possession of the world's third largest nuclear arsenal, the process probably would have been longer.

By 1994, leading Western powers had begun to treat the ex-Soviet republics as entities in their own right rather than inconvenient by-products of the Soviet collapse. But even ten years later, on the eve of Ukraine's Orange Revolution, the West was still underestimating the impact this abandonment of "Russia first" was having on Russia's thinking. Russia's liberals simply could not understand why the West would risk damaging relations with a country of such obvious importance as Russia for the sake of countries that never possessed the attributes of statehood. To the "great power" *derzhavniki*, who by the mid-1990s were displacing liberals at the helm of policy, the West's cultivation of "partnerships" with Ukraine, Georgia, and Azerbaijan were anti-Russian policies pure and simple. Fear of "chaos" receded. Fear of the near abroad becoming a Western *platsdarm* (bridgehead) increased. As NATO embarked on enlargement, the space for reasoned argument in Russia contracted, as did the gap between military and Kremlin thinking. Two months after NATO's inauguration of Partnership for Peace in February 1994, Boris Yeltsin informed senior officers of the SVR (Foreign Intelligence Service).

[t]here are forces abroad that would like to keep Russia in a state of controllable paralysis .... Ideological conflicts are being replaced by a struggle for spheres of influence in geopolitics.[8]

It is in this context that Eduard Shevardnadze, whose assumption of the Georgian presidency had been backed by Moscow, gradually lost confidence in the possibility of retaining Russia's trust and preserving Georgia's independence. In Azerbaijan, where Russia's position over Karabakh was having much the same effect as its position over Abkhazia had in Georgia, President Heydar Aliev, former KGB Major General and member of Yuriy Andropov's Politburo, underwent a similar and equally reluctant evolution.

Given this worsening climate, Moscow's readiness to concede to the CSCE the leading role in brokering the Nagorno-Karabakh cease-fire requires explanation. To all appearances, the role assumed by the Minsk Group after March 1992 seemed likely to put it at cross purposes with Yeltsin's February 1993 appeal to "responsible international organizations, including the United Nations [to] grant Russia special powers as guarantor of peace and stability in the former Soviet Union."[9] Moreover, the new Clinton administration in Washington had already mapped out an ambitious course of "democratic enlargement" in the region, and it assigned an ambassador to the Group who was critical of Russian policy.[10]

The fact is that Moscow had no realistic alternative. Having absorbed hundreds of thousands of Armenian refugees from the conflict—creating in Sergey Markedonov's words, an "internal Southern Caucasus" in the Russian Federation—it dreaded a resumption of conflict.[11] Defying the CSCE would have put it on a course of confrontation that it then lacked the means to pursue. In the mid-1990s, Russia remained dependent on Western goodwill. Despite mounting irritations in both directions, the relationship was not adversarial, and there was nothing to be gained from making it so. More valuable to Moscow than a blatantly independent course was CSCE constraint of US unilateralism. Moreover, the interest of most Western participants was *pro forma*. In terms of expertise and commitment to the process, Russia was head and shoulders above the rest, and its ambassador, Vladimir Kazimirov, gradually took the *de facto* lead. The Americans were neophytes in the region, torn between the power of the Armenian lobby and the potential of Azerbaijani oil. Despite the efforts of Ambassador John Maresca, Washington gradually lost interest. Not least significantly, Moscow was coming to realize that a frozen conflict was not a lesser evil, but a tool of leverage over the protagonists and the region as a whole. Whatever its drawbacks, the obstructions to communications between the Black and Caspian seas would further constrain Georgia's options and, it was hoped, deepen its dependency on Russia. Finally, Russia was the only country that could contribute a peacekeeping force to the region, a course that Pavel Grachev pursued aggressively and that Aliyev alone had the strength to resist. Russia's work in the Minsk Group between 1992 and 1994 persuaded it to embrace the OSCE (as the CSCE became in October) as its Pan-European security structure of choice.

THE GEOPOLITICS OF TENSION: 2000–13

For 17 years after the collapse of the USSR, Western establishments maintained that as Russia became more prosperous, self-confident, and integrated into the global economy, its geopolitically deterministic outlook and need for dominance in the former Soviet world would recede. The events of 9/11 and the emergence of presumptive "common enemies" rejuvenated these convictions. In practice, these views (which in some quarters had become a catechism) dulled awareness of the impact of Western policies on Russia and distorted assessments of changes occurring in Russia itself.

Initial Western perceptions of Vladimir Putin said more about the West than about him. Although Putin's promise to "revive Russia as a strong state, a great state" was duly noted, three notes articulated at the outset of his first term rekindled hopes in Russia's "far abroad:" a robust and outwardly reformist economic policy, a determination to replace oligarchic impunity with the "dictatorship of law" and, above all, a policy based on "pragmatism," one that "better conforms with the general capabilities and resources of this country."[12] In the West, where pragmatism is juxtaposed to dogma and where Russia's "general capabilities" were weak, these formulae inspired cautious optimism. But in Russia's near abroad, where pragmatism implies cynicism and where, even in 2000, Russia's general capabilities were strong, it was clear that a harder policy was about to emerge. In the South Caucasus, that presentiment was underscored by the rigorous prosecution of the second Chechen war.

Whereas everyone understood that in genealogical terms, Putin was the product of the KGB, fewer grasped that in sociological terms, he was the product of the new class that emerged in the Darwinian conditions of the 1990s: business-minded, ambitious, nationalistic, and coldly utilitarian about norms and rules. Putin not only reflected the self-confidence of this new class, but also its resentments and its belief that Yeltsin-era "chaos" and the West's "unipolar moment" were consciously and organically connected. Putin's generation is not Gorbachev's generation. This sociological difference presents a telling discontinuity with the low-risk, consensus seeking political cultures of the post-Cold War West. Moderation, compromise, and respect for others have not been the hallmarks of Russia's new class. On coming to power, their instincts lent themselves to a tough and "pragmatic" geo-economic policy, backed by a revival of state power.

Yet geo-economics was unlikely to be the end of it. NATO's first eastern enlargement occurred in June 1999. Then and since, Russia's fundamental indictment of NATO was tautological. Because NATO was deemed to be an anti-Russian alliance, its expansion proved its aggressiveness. Even in Yeltsin's time, mere handfuls of people in Russia gave credence to the sincerity of NATO's post-Cold War transformation. Enlargement put the issue beyond the range of rational argument. The fact that NATO's model of defense reform in new member states did not emphasize territorial defense but soft security and expeditionary capabilities far from national borders was deemed neither noteworthy nor relevant.

It is fateful that this initial enlargement coincided with Operation Allied Force, NATO's military intervention in Yugoslavia. From the moment the first NATO bomb fell on Serbia, NATO could no longer claim to be a "strictly defensive alliance": a shift that Moscow not only noted but also subjected to worst-case analysis, enhanced by the dogmas that the Serbs were a kindred people and that Yugoslavia lay "in the vicinity of Russia's borders." Even five years earlier, during NATO's *United Nations Security Council-sanctioned* intervention in Bosnia-Herzegovina, 66 percent of Russians said they would regard a NATO air strike on Serbia as tantamount to a strike on Russia.[13] Not surprisingly, thoughts in Russia's military establishment turned to how NATO's new tools—civil society mobilization, "coercive diplomacy," and "humanitarian intervention"—could be used to break up other "problematic" states, not least on the borders of the Russian Federation itself. In the words of the Armed Forces newspaper, *Kasnaya Zvezda*, "today they are bombing Yugoslavia but thinking of Russia."[14] In the words of Lieutenant General Leonid Ivashov, then Head of the Ministry of Defense's International Cooperation Directorate, "[i]f the world community swallows this large-scale aggression, this barbarity, then it is today difficult to say who will be next, but there will be a state that is going to be next in line without fail." In April 2000, the first Military Doctrine of the Putin era defined "employment of military force military-force for 'humanitarian intervention'" as a "destabilizing factor" in the military-political environment.[15]

It is equally fateful that in 2004, the first wave of European Union (EU) enlargement coincided with Ukraine's Orange Revolution, which the Kremlin regarded as a US special operation from beginning to end. The Orange Revolution was instrumental in solidifying the conviction that the United States and its allies wished to emasculate Russia's influence, damage its security, and undermine its political order. In this dramatically changed context, the 1990s view of the EU as a geopolitical counterbalance to the United States was gradually but comprehensively revised. After the treaties of Amsterdam, Nice, and the 2003 Treaty of Accession, Russia already was coming to terms with the fact that the EU, in its essence, was an integration project, designed to institutionalize norms of business, law, and administration—not to say political and social life—at variance from those that prevailed in the post-Soviet world. To Moscow the Orange Revolution demonstrated that the EU was a geopolitical project every bit as much as NATO. NATO increasingly defined as a "military-civilizational" force, provided the military component to this new "civilizational schism." Public acceptance that Russia was under civilizational attack soon followed. In March 2007, a plurality of Russians (45 percent) described Russia as a "distinctive Eurasian civilization."[16]

The Orange Revolution stimulated Moscow to launch a counter-revolution designed to inoculate Russia against a colored revolution on its own territory as well as undermine those that had already taken place. In Ukraine, energy had already been deployed as a coercive tool of influence as early as the gas crisis of December 1999–April 2000 (which, unlike the subsequent crises of 2006 and 2009, largely escaped the West's attention). It was not only a coercive tool, but a means of binding and enriching local elites wedded to a "networked" as opposed to rules-based modes of business in what remained a collusive, opaque, and Russian dominated sector. Other sectors—banking, defense, and much of heavy industry— had a similar collusive quality, enhanced by the commercialization of "special services" and their prominence in leading economic entities with interests and investments abroad. As Agnia Baranauskaite noted some years later, even EU membership would afford limited protection against entrenched *nomenklaturist* networks, weak regulatory structures, corruptible politicians, and law enforcement.[17] Even before the Orange Revolution, business was already becoming a potent means of advancing what Dmitry Trenin called the "CIS Project," whose "main instrument would be the securing of understandings with the governing elites of CIS countries." This would demand:

> long-term and detailed work in forming and promoting groups of influence in neighboring countries oriented to Moscow and the gradual weakening and neutralization of pro-Western circles.[18]

None of these developments persuaded the EU that the time had come to view itself as a geopolitical entity. The technocratic mindset, the "win-win" ethos, and the absorption with programs and process were just too strong. The conviction that what was good for Central Europe would prove beneficial to Russia ignored the immutable reality that it could not prove beneficial to the stake-holders of the clientelist, vertically managed system that Putin and his inner circle had constructed. For its part, NATO took Russian anxieties more seriously. But the steps that induced Russia to prime the mechanism of conflict with Georgia—the Western recognition of Kosovo's independence (February 2008) and the NATO Bucharest Summit (April 2008)—were responses to more immediate interests. Nine years after the Kosovo conflict, most NATO allies were persuaded of the merits of a clean break with a post-conflict status quo that appeared unsustainable. Two months later, but not for the first time, NATO put Alliance unity ahead of geopolitical foresight. No one doubted that the Bucharest Summit declaration—Georgia and Ukraine "will become members of NATO"—would dissatisfy Russia. But Russia had been dissatisfied before without devastating consequences.

The miscalculation on the West's part was fourfold. First, it underestimated the significance of the change that had taken place in Russia. Russia was no longer a partner with manageable grievances, but a proud, resentful, and self-confident power that was no longer seeking Western approval. Second, the West underestimated the extent to which its own power had become overstretched and attenuated by years of inconclusive war in Afghanistan and Iraq. Third, it failed to appreciate that Russia had acquired usable military power and was prepared to use it. Fourth, it failed to grasp that six years of Train and Equip and Sustainment and Stability Operations had done nothing to address Georgia's prime security requirement: defense of national territory.[19] On the outbreak of hostilities, the most combat capable of Georgia's four brigades was on deployment in Iraq.

Between August 8–12, 2008, Russia conducted a 1940s-style combined arms operation with 1970–80s technology. Despite 25 percent per annum growth in nominal (15 percent in real) defense expenditures between 2002 and 2005, striking deficiencies emerged in execution. But these deficiencies were secondary to the fact that a Distinctive Partner of NATO was defeated without reprisal and that NATO's edifice of partnerships was shown to be lacking in mettle. By rights, the West's post-Cold War orthodoxies should have fallen to the ground. But this did not happen. Instead, three changes prolonged their life.

The first was Dmitry Medvedev's presidency. Although Medvedev took up office three months before the war with Georgia, the West with some justice did not regard this as "his" war. The five-day conflict crudely mauled his diplomatic offensive for a new European Security Treaty, assiduously launched in Berlin on June 5. War or no war, the West could not possibly have embraced a treaty that, however cordially presented, would effectively neuter NATO and legitimize Russia's "privileged" interests in the former USSR. Yet the tone of Medvedev's diplomacy, his evident lack of animus toward the West, and his sponsorship of non-commodity based "modernization" kept the cause of "normalization" alive in Western capitals. The second change was the decision to "reset" relations by the incoming Obama administration. That the Kremlin plainly regarded the reset as a policy of atonement was secondary in Washington to the presumptive common interests the two parties shared, the conviction that Russia's recent course was not economically "sustainable" and the conclusion, *pace* Vice President Biden, that Russia "needed" to take "calculated decisions" (i.e., new ones) about where its own long-term interests lay.[20] The third change was the events of the Arab spring, which reinforced the preceding postulates until the slaying of Qaddafi produced an explosion of indignation in Moscow.

Thanks to these preoccupations, Western attentiveness to the South Caucasus soon returned to its pre-war level. Yet the war in Georgia had shifted the tectonic plates. Not all of these shifts benefited Russia as much as it had hoped. Georgia was not simply a Black Sea state on the divide between East and West; it was a major trade artery, a strategic energy transit corridor, and a state enjoying a close defense partnership with Ukraine in and outside the ambit of the GUAM organization.[21] GUAM became a non-entity, but Georgia lost none of its geopolitical significance. By detaching Abkhazia and South Ossetia—and, what is more, cutting previous transport arteries—Russia had defeated Georgia and damaged it. But as Sergey Markedonov notes, "the events of August 2008 left Russia without the tools it previously possessed for exerting pressure upon Georgia, and thereby pushed Tbilisi closer to the United States."[22] Yet while the two countries concluded a Charter on Strategic Partnership in January 2009, Markedonov fails to appreciate that from this point forward, American prestige was decidedly lower than it had been before the conflict.

The seismic disturbances generated by the conflict were felt immediately by Armenia, whose lines of communication with Russia had run through Georgia. This was an ironic result for Russia, even though it underscored to Armenia just how dependent it was. The destruction of the Grakali railway bridge cost Armenia $500 million in revenue and, until its restoration was complete, 80 percent of its imports.

The lessons for non-aligned Azerbaijan were all to Russia's favor, but not immediately. The Western alliance on which Baku had placed a modicum of confidence now looked like a fair weather friend. More ominously, an explosion in Turkey three days before the war shut the Baku–Tbilisi–Ceyhan pipeline for 19 days. Its closure diminished global energy supply by only 1 percent. Yet the pipeline is not a purely commercial project: it is a lynchpin of what was then more than a decade-long US-led strategy designed to diminish energy dependency on Russia. For Azerbaijan, the result of a prolonged closure would have meant economic wreckage and geopolitical bankruptcy. Russia's message to governments and investors was therefore clear: energy projects that exclude Russia in the "former Soviet space" are inherently unsafe. To NATO, which committed itself in November 2006 to "promote energy infrastructure security," the message was equally clear: best of luck.

Russia took its setbacks in its stride and wasted no time capitalizing on its gains. The day after Medvedev and Sarkozy (on behalf of the EU) signed the September 8 agreement mandating the "complete withdrawal" of Russian "peacekeeping forces," Russia's Minister of Defense, Anatoly Serdyukov, announced that Russia would base two contingents of troops, 3800 each, in the territories. To pre-empt any charge that Moscow was violating what had just been concluded, Lavrov stated, "[t]hey are not peacekeepers. They are military contingents."

Of no less import, Moscow sought to recalibrate the contours of Azerbaijan's multi-vector policy. Yet despite the conclusion of a Treaty of Friendship in July, this undertaking did not initially produce positive results. Despite NATO's loss of prestige, the immediate lesson of the war for Baku was the danger of dependency upon Russia. Rather than deepen energy ties with Russia, Azerbaijan focused its efforts more intensively on its core market, Europe, and the EU's core project in the region, the Southern Gas Corridor. No less ambitiously, Azerbaijan re-positioned itself as Georgia's energy patron. At the peak of the Caspian oil boom, Ilham Aliyev was confident that Azerbaijan had options denied to its neighbors.

Moscow wisely decided that all things come to those who wait. As Azerbaijan's confidence in the Obama administration waned, its reinsurance policy with Russia expanded. Moscow wisely decided to facilitate this by underscoring its support for Azerbaijan's territorial integrity in May 2010 (and reminding Baku of its non-recognition of Nagorno-Karabakh's independence) and by concluding a delimitation and demarcation agreement of the 390 km border in September, to the arguable detriment of the minority Lezgin population in both Dagestan and Azerbaijan (where they number 473,000 and 186,000 respectively).[23]

Russia's most noticeable, if least strategically significant, effort was its fresh mediation effort over Karabakh. It failed like the others. But Medvedev, who grabbed and guided the process, radiated a desire to overcome obstacles and secure agreement. His efforts produced dividends for Russia, not to say a modicum of goodwill, and this reinforced Washington's perception that the crisis was over. And yet the problem was worsening.

THE NEW GEOPOLITICS

In June 2009, this author summed up the lessons of the Russia-Georgia war in the following terms:

- War is possible;
- The former Soviet borders are no longer sacrosanct;
- Questions long regarded as settled (e.g. the status of Crimea and Sevastopol) can be reopened at any moment;
- "Civilizational" and "humanitarian" factors (e.g. the status of the Russian diaspora) can constitute a *casus belli*;
- Where there is no Article 5, there is no collective defense.[24]

In Ukraine at least, any veracity contained in this forecast was occluded by Viktor Yanukovych's election in February 2010. The new president moved swiftly to address, not to say pre-empt, Ukraine's two most acute sources of friction with Russia: the Black Sea Fleet (whose withdrawal from Crimea by 2017 had been mandated by the intergovernmental agreements of 1997) and the relationship with NATO, membership of which was a top priority of Viktor Yushchenko's administration. At the Kharkiv summit of April 21, 2010, Yanukovych and Medvedev agreed to extend the Fleet's lease until 2042. In July, the *Verkhovna Rada* (parliament) adopted a law on Ukraine's "non-bloc" status. Having made these core concessions, Yanukovych concluded that Russia would not obstruct his path to a closer relationship with the EU.

He could not have been more mistaken. As early as the following month, it became clear that instead of diminishing Russia's ambitions by pre-emptive concessions, he had only whetted them. Yanukovych immediately found himself parrying Russian demands for inter-sectoral integration, the very thing he was trying to avoid. When he protested, Medvedev replied, "it's only the beginning."[25]

If to the West the new geopolitics arrived when Russia's "polite little people" appeared in Crimea, to Russia the threshold was crossed when the EU resolved to conclude Association Agreements (EUAA) with Armenia, Georgia, Moldova, and Ukraine. The first twist of the coil was the creation of the EU's Eastern Partnership, through which its Polish and Swedish sponsors hoped to reinvigorate the integrationist and democratic impulse blunted by the Russia-Georgia war and Russia's ambitious integrationist projects in the former USSR.[26] By means of these Agreements and, integral to them, Deep and Comprehensive Free Trade Areas (DCFTA), the four interested countries would benefit from 80 percent of the EU *acquis* without having to endure the rigors and political hazards of a membership process. If successful, the enterprise would circumvent EU enlargement fatigue while augmenting the EU's economic sway and political influence in east-central Europe. This was a geopolitical project in everything but name.

That it was also strongly welcomed by the recipient states was immaterial to, indeed grist to the mill of those who now assessed threats and responded to them in Moscow. This was a far narrower circle than the governing elite in place during the years of the Medvedev-Putin tandem. On returning to the presidency in May 2012, Putin reconstituted the leadership structures in a defensive and illiberal direction. The once conspicuous role of Russia's *siloviki* in the governing matrix became dominant and effectively uncontested.

This shift in regime chemistry is scarcely irrelevant to the dynamic of Russian foreign policy in the months preceding the Ukraine conflict. Between 2009 and 2011, Russia voiced displeasure with the Eastern Partnership. In 2013, it "took measures." On September 3, Deputy Prime Minister Dmitry Rogozin (who doubled as Special Presidential Representative for Transnistria) reminded his Moldovan interlocutors that "energy supplies are important in the run-up to winter—I hope you won't freeze."[27] Confident that the EU could maintain its energy security in the face of Russian pressure, Moldova's pro-European coalition disregarded Rogozin's warning and, in the event, signed the EUAA and DCFTA on June 27, 2014. Georgia also did so on the same day.

But the positions of Armenia and Ukraine were decidedly different, each in their own distinctive way. Both envisaged geopolitical, economic, and domestic political benefits from EU Association. But whereas Yanukovych primarily regarded the EUAA as a political resource to secure re-election in a strongly Europhile country, Armenians viewed it as their one alternative to a dependency upon Russia that was a source of demoralization. For this reason, Russia was determined to remove this alternative from the equation. On July 8, one of Russia's most senior envoys in the region, Vyacheslav Kovalenko, publicly reminded Armenia of the old axiom: "Armenia can only live with Russia or not at all." He went on to warn that if Armenia signed the accord as scheduled in November, "allied relations between Russia and Armenia have their boundaries."[28]The latter phrase was graphically substantiated when Putin met Armenian President Serzh Sargsyan, carrying a draft arms accord with Azerbaijan. Hours later, the latter announced Armenia's intention to join the Eurasian Economic Union (EEU).

But Ukraine's importance overshadows all else. West of the Urals, most Russians would invert Zbigniew Brzezinski's celebrated maxim: Russia *can* remain an empire without Ukraine, but it cannot remain Russia. One need not inhabit the Kremlin's febrile world to understand that Ukraine's successful incorporation into the European system would have profound consequences inside the country. Moreover, Ukraine is pivotal to the Russian-sponsored EEU—and not only in civilizational terms. As Arkady Moshes wrote in 2013, the "stagnation of Eurasian integration" makes Ukraine's inclusion "more critical than ever."[29] As a transit hub for energy and a potential *platsdarm* of the West, Ukraine's strategic importance is an article of faith. In the words of Leonid Reshetnikov, director of the President's Administration's analytical center:

> From Lugansk or Kharkov, tactical cruise missiles can reach beyond the Urals, where our primary nuclear deterrent is located. And with 100 percent certainty they can destroy silo or mobile-based ballistic missiles in their flight trajectory.[30]

The reason Lavrov omitted the EU when he stated (in April 2008) that Russia would take "all possible measures" to prevent Ukraine and Georgia from joining NATO is that then, their admission to the EU was beyond the bounds of realism, even *de facto*. By summer 2013, as the Vilnius European Partnership summit approached, it was becoming all too realistic.

The subordination of Ukraine was never going to be as simple a matter as corralling Armenia. Yet Yanukovych's ham-handed and predatory policies (which by summer 2013 were pushing Ukraine's economy to the abyss) greatly facilitated the task. On November 12, Putin presented Yanukovych with an elaborate raft of countermeasures that went well beyond the EEU's statutory provisions and which were plainly designed to inflict the maximum amount of damage not only on Ukraine's economy as a whole, but also on the financial and business interests tied to Yanukovych personally. On November 21, Moscow secured its Pyrrhic victory: Ukraine's withdrawal from the EUAA negotiations. On December 17, Yanukovych handed Russia every economic concession it had sought. The *Maidan* of 2013 no more featured in the Kremlin's calculus than the *Maidan* of 2004. One minute, Russia had secured almost everything it had sought in Ukraine since 1992. The next minute, it had no influence at all. The Crimean operation was a foregone conclusion.[31]

Yet it was also a culmination and a turning point. When Russia attacked Ukraine in 2014, it also attacked the legal and treaty regime of Europe. Before and since, it declared many landmarks of the Helsinki system—the Conventional Forces in Europe (CFE) treaty, the Budapest memorandum, the 1997 interstate treaty with Ukraine—null and void. It has thrown the 1990 Paris Charter overboard. It also has put itself in clear violation of a key component of European security since 1987, the Intermediate Nuclear Forces (INF) Treaty.

Little of this is denied. Formerly, Russia pursued "hard diplomacy and soft coercion" in the former USSR within the framework of post-Cold War rules emphasizing state sovereignty and freedom of choice.[32] In 2014, it called for "new rules" based on the Yalta principles of "balance of power" and "respect." Russia no longer conceals its ambition to transform a European and global system that its president calls "weakened, fragmented and deformed."[33] Three weeks before the line was crossed, State Duma Speaker Sergey Naryshkin warned that Europe either "relearn the lessons of Yalta" or risk war.[34]

Underpinning this change, since 2008, Russia has made a steady, cumulative investment in the capacity to wage local and regional war throughout the interior and on the periphery of the former USSR. This means full spectrum "non-linear" war, from non-attributable attacks by "polite little men" to first use of nuclear weapons. It also means information war, from disinformation to cyber-attacks, as well as a coordinated effort to "mobilize" the state.[35]

These developments have a systemic character that far exceeds the impact of the Russia-Georgia war, and they have a dynamic that has only begun to unfold. Already, they are unsettling the tectonic plates that for 22 years maintained the Nagorno-Karabakh conflict in its deceptively frozen state.

First, Crimea is not only incorporated into Russia, but is also swiftly being transformed into a rear and forward staging area of a defense system stretching from the Caspian to the eastern Mediterranean. To all intents and purposes, it is also under the jurisdiction of Russia's Ministry of Defense. In the Black Sea alone, Russia's ever more densely networked A2 AD (anti-access/area denial) capabilities have removed an important constraint against Russia's prosecution of war in the Caucasus, a point that is bound to bear on Georgia's membership prospects in NATO. As if to underscore this point, on July 10, 2015, Russia chose the occasion of a NATO-Georgia exercise to move the border of South Ossetia 1.5 km further into Georgian territory, incorporating one kilometer of the Baku–Supsa pipeline in the process. NATO's exercise ended on schedule, as if nothing had happened. If Russia was conducting a *razvedka boem* (reconnaissance by combat), then this quiescence doubtless advanced Russia's aim of showing Georgia that NATO is irrelevant to its security.

Second, by a combination of design and inadvertence, the war in Syria has sharply altered the relationship between Russia and Turkey. Twenty years of expanding trade and political cooperation have been swiftly reversed, if not undone. Turkey is, apart from Saudi Arabia, the only regional player of note whose core interests in the Syria conflict are at cross purposes to Russia's own. Unlike Saudi Arabia, it is also a NATO ally, a fact which in the post-2014 context affords Russia the opportunity to test the cohesion of NATO and weaken it. Prior to the downing of a Russian Su-24 on November 24, 2015, Turkey faced a Hobson's choice: either to allow Russia a *de facto* operations corridor across its territory—for the purpose of bombing the Turkmen tribes in northern Syria that Turkey is supporting—or to "escalate" the conflict. NATO's *pro forma* response scarcely concealed the extent of division and apprehension in the Alliance. As in the Ossetia episode, Moscow learned more than it deserved to know about NATO's cohesion.

For these reasons, the South Caucasus might acquire "uses" that transcend Russia's regional interests. Deterrence against what the West terms "hybrid war" rests on the perception that threats of potentially strategic importance, however indirect or small in scale, will be countered swiftly and effectively. The Baku–Supsa pipeline was built as a component of the West's strategic energy infrastructure. It would be surprising if the target of Russia's border latest revision in South Ossetia were not NATO as much as Georgia. NATO's failure to respond would not have strengthened deterrence.

For Armenia, Azerbaijan, and Nagorno-Karabakh, the more salient question is how Turkey's transformed position will affect the likelihood and course of future conflict. Nine years ago, the emergence of the unified AKP government coincided with a marked turning away from a pro-American orientation and the development of an ambitious regional policy. With all its incipient difficulties, the latter emerged in the context of burgeoning trade with Russia and expanding political cooperation. In 2008–10, there was no synchronization between Medvedev's Nagorno-Karabakh mediation effort and Turkey's football diplomacy with Armenia. But the two efforts ran in parallel, because neither Turkey nor Russia viewed their respective aims as inherently conflictual. The Turkey–Russia relationship had become a factor of regional stability.

Today it is not. Were Turkey's position over Syria strong and firmly backed by NATO, then its ties to Azerbaijan might pose a considerable worry to Russia. But in conditions where Turkey and NATO are perceived to be weak and working at cross purposes, then Turkey's role in the region presents possible opportunities. For one thing, Ankara's influence over Baku is not what it was. Neither is Washington's. Between 1992 and 2010, the United States provided $327 million in defense and security assistance to Azerbaijan. During Putin's state visit to Azerbaijan in August 2013 (which included "a large delegation of ministers and other officials"), military cooperation agreements were signed that included arms transfers of some $4 billion (according to the Congressional Research Service).[36] Already in June 2013, Russia had begun delivering an earlier arms package of $1 billion (according to the respected Russian defense think tank, CAST).[37] Between 2010 and 2014, Russia supplied Azerbaijan with 85 percent of its arms imports.[38]

Moreover, President Recep Tayyip Erdogan's temperament is a problematic factor in the pursuit of Turkey's interests. Like Georgia's erstwhile president, Mikheil Saakashvili, he wraps his ego around every problem. Moscow's exploitation of Saakashvili's psyche during the 2008 crisis amounted to a classic application of "reflexive control." Should the Kremlin be tempted to "cut Turkey down to size" (and wrong-foot NATO as well), it might embark on another such enterprise. The risks and consequences, for Russia as well as Turkey (which unlike Georgia, is a NATO ally), might prove vastly more dangerous than those that followed the events in South Ossetia.

The resurgence of conflict between April 1 and April 5, 2016, is indicative of what has changed and what might still change for the worse. If there was a mastermind behind the violence that most outside analysts blamed on Azerbaijan, there is no certainty about it, and if there was no mastermind, there is no clarity about where the orders came from. What is clear is that there is no clarity. On March 31, US Vice President Joseph Biden to all accounts had a highly constructive meeting with the two national presidents in Washington. While the possibility cannot be excluded, it seems most unlikely that Ilham Aliyev would have attended the meeting in utterly bad faith. Both he and President Sargsyan were still in transit when the attack began. Some have argued that such an attack would have required much advance planning, and that it could only be authorized by the highest authority in Baku. Yet "planning" and "authorization" are two different phenomena (as the Crimea operation most recently showed). Moreover, it was a flank attack, not a drive on Stepanakert, and it is at least possible that someone else in the command chain authorized it.

There is more clarity about what happened afterwards. Putin immediately entered into intensive discussion with both presidents, and a similar process took place between Lavrov, Minister of Defense Sergey Shoygu, and their respective counterparts. The April 5 cease-fire was brokered by Shoygu. Notably, the Minsk Group co-chairs played no role in this process. According to Matthew Bryza, Putin followed these steps "by pressing Azerbaijan to join the Eurasian Economic Union and the CSTO."[39] That Russia somehow initiated the events of April may not be likely. That it had foreknowledge of them certainly is. Yet even if it had no foreknowledge, the plain fact is Moscow grasped their significance and produced an immediate, robust, and coordinated response. Whatever Washington grasped, it did next to nothing. In consequence, Russia has "reaffirmed and reinforced the local perception that [its] involvement is essential, largely to the diplomatic detriment of the two other Minsk Group co-chairs." Moreover, Baku now "views Moscow as the key to any change in what is sees as an unacceptable 'status quo.'"[40]

Since the final days of the Soviet Union, Russian, Western, and regional experts have agreed on the perils of treating the conflict in Nagorno-Karabakh as a faraway local difficulty of little import to the world around it. Yet for 30 years, more portentous and dramatic issues elsewhere have kept the issue in the margins of consciousness for all but a handful of people outside. This geopolitical configuration also supported a remarkable degree of East-West working level cooperation and accord. Russia's assault on the "weakened, fragmented and deformed" security order, beginning with Ukraine and proceeding to Syria, has brought this era to an end. Yet like the lady in the famous 1914 Lowe cartoon, we risk adhering to the comforting certainty that if things go wrong, "the powers will intervene." Such complacencies invite little wars, even big ones.

Notes

1. Thomas de Waal, *Black Garden: Armenia and Azerbaijan Through Peace and War* (New York and London: New York University Press, 2003/2013), 307.
2. Deputy Foreign Minister Fedor Shelov-Kovedyayev, "Strategy and Tactics of Russian Foreign Policy in the New Abroad" [Strategiya i taktika vneshney politiki Rossii v novom zarubezh'ye], September 1992, 2 and 4.
3. Long-standing tensions between the Autonomous Republic of Abkhazia and the Georgian Soviet Socialist Republic erupted into violence in March 1989, a month before the "massacre of spades" in Tbilisi. The Pridnestrovian Moldovan Socialist Republic was established in September 1990, and conflict between right and left bank Moldova broke out two months later.
4. Shelov-Kovedyayev, "Strategy and Tactics of Russian Foreign Policy in the New Abroad."
5. As relayed to Thomas de Waal by Igor Muradian, who added, "we weren't interested in their fate, and we're not interested now," de Waal, *Black Garden: Armenia and Azerbaijan Through Peace and War*, 22.
6. *Moskovskiye Novosti*, no. 13, 1992, 9. Cited in J.C. Oliphant, *Nationalities Problems in the Former Soviet Union* (Sandhurst: Soviet Studies Research Centre, Royal Military Academy, June 1992), 11.
7. Cited in Michael Orr, "Peacekeeping: A New Task for Russian Military Doctrine," *Jane's Intelligence Review—Europe*, July (1994).
8. *ITAR-TASS* (cited by *BBC Summary of World Broadcasts*), April 27, 1994.
9. Speech to the Civic Union, February 28, 1993.
10. Two months before Yeltsin's appeal to the UN, Clinton's National Security Advisor, Anthony Lake, stated that "the successor to a doctrine of containment must be enlargement of the world's free community of market democracies." Cited in Julien Zarifian, "U.S. Foreign Policy in the 1990s and 2000s, and the Case of the South Caucasus (Armenia, Azerbaijan, Georgia)," *European Journal of American Studies* 10, (2015): 3.
11. Sergey Markedonov, "The Cold War Legacy in Nagorno-Karabakh: Visions from Russia, the United States and Regional Actors," in *Europe's Next Avoidable War*, eds. Michael Kambeck and Sargis Ghazaryan (Basingstoke: Palgrave Macmillan, 2013), 133.
12. Vladimir Putin, "Russia at the Turn of the Millennium," December 1999. Press conference of Sergey Ivanov (then Secretary of the RF Security Council) previewing the new Concept of Foreign Policy, *BBC Summary of World Broadcasts*, March 28, 2000.

13. *Izvestiya*, February 5, 1994.
14. *Krasnaya Zvezda* [Red Star], March 27, 1999.
15. Voyennaya Doktrina Rossiyskoy Federatsii, ukazannom prezidenta No. 706, April 21, 2000.
16. VTsIOM [All-Russian Centre for the Study of Public Opinion], March 16, 2007.
17. Agnia Baranauskaite, "Russian Influence in the Baltic States: Legacies, Coercion, and Soft Power," *Chatham House Briefing Paper*, February 2012.
18. "Moscow's Realpolitik: Russia Withdraws into Post-Soviet Space" [*Realpolitik Moskvy: Rossiya zamiykaetsya v postsovetskom prostranstve*], *TsentrAzia*, February 9, 2004.
19. The 18-month Georgia Train and Equip Programme (GTEP) was established in 2002 in response to the crisis in the Pankisi gorge and, initially, with the endorsement of President Putin. Its successor, established in a far less friendly climate, was a small command (subordinate to a lieutenant colonel), providing training for unit level (as opposed to combined arms) "crisis response operations" in multi-national peace-keeping operations rather than territorial defense.
20. Interview with *Wall Street Journal*, July 25, 2009.
21. GUAM stands for Georgia, Ukraine, Azerbaijan, Moldova. It is officially known as the Organization for Democracy and Economic Development—GUAM.
22. Markedonov, "The Cold War Legacy in Nagorno-Karabakh: Visions from Russia, the United States and Regional Actors," 130.
23. Mairbek Vatchagaev, "Lezgin Leader Assassinated in Dagestan," *Eurasia Daily Monitor* 13, no. 63, March 31 (2016).
24. Sherr, "Living Through Bad Times," in *National Security and Defence*, no. 2 (106) (Ukrainian Centre for Economic & Political Studies, 2009), http://www.uceps.org/eng/files/category_journal/NSD106_eng.pdf
25. "Medvedev: It's only the beginning" [*Medvedev: 'Eto tol'ko nachalo'*], *Glavred*, May 17, 2010, www.glavred.info; "Yanukovych: "it's impossible to work so quickly," Medvedev: "we must"" [Yanukovich: 'tak bystro rabotat' nel'zya' Medvedev: 'Pridyetsya'], *Glavred*, July 17, 2010.
26. The proposal for an Eastern Partnership was tabled by Swedish Foreign Minister Carl Bildt and Polish Foreign Minister Radek Sikorski in May 2008, and the Partnership came into effect in May 2009.
27. Laurence Peter, "Armenia Rift Over Trade Deal Fuels EU-Russia Tension," *BBC News*, September 5, 2013, http://www.bbc.co.uk/news/world-europe-23975951
28. "Ex-Russian Envoy Warns Armenia Over European Integration Drive," *RFE/RL*, July 8, 2013.

29. Arkady Moshes, "Will Ukraine Join (and Save) the Eurasian Customs Union?," Policy Memo 247, *PONARS Eurasia*, April (2013).

30. http://world.lb.ua/news/2012/07/10/160111_zatulin_putin_edet_krim_smenu.htm. Note the revealing addition: "At present, this region is inaccessible to them [U.S. anti-missile systems] from Poland, Turkey or Southeast Asia."

31. For a fuller analysis of the Russia-Ukraine conflict, see James Sherr, "A War of Narratives and Arms," in *The Russian Challenge*, eds. Keir Giles, Philip Hanson, Roderic Lyne, James Nixey, James Sherr, and Andrew Wood (London: Chatham House Report, June 2015).

32. For a full exposition, see James Sherr, *Hard Diplomacy and Soft Coercion: Russia's Influence Abroad* (London: Chatham House, 2013).

33. President Putin, "Speech to 9th Session of the Valdai Club," October 24, 2014. Also Foreign Minister Lavrov's March 2015 annual statement, where he emphasized the dangerous contradiction between an increasingly "polycentric" world and "persistent attempts by the 'historical' West to preserve global leadership at all costs," http://en.kremlin.ru/events/president/news/46860

34. "Dialogue rather than War: Sergey Naryshkin calls upon Western leaders to study the 'lessons of Yalta'" [*Dialog a ne voyna: Sergey Naryshkin prizva liderov Zapada uchit' "uroki Yalty"*], *Rossiyskaya Gazeta* (hereafter RG), February 5, 2015.

35. James Sherr, *The New East-West Discord: Russian Objectives, Western Interests* (The Hague: Netherlands Institute of International Relations, Clingendael report, December 2015); Written Evidence to House of Commons Defence Committee, February 2016; Keir Giles, "Russia's 'New' Tools for Confronting the West: Continuity and Innovation in Moscow's Exercise of Power," *Chatham House Research Paper*, March (2016); Andrew Monaghan, "Russian State Mobilization: Moving the Country on to a War Footing," *Chatham House Research Paper*, May (2016).

36. Jim Nichol, "Armenia, Azerbaijan, and Georgia: Political Developments and Implications for U.S. Interests," *Congressional Research Service*, April 2, 2014, 11 and 45, https://www.fas.org/sgp/crs/row/RL33453.pdf

37. "Russia Starts Delivering $1 Billion Arms Package to Azerbaijan," *Reuters*, June 18, 2013, http://www.reuters.com/article/us-russia-azerbaijan-arms-idUSBRE95H0KM20130618

38. Marko Marjanović, "Armenian Complaints Are Misguided: Russia–Azerbaijan Arms Trade Is to Yerevan's Advantage," *Russia Insider*, April 17, 2016, http://russia-insider.com/en/politics/armenians-are-wrong-complain-moscow-arming-azerbaijan-really-their-advantage/ri13929

39. Matthew Bryza, "The Nagorno-Karabakh Conflict Is Too Dangerous for the US to Ignore," *Washington Post*, April 11, 2016.

40. Richard Giragosian, "The Nagorno-Karabakh conflict: Ceasing Fire Is Not a Ceasefire," *LSE Comment*, April 11, 2016, http://blogs.lse.ac.uk/europpblog/2016/04/11/the-nagorno-karabakh-conflict-ceasing-fire-is-not-a-ceasefire/

CHAPTER 4

Russia: A Declining Counter-Change Force

Pavel K. Baev

Two-and-a-half decades on, the lack of any resolution to the Armenia-Azerbaijan conflict is met with fatigue and irritation in many international quarters. Indeed, this first of the post-Soviet conflicts has not only frustrated many efforts aimed at finding a resolution, but also prevented many initiatives on establishing security institutions in the South Caucasus region, and hindered the management of Armenian-Turkish controversies from advancing to meaningful results. In Moscow, by contrast, there is an underlying satisfaction with its not-quite-frozen status, and this content was only momentarily disturbed by the escalation of fighting in April 2016. From the Russian perspective, this deadlock prevents many external powers (and first of all, the United States, and also Turkey) from gaining influence in this troubled region, and secures for Russia a position of effective dominance. The problem with this low-cost conflict management, aimed at preserving the status quo, is that the balance of local forces and the interplay of regional interests are fast changing, particularly in the course of the Russian-Turkish conflict caused by the Russian intervention in Syria. Moscow is lagging behind the shifting dynamics, clinging instead to habitual instruments that are hardly suitable for the task of maintaining a status quo which may very well have become unsustainable.

The root causes and the trajectory of the Armenian-Azerbaijani conflict over Nagorno-Karabakh have been examined in great detail in the existing literature on the subject. Thomas de Waal's book *Black Garden* especially stands out in terms of the depth of analysis of amassed unique material.[1] There is no need, therefore, to re-examine the making of Russia's policy toward this conflict or the actions of the two main protagonists to it in the post-Soviet period up until

P.K. Baev (✉)
Oslo, Norway

S.E. Cornell (ed.), *The International Politics of the Armenian-Azerbaijani Conflict*, DOI 10.1057/978-1-137-60006-6_4

recently. However, the explosion of the Ukraine conflict since the beginning of 2014 has led to a profound impact on all Eurasian conflicts—an impact which remains under-researched as Russia engages deeper in the evolving confrontation with the West as well as with Turkey. This chapter aims at examining this impact in the particularly demanding and mostly overshadowed case of Nagorno-Karabakh. It starts by siting the conflict within the shifting geopolitical landscape of the Caspian/Black Sea area, before assessing the influence of the counter-revolutionary impetus on Russian conflict management in this case. It further examines the particularity of this conflict in the category of "frozen conflicts," which has undergone radical change with the addition of Crimea and the Donbass region of Eastern Ukraine, and continues by evaluating the impact on this conflict of the even greater changes in the geo-economics of Caspian hydrocarbons. The conclusion argues that Russia is underestimating the risks of shifting dynamics at play.

A Small "Black Hole" in the Big Geopolitical Picture

Grand geopolitical perceptions, particularly that of the "multi-polar world" in which Russia is destined to be one of the "emerging powers" challenging the dominance of the West—and principally the hegemony of the USA—have been gaining in popularity among the Russian political class since the beginning of the 2000s. While correlating to a certain extent with the reality of global processes, this picture has become seriously misleading. Russia's role in the world has changed beyond its own capacity to comprehend with its aggressive move of annexing Crimea; this role continues to evolve as the Ukraine crisis drags on and as the Syrian intervention indicates. The confrontation with the West has become a crucial condition of Putin's regime survival—and it remains to be seen for how long Moscow can sustain this confrontation.[2] The problem certainly goes far beyond the limited scope of this analysis, but what is relevant here is the huge concentration of Russian efforts and thinking on engaging in this confrontation—to the degree that opposing Western, particularly USA and also Turkish, encroachments into Russia's immediate neighborhood is now the prime political aim in the Caucasus and the wider Black Sea area.[3] This preoccupation fits perfectly with the pronounced tendency of Caucasian elites, as well as among the general public, to place their particular problems into grand geopolitical contexts and to see local conflicts as driven by clashes of major global interests allegedly focused on the Caucasian crossroads.[4]

What makes the geopolitical setting of the Armenia-Azerbaijan conflict particularly complicated for Russia is the perceived need to keep both protagonists—Armenia and Azerbaijan—within the Russian sphere of influence and to check any drift toward the West. In the autumn of 2013, Moscow effectively prevented Armenia from signing an Association Agreement with the European Union (EU). But while a similar Russian action triggered the *Maidan* uprising in Kiev, it encountered little opposition in Yerevan, and so Armenia proceeded smoothly with joining the Eurasian Economic Union.[5] Nevertheless, this confirmation of geopolitical loyalty to Russia has not erased suspicions concerning Armenia's ties with the West, and Moscow continues to watch anxiously every step in Yerevan's relations with Brussels.[6] For its part, Azerbaijan had never contemplated an Association Agreement with the EU and keeps a low profile in the Eastern Partnership; but neither has it ever expressed interest in joining the Eurasian integration process.[7] Moscow is suspicious about Baku's connections with the North Atlantic Treaty Organization (NATO), but generally assumes that the maturing of an authoritarian regime in Azerbaijan, which it sees as a perfectly natural development, sets a rather low limit to these ties.

One crucially important and significantly ambivalent power in the geopolitical puzzle of the South Caucasus is Turkey. Moscow had, until the Turkish downing of a Russian bomber on November 24, 2015, paid great attention to engaging Ankara in a special relationship. Moscow viewed Turkey's long-established membership in NATO (despite all the anti-Alliance rhetoric) as much less of a problem than its close ties with Azerbaijan, which are seen as a major driver in the conflict over Nagorno-Karabakh. At the same time, Moscow viewed the possibility of the normalization of relations between Turkey and Armenia as a hostile US intrigue aimed at eroding Russia's influence in the region.[8] Seeking to prevent any breakthrough in this old deadlock, Putin paid a visit to Yerevan in May 2015 and spelled out the loaded word "genocide," knowing full well that it would reverberate strongly in Turkey.[9] Indeed, his meeting with President Erdogan in Baku during the European Games in June 2015 was rather strained and showed few signs of their good personal relations.[10] Erdoğan's visit to Moscow in September 2015 further failed to resolve any disagreements, and the crisis in bilateral relations triggered by the November 24 incident has acquired an intensely personal character. Azerbaijan sought to stay out of the quarrel, but its position between the two antagonists is precarious indeed.[11]

Georgia is a major target for, and a serious complication in, Russian geopolitical power play in the South Caucasus, with the legacy of the Russia-Georgia War of 2008 continuing to affect regional security. Since the start of the Ukraine conflict, Georgia has been cautious not to provoke Moscow's ire but has nevertheless proceeded with the implementation of its Association Agreement with the EU. Russia has also refrained from overtly aggressive moves, assuming that the "Georgian Dream" coalition is far better from a Russian perspective than Mikheil Saakashvili's government. Nonetheless, Moscow is clearly irritated by the establishment of a NATO Training Center in Tbilisi.[12] Neither diplomatic intrigues nor direct pressure can change the geopolitical fact that Georgia blocks Russia's military access to Armenia, and thus limits its ability to project power toward the Nagorno-Karabakh theater.

The de-escalation of tensions between the West and Iran in the course of the implementation of the nuclear deal and its impact on geopolitical interactions in the South Caucasus did not prove immediately clear to policy-makers in Moscow. The pattern of Russian-Iranian military partnership in Syria is also far from certain.[13] The United States will presumably lose interest in acquiring a military "foothold" in Azerbaijan, even if the proposition for making it a part of an anti-Iranian coalition was always far-fetched. It is doubtful whether a re-energized Iran would be able to increase its influence in Azerbaijan, but it would definitely prefer and even insist upon the reduction of tensions regarding Nagorno-Karabakh.[14]

Overall, Russia has had no reason to suspect a sudden increase of Western geopolitical stakes in the enduring rivalry between Armenia and Azerbaijan. However, this hardly grants Moscow greater freedom of maneuver because, having ensured the ineffectuality of the Minsk Group, it has to contain the escalation of tensions by its own efforts. Recycling the old proposition for peacekeeping forces is definitely not enough for such a containment, while Moscow's policy of supplying weapons to both parties works against it.

TURNING BACK THE TIDE OF "COLOR REVOLUTIONS"

Geopolitical constructs in Russian foreign policy are combined in a far from coherent way with a major ideological imperative: the determination to withstand and turn back the tide of "color revolutions." This counter-revolutionary stance has shaped Russia's aggressive policy toward Ukraine, and it also has high salience in the Caucasus, where Georgia is seen as a dangerous propagator of revolutionary ideas.[15] It is certainly the West, and principally the United States, that is seen as the instigator and manipulator of revolutionary movements, but Russia's goals in countering these "conspiracies" are significantly different from a classical geopolitical competition.[16]

Despite being a fully committed security ally, Armenia is actually perceived in the Kremlin with some suspicion regarding its readiness to stand firm against the threat of "color revolutions" and eliminating opposition to the ruling regime. The explosion of street protests in Yerevan in June and July 2015, for instance, was interpreted by the Russian leadership as a coup attempt, and portrayed by the Kremlin-controlled propaganda machine as directed by the inherently hostile West. The rejection of this narrative by the Armenian leadership, which sought to address the economic causes of the leaderless protests, was seen in Moscow as showing softness toward a potential "*Maidan*."[17] President Putin has good reason to see Armenia's track record in applying force against public uprisings as dubious, and probably for this reason has never developed a useful personal rapport with President Serzh Sargsyan, or with Robert Kocharyan in the first half of the 2000s.

By contrast, the Putin regime views Azerbaijan as a solid force in the struggle against the threat of revolutions, and unlike Azerbaijan's Western partners, Moscow finds the repressive measures deployed by the Azerbaijani government perfectly agreeable.[18] Azerbaijan scores top marks in Russian assessments of political stability in the Caucasus, there having hardly been any concerns about the hidden pool of discontent in times of economic slowdown.[19] Despite all the differences in family upbringing and career development, Vladimir Putin and

Ilham Aliyev have always enjoyed good personal relations, even if this chemistry does not necessarily translate into congruence of political aims.

Russia finds it important to build a coalition of like-minded post-Soviet regimes against the menace of "color revolutions" and seeks to make the security institutions, namely the Collective Security Treaty Organization (CSTO), into structures of such a coalition.[20] The problem with this joint effort is that Armenia, which tends to focus on the root causes of protests rather than label them Western "instigations," is a full member of the CSTO while Azerbaijan is not.[21] In any case, it has become painfully clear that none of the authoritarian regimes in the former Soviet space are going to support in any meaningful way Russia's fight against the revolutionary influence spreading from Ukraine. At the same time, the need to provide support to fellow regimes in distress might become a challenge for Russia's already overstretched power-projection capabilities.

Russia also sought to find a common approach with Turkey in opposing revolutionary chaos, assuming that the Erdoğan regime was evolving along the same trajectory as Putin's and expecting a blossoming of the two leaders' "beautiful friendship." These expectations never quite came true, even while both leaders tried to bracket out their disagreements over Syria until late 2015. Presently, the desire in the Kremlin to exact revenge on Erdoğan is so intense that Moscow shows readiness to support any opposition, including even the Kurdish extremists.[22]

What has happened instead is the maturing of personal ties between Presidents Erdoğan and Aliyev. Aliyev successfully dissuaded Erdoğan from looking for opportunities to revive ties with Armenia, and both were keen to exploit the summer turmoil in Yerevan in 2015 for increasing the pressure in the Nagorno-Karabakh cauldron of conflict.[23] Russia was taken by surprise with the escalation of hostilities along the cease-fire line in August 2015, and had to resort to some emergency shuttle diplomacy in order to ensure that it remained relevant in managing the conflict.[24] The meeting between Aliyev and Sargsyan in Bern in December 2015 was fruitless, however, and Moscow saw no reason to worry about a new escalation of firefights in February 2016.

Overall, Russia's propensity to over-react to the threat of revolutionary uprisings is set to increase as its own domestic Putin-centric stability is eroding under the inescapable pressure generated by the deepening economic crisis.

MILITARY BUILDUP AND THE TRANSFORMATION OF SECESSIONIST CONFLICTS

Nagorno-Karabakh used to be treated as a quintessential "frozen conflict"— one which was habitually discussed in various international fora (including in the EU Eastern Partnership framework) without much hope for achieving a breakthrough. The explosion of the Ukraine conflict has not just added two new cases to the list—Crimea effectively annexed by Russia and "rump

Novorossiya" in the Donetsk and Luhansk regions secured by the Minsk agreements—but altered radically the whole context of this European problem. What had been seen as an undesirable but bearable fact has started to be recognized as an acute security challenge that must be treated accordingly. It appears entirely probable that this change of attitude constitutes one of the key factors driving the renewed efforts at finding a solution for the problem of divided Cyprus and thus resolving the oldest of the "frozen conflicts" in Europe.[25]

Policy-makers in Moscow do not appear to have fully comprehended the scope of change in the context of this old problem. While resolutely insisting that Crimea cannot be treated as part of it, since it is formally incorporated into the Russian Federation, the Kremlin remains ambivalent about the status of the rebel "republics" in Eastern Ukraine. Moscow also asserts that Abkhazia and South Ossetia are not Georgia's secessionist provinces but sovereign states, while proceeding with their effective incorporation into Russia's state structures.[26] By mid-2015, it had become clear that the plan for blazing a "corridor" across Southern Ukraine reaching toward Transnistria involved a long leap of strategic imagination, so the existence of this quasi-state in Moldova is just a function of sustaining the deployment of a very limited contingent of Russian troops, while Ukraine has resolutely stopped all military transit.[27]

This leaves Nagorno-Karabakh as a unique case in the deconstructed category of "frozen conflicts," and as events in April 2016 showed, the intensity of violent clashes arguably merits it inclusion in the group of ongoing violent conflicts. What only a few years ago to many Europeans seemed to represent a typical ethno-political conflict caused by the collapse of the USSR is now, post-Crimea, an attempt to redraw Azerbaijan's state borders by force. Moreover, what may have been considered justifiable from the point of view of the self-determination of an oppressed minority is now unacceptable as an attempt to camouflage an annexation of a part of territory of a neighboring state by referring to the "people's will."[28] In this context, the statements of Azerbaijan's top officials regarding the readiness to solve the Nagorno-Karabakh problem by force cannot now be dismissed as usual hollow bravado but have to be taken seriously as an expressed intention to restore violated state sovereignty.[29]

Azerbaijan's capacity for such a *reconquista* is by no means assured. Despite Baku's officially established policy of spending on its military more than Armenia's whole state budget, a policy now sustained for many years, there are doubts whether this can be sustained given the dip in global oil prices. Russia has actually been a major contributor to (as well as beneficiary of) this policy, selling modern armaments to Azerbaijan that range from T-90S tanks and Mi-35 M attack helicopters to S-300PMU-2 surface-to-air missiles.[30] It is remarkable that Baku decided to turn to Russia for acquisitions of heavy weapons only in 2009, immediately after the Russia-Georgia war. By 2014 the Russian share in its import of arms had reached an impressive 85 percent, amounting to $3.5 billion.[31] Armenia is not able to match this scale of rearmament (the largest known arms deal with Russia involved 35 T-72B tanks) and has expressed concern about the large-scale arms deals between Russia and Azerbaijan. Baku, for its part, protested against a new $200 million loan for purchasing weapons provided by Moscow to Yerevan in February 2016.[32] Russian officials maintain, however, that the arms deliveries are carefully calculated in order to preserve the "parity."[33]

Azerbaijan disregards any notion of military parity, and is keen to test the fortified Armenian defenses around Nagorno-Karabakh. In August 2014, there was a surge in exchanges of fire along the cease-fire line, followed by a hit on an Armenian helicopter on November 12. The 72 registered casualties on both sides made 2014 the worst year since the freezing of the conflict in 1994.[34] August 2015 saw the escalation of fighting reaching yet a new high, with some 150 fire exchanges reported every day and casualties mounting accordingly.[35] This spasm of fighting started soon after the visit to Moscow of Azerbaijani Defense Minister Zakir Hasanov and his reportedly cordial talks with his Russian counterpart, Sergei Shoigu.[36] While Moscow dispatched Foreign Minister Sergei Lavrov to Baku, it generally remained unconcerned about the situation assuming that the conflict remained safely "frozen" and that President Aliyev would not dare launch a real offensive.[37] Winter 2016 saw even greater indifference from the Russian leadership to the constant exchanges of heavy gunfire, which culminated in the "four-day war" of April 2016. These assumptions might underestimate, however, the impact of the downward shift in the economic situation, which affects Russia's own foreign policy-making as well as its conduct of the "hybrid war" in Ukraine and intervention in Syria.

THE OIL FACTOR IN CONFLICT DYNAMICS

The downturn in economic fortunes in Russia, as well as in Armenia and Azerbaijan, since the middle of 2014 has been very sharp. Policy-makers do not appear to have grasped yet the consequences of the recession, which according to the steadily worsening forecasts could be both deep and long-lasting. In fact, Russia's economy never regained the strong growth of the early 2000s, interrupted by the severe crisis of 2008–09, and showed a clear propensity to stagnation already in 2013. Thus, the combined effect of Western economic sanctions and the drop in oil prices to a new plateau less than half the average price in 2010–13, pushed it in 2015 deep into "negative territory" that was set to continue through 2016. This new reality calls for a profound revision of political ambitions and guidelines, but the Kremlin has remained essentially in denial of this paradigm change, instead insisting that oil prices will return to "normal" in a year or two, thus erasing the need for structural reforms.[38]

Russia's decline, and in particular the shocking weakening of the ruble, affects very strongly the Armenian economy, which depends heavily upon trade with and remittances coming from Russia. It is common knowledge that the increase in electricity prices, which triggered protests in Yerevan in summer 2015, was executed by Russian investors who owned the Armenian energy grid.[39] The expectations and official promises regarding the benefits for Armenia of joining the Russia-led Customs Union and Eurasian Economic

Union have been disappointed as the structures of economic cooperation have instead become transmitters of contraction and capital flight; and even the granted reduction of price for imported gas cannot compensate for this.[40]

Azerbaijan is also hit by the disruption of economic ties with Russia (including remittances), but a greater disaster for its economy is delivered by the collapse of oil prices, which has caused chaos in the financial sector.[41] The plans for diversifying the economy, particularly by becoming a key transit hub for China's Silk Road Economic Belt, will only deliver dividends slowly, while the cost-inefficiency of many high-prestige projects has become undeniable and the possibility of social unrest caused by the fall of household income is rising.[42] One direct consequence of the contraction of petro-revenues will be the shrinking of the overblown defense budget (estimated at about $5 billion for 2015, before the twin devaluations of the manat) and the reduction of funding for arms imports by as much as half.[43] This inability to sustain the military buildup may determine a change of course toward the conflict over Nagorno-Karabakh. On one hand, it could lead the Azerbaijani leadership to conclude that the best opportunity to score a military victory is now, in a situation where the combat readiness of the armed forces will be undercut by diminished funding in the near future.[44] *This may have played a role in the Azerbaijani offensive in April 2016.* On the other hand, it may lead an elite busy with pocketbook issues to further postpone high-risk military action.

For many years, it was the work on constructing an energy link between the Caspian area and European markets, and even more so the designs for expanding the modest flow of oil and gas to a wide "corridor," that effectively blocked any escalation of conflicts in the South Caucasus in general, and in Nagorno-Karabakh in particular. Since the start of this decade, however, the significance of Caspian hydrocarbons for Europe has steadily declined. The fiasco of the much-advertised Nabucco gas pipeline project became a major manifestation of this trend, while the follow-up fiasco of Russia's rival South Stream project was also entirely predictable.[45] Azerbaijan engaged in furious lobbying with Turkey in order to secure the transportation to Southern Europe of the new volumes of natural gas from the off-shore Shah Deniz field. It succeeded in creating the combination of TANAP/TAP pipelines, which has been further accelerated as a result of the Russian-Turkish confrontation.[46] The proposition for linking Turkmenistan to this "corridor" via a Trans-Caspian pipeline is still under discussion, but it looks increasingly far-fetched, as a more interesting prospect shapes up with the opening of a route connecting Iranian gas fields with Europe.[47] Azerbaijan has a slim chance to link with these new designs (which are still quite uncertain) and faces a bitter reckoning with the reality of its position as a minor supplier in a saturated market, in which Russia will be struggling to keep its share. Moreover, its reputation as a reliable supplier suffered from a fire on the Guneshli off-shore oil platform in December 2015, which revealed serious problems in the state-owned SOCAR corporation.[48]

Overall, the oil-and-gas projects may no longer be a significant deterring factor in the Nagorno-Karabakh conflict transformation, but the accumulated petro-revenues in the form of the arsenal of modern weapons in Azerbaijan are a major driver for a probable new eruption of hostilities.

Conclusion: Can Russia Control the Conflict Dynamics?

There are so many factors of change at work in the South Caucasus that Russia finds it all but impossible to reconcile its own diverging interests. It used to see oil and gas flows as the main driver of political activities, but in fact, the significance of energy has been on the wane for several years, and the sustained drop in oil prices has reduced it even further, with negative prospects for recovery. The Kremlin is obsessed with the threat of "color revolutions" and is determined to lead the struggle against this menace, which brings it closer to Azerbaijan, and the personal rapport between Putin and Aliyev works to reinforce this counter-revolutionary "axis." At the same time, the single most important material fact on the South Caucasian ground is the presence of the 102nd Russian military base in Armenia, which hosts some 5000 troops and two Air Force squadrons (including Mig-29 fighters and Mi-24 helicopters).[49] Russia may have no intention to get directly involved in the next spasm of hostilities around Nagorno-Karabakh, and seeks to limit the strategic tasks of its grouping to counter-balancing Turkey's engagement with Azerbaijan, but the loyalty of this "lost legion" is far from rock solid, and its behavior in a crisis situation could turn maverick.

One strong determinant of Russia's interests is the scope of Western engagement. Had the EU and the USA shown a propensity to increase their activities in the South Caucasus, Moscow would likely have responded in kind. The West, however, is clearly cutting down on its engagements, and so the Russian leadership feels no need to countervail.[50] Moscow does still monitor every trip EU or US officials undertake to the region, but generally Moscow tends to assume that suggestions about introducing a peacekeeping force into the conflict zone in and around Nagorno-Karabakh is merely a diplomatic charade aimed at keeping up the pretense that the Minsk Group is still involved in meaningful work.[51] Russia maintains the Minsk routines but prefers its own formats, such as the trilateral Sochi meeting between Putin, Aliyev and Sargsyan in August 2014.[52] The lack of success does not bother Moscow much as long as nothing else brings a chance of a breakthrough. Indeed, Lavrov was perfectly comfortable with recycling old plans for deploying Russian peacekeepers that are plainly unacceptable for both Armenia and Azerbaijan, and Putin had nothing to say to Sargsyan in response to his warnings about the rise of tensions in their September 2015 meeting.[53]

In the super-centralized system of decision-making that has rigidified in Russia, the amount of attention accorded to strategic non-priority issues (and the Caucasus falls into this category) is extremely limited, particularly given the need to prioritize petty squabbles between the Kremlin courtiers, none of whom has any stakes in the South Caucasian conflicts. Putin presently has to add the Middle Eastern intrigues to three key strategic matters—the Ukraine conflict, the confrontation with the West, and the "pivot" to China, which leaves Armenia and Azerbaijan far outside the Kremlin's proverbial "radar screen." Furthermore, whereas violent instability in the North Caucasus had previously drawn utmost attention, this problem is presently perceived as solved. This was symbolized by the Sochi Winter Olympics in February 2014, the staging of which had been a long-prepared political triumph. Of course, there are in fact many forces at work against the "pacification" of that region. The murder of Boris Nemtsov on February 27, 2015, brought into focus Moscow's astounding lack of control over Ramzan Kadyrov's despotic regime in Chechnya, and the outbreaks of clan infighting in Dagestan in summer 2015 indicated that the tensions in this malignant seat of conflicts are on the rise.[54] The FSB is monitoring the flow of volunteers to the ranks of ISIS in Syria (Azerbaijan is also facing this problem), but Putin prefers to address this challenge through projecting air force in Syria and spinning political intrigues in the Middle East.[55] It is the inevitable reduction in the transfers of federal funds that determines the growth of discontent in the North Caucasus, and Moscow could experience a rude awakening to yet another explosion of hostilities in this troublesome "underbelly."

The Russian leadership is clearly not prepared to contemplate the consequences of the deepening economic crisis for political stability in the South Caucasus, much the same way as it tends to take the continuation of political inertia in Russia for granted. There are, nevertheless, strong indications that the potential for conflict is increasing, which might yet bear out the multiple predictions of a new round of war occurring around Nagorno-Karabakh.[56] In Armenia, the government is challenged not so much by street protests as by the growth of uncontrollable social networks, and it seeks to re-establish its monopoly on shaping the political agenda by boosting the security discourse. In Azerbaijan, deeper problems could lead to a shift of focus toward the external threat. The stability of the regime was, but no longer is, underpinned by steady economic growth and trickling-down of petro-revenues, and the power-holders have little way of estimating the possible reaction in seriously over-populated Baku on the reduction of incomes, remittances and social benefits. They are also concerned about the increase in influence of a re-energized Iran, which is one reason Aliyev paid a visit to Tehran in February 2016.[57] One pertinent lesson of the Ukraine crisis for Azerbaijan is that "patriotic" mobilization works perfectly well in upholding Putin's popularity in times of serious economic troubles. This certainly increases the pressure on the leadership to deliver on the many promises to resolve the Karabakh problem by force, since diplomacy has obviously been unable so far to produce anything resembling a solution. The escalation of hostilities in April 2016 released some of this pressure, but it has also generated a new momentum in experimenting with the use of military instruments.

President Aliyev cannot, of course, hope to secure Moscow's consent for a large-scale offensive on the Karabakh front but he discovered in April 2016 that such consent may be not necessary. Indeed, it is not difficult to envisage some turns of events that would make Russia indifferent to an escalation of the on-going clashes to a small-scale war, in which it actually has no direct stake. One such development could be yet another explosion of street protests in Yerevan, which the Kremlin could interpret as a recurrent "color revolution," in which case Azerbaijan could exploit the uncertainty and argue through high-level channels to the Kremlin that a revolutionary Armenia has lost its value for Russia as a strategic ally. Another opportunity could arise in the case of a possible spread of violent clashes across the North Caucasus, which would effectively tie Russia's hands and make it impossible to provide any effective support to Armenia. Finally, a scenario of serious violent turmoil in Moscow is now also within the realm of the possible. Putin's regime may turn out to be far less stable than it seems—and it cannot afford to give up the grasp on power without a fight. It might be informative to reflect on the coincidence of the escalation of fighting around Sukhumi in October 1993 with tanks deciding the outcome of a severe political crisis in Moscow.

Russia is caught in a self-made trap whereby its resources available for a "muscular" foreign policy are fast diminishing, and yet its ambitions to prove that the confrontation with the West does not diminish Russia's ability to make a difference on the global arena are increasing. The conflict over Nagorno-Karabakh may well be the place where the workings of this trap become clear, as Moscow would be paralyzed by the dilemma of abandoning Armenia, a security ally in distress, or confronting Azerbaijan, another friendly regime. Much the same way as the collapse of the USSR triggered a chain reaction of conflicts in the Caucasus, Russia's sinking into troubles could generate a new destabilizing resonance in which Nagorno-Karabakh constitutes the epicenter of this security quake.

NOTES

1. The revised edition has many updated additions; see Thomas de Waal, *The Black Garden: Armenia and Azerbaijan Through Peace and War* (New York & London: New York University Press, 2013). Noteworthy also is Chapter 6 ("The war over Karabakh") in Christoph Zürcher, *The Post-Soviet Wars: Rebellion, Ethnic Conflict and Nationhood in the Caucasus* (New York & London: New York University Press, 2007). For a perspective from the Azerbaijani side, there are no peers to Thomas Goltz, *Azerbaijan Diary* (London: Routledge, 1999). One recent theory-informed analysis is Laurence Broers, "From 'frozen conflict' to enduring rivalry: Reassessing the Nagorny Karabakh conflict," *Nationalities Papers* 43, no. 4 (2015): 556–576.

2. My examination of this change is in Pavel K. Baev, "Russia reinvents itself as a rogue state in the ungovernable multi-polar world," in *The State of Russia: What Comes Next?*, eds. Maria Lipman and Nikolai Petrov (London: Palgrave Macmillan, 2015).

3. This preoccupation is evaluated in Stephen Blank, "US policy, Azerbaijan, and the Nagorno Karabakh conflict," *Mediterranean Quarterly* 26, no. 2 (2015): 99–114.

4. A useful updated analysis of the conflict dynamics is Fiona Hill, Kemal Kirişci, and Andrew Moffatt, *Retracing the Caucasian Circle: Considerations and Constraints for U.S., EU, and Turkish Engagement in the South Caucasus* (The Brookings Institution: Turkey Project Policy Papers Series), No. 6, July 2015, http://www.brookings.edu/research/reports/2015/07/south-caucasus-engagement. A careful Russian review of this report is Sergei Markedonov, "The Geometry of the Caucasian Circle," *RIAC Analysis*, August 18, 2015, http://russiancouncil.ru/inner/?id_4=6473#top-content.

5. On Putin's visit to Yerevan in December 2013, see Yuri Simonyan, "Putin has ruled" [in Russian], *Nezavisimaya Gazeta*, December 4, 2013, http://www.ng.ru/cis/2013-12-04/3_kartblansh.html. Note: titles of articles from Russian-language news sources have been translated by the author into English.

6. A positive view on these ties is Richard Youngs, "Armenia as a showcase for the new European Neighborhood policy?," *Strategic Europe*, April 2, 2015, http://carnegieeurope.eu/strategiceurope/?fa=59617; for a more skeptical view on Donald Tusk's visit to all three South Caucasian states in summer 2015, see Irina Dzhorbenadze, "To tick the Caucasus agenda," *Rosbalt*, July 24, 2015, http://www.rosbalt.ru/exussr/2015/07/24/1421924.html

7. The "never say never" message from Azerbaijan's Foreign Minister Elmar Mamadyarov was merely a diplomatic joke; see Sohbet Mamedov, "Baku is in no rush to join the Eurasian Union," *Nezavisimaya Gazeta*, October 2, 2015, http://www.ng.ru/cis/2015-10-02/7_azerbaijan.html

8. A sharp view on these prospects is Armen Grigoryan, "Turkey-Armenia relations and Turkey's elections," *CACI Analyst*, May 27, 2015, http://www.cacianalyst.org/publications/analytical-articles/item/13225-turkey-armenia-relations-after-turkey%E2%80%99s-elections.html

9. See Igor Gerasimov, "The Kremlin rejected Turkish complains about Putin's words on Armenian genocide," *RBC.ru*, April 24, 2015, http://top.rbc.ru/politics/24/04/2015/553aa7599a79471b6d6d4fe5

10. On the context to that meeting, see Orhan Gafarli, "Putin and Erdogan meet in Baku: Will the balance of power change in the South Caucasus?," *Eurasia Daily Monitor*, June 25, 2015, http://www.jamestown.org/

programs/edm/single/?tx_ttnews%5Btt_news%5D=44079&cHash=c
d6bc6f5131756bc9ba5dfaf0512780b#.Vvzda_mLTIU

11. See on this Vugar Gasanov, "Baku in the clutches of conflict between
Ankara and Moscow," *Nezavisimaya Gazeta*, February 16, 2016,
http://www.ng.ru/cis/2016-02-16/3_kartblansh.html

12. See Liz Fuller, "Georgia-NATO relations in thrall to previous miscalculations," *RFE/RL Caucasus Report*, September 3, 2015, http://www.
rferl.org/content/georgia-nato-relations-thrall-past-
miscalculations/27224738.html

13. See M.K. Bhadrakumar, "Russia, Iran coordinate moves on Syria," *Asia
Times*, February 17, 2016, http://atimes.com/2016/02/russia-iran-
coordinate-moves-on-syria/

14. Armen Grigoryan, "Armenia and the Iran Deal," *CACI Analyst*,
August 31, 2015, http://www.cacianalyst.org/publications/analytical-
articles/item/13263-armenia-and-the-iran-deal.html. On the modest
positive results of Aliyev's visit to Tehran in February 2015, see Sohbet
Mamedov, "Iran and Azerbaijan launch the North-South project,"
Nezavisimaya Gazeta, February 25, 2016, http://www.ng.ru/
cis/2016-02-25/6_azerbaijan.html

15. This perspective can be found in Alexei Fenenko, "Russia's Georgian
prospects," *Nezavisimaya Gazeta*, September 3, 2015, http://www.
ng.ru/cis/2015-09-03/3_kartblansh.html

16. Aleksei Tokarev, "Reaction on colour," *Kommersant-Vlast*, July 24,
2015, http://kommersant.ru/doc/2791306

17. One sober analysis of this manageable crisis of governance is Aleksandr
Artemyev, "The end of barricades: Why protests will not lead to a revolution in Armenia," *RBC.ru*, July 6, 2015, http://top.rbc.ru/politics
/06/07/2015/559a95f89a79473bc3268bac. See also Vadim
Dubnov, "Why protests in Armenia will not turn into a Maidan,"
Carnegie.ru, June 29, 2015, http://carnegie.ru/2015/06/29/
ru-60518/ib5t

18. One good example of European criticism is Jules Boykoff, "European
leaders should boycott autocratic Azerbaijan's mini-Olympics," *The
Guardian*, June 3, 2015, http://www.theguardian.com/commentis-
free/2015/jun/03/azerbaijan-european-games-human-rights

19. On these assessments, see Pavel Tarasenko, "The South Caucasus states
are ranked by political risk," *Kommersant*, August 19, 2015; and Ilya
Karpyk, "The prospects of the South Caucasus," *Polit.ru*, August 20,
2015, http://polit.ru/article/2015/08/20/kavkaz/

20. For a passionate argument in favour of this coalition-building, see
Aleksandr Bartosh, "CSTO targets colour revolutions," *Nezavisimoe
voennoe obozrenie*, April 11, 2014, http://nvo.ng.ru/wars/2014-04-
11/1_odkb.html

21. I have examined the limitations of this institution in Pavel K. Baev,
"The CSTO's role in Russian reintegration efforts," in *Putin's Grand*

Strategy: The Eurasian Union and Its Discontents, eds. S. Frederick Starr and Svante Cornell (Stockholm and Washington D.C.: Central Asia-Caucasus Institute & Silk Road Studies Program, 2014).

22. See on that Simon Tisdall, "Turkey's rising tensions with Russia over Kurds puts Erdogan in a corner," *The Guardian,* February 9, 2016, http://www.theguardian.com/world/2016/feb/09/ever-heightening-tension-putin-puts-turkey-in-a-corner

23. See Alexei Malashenko, "Escalation in the zone of conflict is a gamble with unforeseeable outcome," *Carnegie.ru,* July 3, 2015, http://carnegie.ru/2015/07/03/ru-60597/icxi

24. On Foreign Minister Lavrov's visit to Baku, see Sohbet Mamedov, "Armenia and Azerbaijan are back to the brink of war," *Nezavisimaya Gazeta,* September 1, 2015, http://www.ng.ru/cis/2015-09-01/6_baku.html

25. On these as yet fruitless efforts, see Jacopo Barigazzi, "Cyprus settlement deal 'within reach,'" *Politico,* January 18, 2016, http://www.politico.eu/article/cyprus-settlement-deal-within-reach-reunification-ali-talat-anastasiades/

26. See Robert Orttung and Christopher Walker, "Putin's frozen conflicts," *Foreign Policy,* February 13, 2015, https://foreignpolicy.com/2015/02/13/putins-frozen-conflicts/. Russia has forced Abkhazia to enforce sanctions against Turkey; see Svetlana Samodelova, "Abkhazia and the Turkish gambit," *Moskovsky Komsomolets,* February 4, 2016, http://www.mk.ru/social/2016/02/04/abkhaziya-i-tureckiy-gambit-chem-zhivet-respublika-podderzhavshaya-sankcii-rossii.html

27. See Neil Buckley, "Transnistria shapes up as the next Ukraine-Russia flashpoint," *Financial Times,* June 3, 2015, http://blogs.ft.com/the-world/2015/06/transnistria-shapes-up-as-next-ukraine-russia-flashpoint/; and Svetlana Gamova, "Russian troops in Transnistria are surrounded by police," *Nezavisimaya Gazeta,* August 27, 2015, http://www.ng.ru/cis/2015-08-27/1_ms.html

28. On this shift, see Elena Pokalova, "Conflict resolution in Frozen conflicts: Timing in Nagorno- Karabakh," *Journal of Balkan and Near Eastern Studies* 17, no. 1 (2015): 68–85.

29. For this interpretation of a recent statement of this sort, see Yuri Matsarsky, "Azerbaijan is ready to return the Nagorno Karabakh territory by military means," *Kommersant-FM,* August 7, 2015, http://kommersant.ru/doc/2783505

30. For a competent overview of trends in arms exports to the South Caucasus, see Andrei Frolov, "Military build-up in the South Caucasus: An arms race?," *RIAC Analysis,* July 10, 2014, http://russiancouncil.ru/inner/?id_4=4026#_ftnref9

31. See Sohbet Mamedov, "Azerbaijan has turned to Russian arms," *Nezavisimaya Gazeta,* November 28, 2014, http://www.ng.ru/armies/2014-11-28/2_azerbaijan.html

32. See "Baku made a protest to Moscow about Armenian import of Russian arms," *Lenta.ru*, February 24, 2016, https://lenta.ru/news/2016/02/24/azerbajdzhanmfa/

33. Nikolai Bordyuzha, CSTO Secretary General, feels obliged to stick to this argument; see "Bordyuzha: Russia sells weapons to Azerbaijan preserving parity with Armenia," *RIA-Novosti*, June 18, 2015, http://ria.ru/defense_safety/20150618/1076504936.html. See also Felicity Capon, "Russia 'Arming Armenia and Azerbaijan' as Hostilities Increase," *Newsweek*, February 17, 2015, http://europe.newsweek.com/russia-arming-armenia-and-azerbaijan-hostilities-increase-307443

34. See Thomas de Waal, "The Karabakh truce under threat," *Eurasia Outlook*, February 12, 2015, http://carnegie.ru/eurasiaoutlook/?fa=59049

35. The data on ceasefire violations and casualties from both sides is registered by Kavkazsky uzel; see for instance, "Nagorno Karabakh blamed Azerbaijan in breaking the truce," *Kavkazsky uzel*, September 5, 2015, http://www.kavkaz-uzel.ru/articles/268411/

36. See Stanislav Tarasov, "What were the talks between Russian and Azerbaijani defence ministers about?," *Regnum.ru*, August 2, 2015, http://regnum.ru/news/polit/1948306.html

37. See Pavel Tarasenko and Olga Kuznetsova, "Sorting out keys to Nagorno Karabakh," *Kommersant*, September 2, 2015, http://www.kommersant.ru/doc/2801180

38. On the miscalculations regarding the oil price, see Mikhail Krutihin, "Why oil price will not go up for a few more years," *RBC.ru*, August 25, 2015, http://daily.rbc.ru/opinions/economics/25/08/2015/55dc9e129a7947e58a58e29f; on the need for reforms, see Sergei Aleksashenko, "History repeats itself: Could Putin use the window of opportunity?," *RBC.ru*, August 17, 2015, http://daily.rbc.ru/opinions/economics/17/08/2015/55d1bd159a79476e6478f87a

39. See Victoria Panfilova, "Cold integration shower for Armenia," *Nezavisimaya Gazeta*, June 24, 2015, http://www.ng.ru/cis/2015-06-24/1_armenia.html

40. On the malfunctioning of cooperation, see Arshaluis Mgdesyan, "Economic decline in Armenia: Who is to blame and what to do?," *Kavpolit.com*, August 6, 2015, http://kavpolit.com/articles/ekonomicheskij_spad_v_armenii_kto_vinovat_i_chto_d-18912/. President Sargsyan was uncharacteristically blunt about the economic pains in the meeting with Putin in September 2015; see the transcript of his remarks at http://kremlin.ru/events/president/news/50250

41. See Aydin Mammadov, "Azerbaijan's economy hit by banking crisis," *Silk Road Reporters*, July 23, 2015, http://www.silkroadreporters.com/2015/07/23/azerbaijans-economy-hit-by-banking-crisis/

42. On the opening of the Baku-Tbilisi-Kars rail link and how it fits in with Silk Road designs, see Sohbet Mamedov, "From Beijing to Baku in six days," *Nezavisimaya Gazeta*, July 31, 2015, http://www.ng.ru/cis/2015-07-31/1_azerbaijan.html. On the risk of social unrest, see Nailia Bagirova, "Azerbaijan watches for dissent as economy slows," *Reuters*, March 3, 2015, http://www.reuters.com/article/2015/03/03/azerbaijan-economy-idUSL5N0W41PT20150303

43. Russian assessments of this decline are still rather superficial; see Stanislav Tarasov, "Azerbaijan's oil age is coming to an end," *Regnum.ru*, August 22, 2015, http://regnum.ru/news/polit/1955839.html

44. This reasoning is weighed in Youri Smakouz, "Azerbaijan: Falling economy, rising Karabakh war risk," *Eurasianet.org*, May 14, 2015, http://www.eurasianet.org/node/73426

45. For an early prediction that neither of the two bitterly competing projects would be implemented, see Pavel Baev and Indra Øverland, "The South Stream versus Nabucco pipeline race," *International Affairs* 65, no. 5, May (2010): 1075–1090.

46. This narrow "corridor" still signified an important connection; see on that Margarita Assenova and Zaur Shiriyev, eds., *Azerbaijan and the New Energy Geopolitics of Southeastern Europe* (Washington D.C.: Jamestown Foundation, 2015), particularly the chapter by Vladimir Socor and Matthew Czekaj, "Southeastern Europe energy nexus: A crossroads of pipelines and geopolitics," 3–62.

47. See on this Mikhail Serov, "Turkmen gas comes closer to Europe," *Vedomosti*, June 8, 2015, http://www.vedomosti.ru/business/articles/2015/06/08/595685-turkmenskii-gaz-priblizhaetsya-k--evrope

48. See Filipp Prokudin, "Fire power," *Lenta.ru*, December 7, 2015, https://lenta.ru/articles/2015/12/07/fire/

49. On the profile of this base, see John C. K. Daly, "Armenia clashes with Russia over arms sales," *Silk Road Reporters*, April 7, 2015, http://www.silkroadreporters.com/2015/04/07/armenia-appeals-to-csto-over-russian-arms-sales-to-azerbaijan/

50. The reduction of Western attention is clearly identified and lamented in Svante E. Cornell, S. Frederick Starr, and Mamuka Tsereteli, *A Western Strategy for the South Caucasus* (Stockholm and Washington D.C.: Central Asia-Caucasus Institute & Silk Road Studies Program, Silk Road Paper, February 2015).

51. Reflections on the recent trip to Armenia of U.S. Ambassador James B. Warlick Jr. can be found in Yuri Roks, "The Karabakh prospects," *Nezavisimaya Gazeta*, July 22, 2015, http://www.ng.ru/cis/2015-07-22/6_karabah.html. Aliyev has recently expressed dissatisfaction with the "senseless" activities of the Minsk Group but refrained from any criticism of Russia's stance; see Sohbet Mamedov, "Aliyev has sent

a signal to world politicians," *Nezavisimaya Gazeta*, February 1, 2016, http://www.ng.ru/cis/2016-02-01/6_aliev.html

52. On the atmosphere of that meeting, see Alina Sabitova, "We must show tolerance, wisdom and mutual respect," *Kommersant*, August 10, 2014, http://kommersant.ru/Doc/2542749

53. On Lavrov's platitude see John C. K. Daly, "Possible introduction of Russian peacekeepers into Karabakh is opposed by Armenia," *Eurasia Daily Monitor*, August 31, 2015, http://www.jamestown.org/programs/edm/single/?tx_ttnews[tt_news]=44310&tx_ttnews[backPid] =27&cHash=c6d7f3b2881689380f8b13901dc539b4%20-%20. VeXXv5f3hBw#.Ve2pMJf3hBw; and on the Putin-Sargsyan meeting, Yuri Roks, "Putin and Sarsyan compared notes," *Nezavisimaya Gazeta*, September 8, 2015, http://www.ng.ru/cis/2015-09-08/6_armenia. html

54. This clan struggle is exposed in Alexei Malashenko, "Said Amirov: What is behind the fall of the second most important politician in the North Caucasus," *Carnegie.ru*, August 31, 2015, http://carnegie. ru/2015/08/31/ru-61141/ifdr

55. A concise evaluation of these intrigues is Alexei Malashenko, "Russian-Shia alliance in the heads and in politics," *Vedomsti*, January 26, 2016, http://www.vedomosti.ru/opinion/articles/2016/01/27/625601- rossiisko-shiitskii-alyans. On the quality of expertise in Putin's policy-making in the Middle East, see Georgy Mirsky, "Putin, his consultants and unimportant ISIS," *Moscow Echo*, December 17, 2015, http:// echo.msk.ru/blog/georgy_mirsky/1678716-echo/

56. One very convincing prediction of this kind is Georgi Derluguian, "All quiet on the Karabakh front?," *PONARS Eurasia Memo* 66, George Washington University, September 2009, http://www.ponarseurasia. org/memo/all-quiet-karabagh-front

57. See on these worries Eldar Mamedov, "Azerbaijan: Iran nuke deal would be a mixed bag for Baku," *Eurasianet.org*, April 17, 2015, http://www.eurasianet.org/node/73021

Turkey's Role: Balancing the Armenia-Azerbaijan Conflict and Turkish-Armenian Relations

Svante E. Cornell

In 20 years since the collapse of the USSR, Turkey has established itself as a middle power in the South Caucasus. Turkey's influence has been mainly in the area of energy, transport and trade, while its role in the security issues in the region has been more limited. Two chief factors have limited Turkey's position in the region. A first is the shifting priorities of Turkey's foreign policy, in which the Caucasus has often been an afterthought; the other is the realities of the region, and primary among them, the Armenian-Azerbaijani conflict.

THE CAUCASUS IN TURKISH FOREIGN POLICY

Turkey's location ensures that its foreign policy-makers face a competition for attention between various priority areas, ranging from Europe to the Middle East and beyond. Over the past 20 years, moreover, Turkey has experienced a considerable economic boom—a development which has seen it become a member of the G20, prompting Turkish leaders to consider the country a player on the global scale. Among the many competing priorities in a fast-changing world, the Caucasus has seldom been a top item on Ankara's radar. Its importance has, to a large extent, been the function of the ideological priorities of Turkey's leaders. In fact, the importance accorded to the Caucasus is almost a direct function of the affiliation of Turkish politicians.

S.E. Cornell (✉)
Nacka, Sweden

© The Author(s) 2017
S.E. Cornell (ed.), *The International Politics of the Armenian-Azerbaijani Conflict*, DOI 10.1057/978-1-137-60006-6_5

Turkish nationalists, of course, prioritize relations with their ethnic kin, meaning a particular affinity for Azerbaijan—but one that is not necessarily translated for affinity with the Aliyev administration. In fact, in 1995 Turkish ultra-nationalists were even involved in a coup attempt against Heydar Aliyev, whom they opposed for his role in overthrowing the more pan-Turkic presidency of Abulfaz Elçibey. This episode has largely been forgiven, however, and Turkey's Nationalist Movement Party (MHP) keeps close ties with official Baku. Turkish nationalists, for reasons mainly unrelated to Azerbaijan, also harbor a strong hostility to Armenia, whom they accuse of having territorial designs on Turkey, blaming it also for what they allege to be falsifications of history.

Turkish liberals, by contrast, are focused mainly on Turkey's ties with the West. They feel little affinity for the eastward Turkic republics, which they tend to consider to be authoritarian and nationalistic, and thus too reminiscent of the Kemalist Turkey they have sought to reform. Thus, Turkey's liberals have no particular affinity for Azerbaijan. Instead, they tend to be supportive of the recognition of the Armenian massacres as genocide, something that is part and parcel of their efforts to have Turkey face the darker pages of its history. As a result, they tend to support the opening of the Armenian border, and to oppose the notion of an "Azerbaijani veto" on Turkey's policy toward the Caucasus.

Turkish Islamists are, for the most part, disinterested in the Turkic world, since their identity is focused on religion, not ethnicity. Their main interest lies in the core Islamic lands of the Middle East, whereas they tend to consider the faith of former Soviet Muslims as corrupted by Communist atheism. Most Azerbaijanis, moreover, are Shi'a, unlike the strongly Sunni Turkish tradition, thus creating a further distance for Turkish Islamists. Turkish Islamists also tend to be heavily critical of the Kemalist experience, which they see themselves as victims of, and thus, to be less adamant about opposing Armenian claims regarding events a century ago. As a result, paradoxically, Turkey's Islamists have been less partial to Azerbaijan and more accommodating toward an opening to Armenia.

Turkish mainstream politicians of the center-left and center-right fall in-between these different ideological poles. Generally speaking, they have tended to be focused on Turkey's ties with the West, but receptive also to elements of the nationalist discourse. They have thus espoused a positive, though occasionally condescending, attitude toward the Turkic former Soviet republics, including Azerbaijan. This is counterweighed only by the fact that the hostile relationship with Armenia has proved a diplomatic headache, confronting Turkey with continuous efforts to secure international genocide recognition, as well as obstructing Turkey's relations with key EU members. Yet mainstream Turkish politicians have tended to be influenced by the strategic thinking of the Turkish establishment, which has held that the Caucasus and Central Asia are important strategically to Turkey, not least as a transshipment point for Eurasian energy resources.

The collapse of the Soviet Union in 1991 led to a short period of pan-Turkic euphoria in a Turkey that had just seen its membership bid for the European Communities rejected in 1989. Yet, in large part due to the Armenian-Azerbaijani conflict, it soon became clear that Turkey was in no position to replace Russia as the new dominant power in the Caucasus and Central Asia. Instead, by the mid-1990s, the Turkish leadership settled on a more pragmatic approach that focused on the building of the east-west transportation corridor, particularly for Caspian energy, while simultaneously working to build cooperative institutions. This included Turkic cooperation summits, but also the Organization of the Black Sea Economic Cooperation (BSEC). This policy was based on a rock-solid alignment with Azerbaijan on the Nagorno-Karabakh issue, while simultaneously pledging Turkey's good offices to resolve the conflict—a notion that Armenia, predictably perhaps, rejected.

The arrival of the (initially) softly Islamist AKP government[1] in late 2002 gradually changed matters. Accordingly, the intensity of Turkish interest in the Caucasus markedly declined, as the AKP initially focused its efforts on managing Turkey's ties to the EU. Gradually, however, the AKP abandoned this focus for a relentless, and largely unsuccessful, bid for regional leadership in the Middle East. Throughout this period, attention to the Caucasus remained largely on autopilot, which has allowed the primacy of Azerbaijan in Turkish policy to remain in force—that is, with the notable exception of the aborted effort at Turkish-Armenian reconciliation in 2009–10, discussed in detail below.

This policy is not surprising. Even leaving aside the ethnic and linguistic ties connecting Turkey and Azerbaijan, pragmatic considerations led Turkey to embrace a policy that prioritized not only Azerbaijan but also Georgia, the pro-Western countries of the Caucasus that formed the east-west corridor. Indeed, from lukewarm relations undermined by historical hostility in the early 1990s, Turkey and Georgia had by the end of the decade developed a strategic partnership. The logic behind this rested on the common interest in countering Russian efforts to dominate the Caucasus, and to open the Caucasus as an access point for the Caspian Sea and Central Asia. Furthermore, as a country with an armed separatist movement of its own, it is not surprising that Turkey sided in the conflicts in the region with the defenders of the principle of territorial integrity—Azerbaijan and Georgia—against Armenia, which promoted the principle of self-determination. From Turkey's perspective, Azerbaijan's energy resources increased its strategic importance, and indeed, it was clear by 1994 that Azerbaijan's oil and natural gas would soon make it the economic powerhouse of the region, with a GDP that would soon be worth twice that of Georgia and Armenia combined. What is more, Azerbaijan is the only country bordering both Iran and Russia, and thus inescapable for the east-west corridor to Central Asia—a perspective which renders Armenia and Georgia interchangeable.

Undergirding these pragmatic concerns is the reality that foreign policy is determined by domestic politics; and Turkish policy cannot ignore the heavily pro-Azerbaijani sentiment of the Turkish population. Indeed, the maxim "one nation, two states" has come to be repeated frequently enough to have acquired strong roots in Turkish society. To most Turks, certainly at the popular level, the restoration of relations with Armenia is tied not only to Armenia renouncing claims of genocide, but also to the Armenian withdrawal from occupied territories in Azerbaijan.[2]

NAGORNO-KARABAKH AND TURKISH-ARMENIAN RELATIONS

When Armenia and Azerbaijan became independent in December 1991, Turkey was the first country to officially recognize both, an indication of its interest in establishing positive relations with the two countries. However, this ambition foundered on the rapid escalation of the Nagorno-Karabakh conflict in which Turkey faced considerable pressure to take sides. While the initial position of Turkey's leaders was to offer its good offices to resolve the conflict and mobilize its Western connections to raise attention to the escalating conflict, realities on the ground made this an untenable policy. The massacre of Azerbaijani civilians at Khojaly in February 1992 led to massive anti-Armenian demonstrations across Turkey clamoring for a Turkish military intervention. Following Khojaly, Armenian advances on the battlefield—particularly the fall of Shusha in May—led to growing public outrage as footage of fleeing Azerbaijanis filled Turkish television screens, and pushed Turkish leaders to taking a clear stance in support of Azerbaijan as a victim of Armenian aggression. Turkish opposition leaders demanded a stronger Turkish position, seeing Turkish inaction as a threat to Turkey's ambition to gain influence across the former Soviet space. Main opposition leader Mesut Yılmaz demanded that Turkey deploy troops along the Armenian border. By March 1992, Prime Minister Demirel warned that calls for Turkish intervention had become difficult to resist while President Turgut Özal warned that Armenians needed to be "scared a little bit."[3]

The logic of domestic politics therefore led Ankara to clearly take Azerbaijan's side in the conflict. That said, during 1992 Turkey continued to allow Western aid to Armenia to transit its territory, while inspecting shipments for possible weapons. Turkey and Armenia also worked to establish diplomatic relations, but that effort failed, largely because of factors unrelated to the Armenian-Azerbaijani conflict. Indeed, Turkish-Armenian relations were a factor mainly of Armenian diaspora efforts since 1965 to obtain international recognition of the 1915 massacres of Ottoman Armenians as genocide. These efforts, and the campaign of Armenian terrorism against Turkish targets in the 1970s and 1980s, had generated ferocious Turkish resistance mainly because of fears—whether exaggerated or not—that such recognition would result in Armenian territorial claims on Turkey. Indeed, both diaspora organizations and Armenian parliamentarians issued such demands. As a result, the Turkish government sought a formal recognition by Armenia of the common border in order to open diplomatic relations.[4] Armenian leaders, however, refused to include what they termed a "superfluous" declaration to that effect, arguing that such mutual recognition was implicit in the establishment of diplomatic relations.[5] Yet Armenian leaders also knew that the general public—not to speak of the diaspora—would not look kindly on an official recognition of its border with Turkey, as it would imply renouncing Armenia's moral right to what was largely seen as historical Armenian lands.[6] This problem would return in 2009, when the Armenian National Committee of America opposed Turkish-Armenian protocols on the grounds, among others, that they constituted "renouncing the rightful return of Armenian lands."[7]

In early 1993, Turkey closed its border with Armenia. The border issue had little, if anything, to do with that of diplomatic relations. Turkey closed the border as a response to the Armenian army's direct intervention in March and April 1993 to capture the Azerbaijani district of Kelbajar, a largely Azerbaijani- and Kurdish-populated region wedged between Armenia and Nagorno-Karabakh. Following this event, President Özal stated that "all communications and transport links between Armenia and Turkey had been severed and would remain so until Armenia withdraws from all territory in Azerbaijan."[8] This event marked the first major instance of Armenian occupation and ethnic cleansing of Azerbaijani territories outside Nagorno-Karabakh.

Thus, the reasons for the want of Turkish-Armenian diplomatic relations and for the closure of the border are different—one having to do solely with the acrimonious Turkish-Armenian history, and the other with the Armenian-Azerbaijani conflict. Indeed, this commonly overlooked fact elucidates the linkage between the Turkish-Armenian relationship and the Armenian-Azerbaijani conflict.

Turkey's siding with Azerbaijan prevented it from being a major force in the international efforts to resolve the conflict. Ankara did become a member of the Commission on Security and Cooperation in Europe's (CSCE) Minsk Group, though Armenian objections ensured that Turkey never took an active role in the negotiations, and was never seriously considered as a co-chair of the group.

Turkish-Azerbaijani Relations and the East-West Axis

As noted, Turkey defined Azerbaijan as the strategically most important country in the Caucasus. Azerbaijan was a logical strategic pillar for influence in the wider region because of the close ethnic affinity, linguistic proximity, petroleum wealth and its strategic location as the only Caucasian state on the Caspian Sea. As Süha Bölükbasi has noted, Turkey's foreign policy priorities toward Azerbaijan have included: support for Azerbaijan's independence; support for Azerbaijan's sovereignty over Nagorno-Karabakh; a desire to limit Russian dominance in the South Caucasus; to ensure Turkish participation in the production and export of Azerbaijani oil through Turkey; and the preservation of a friendly, though not necessarily pan-Turkist, government in Baku.[9]

These goals were pursued with relative success by successive Turkish governments, in spite of continuing political instability in Turkey that included a short-lived Islamist-led government in 1996–97, and an ensuing military intervention in 1997. Most important in this regard were two partnerships: first, the trilateral partnership between Turkey, Azerbaijan and Georgia; and second, Turkey's strategic partnership with the United States. In combination, through these Turkey worked to support the economic and political independence of countries in the Caucasus, and specifically through the development of the energy and transportation corridor through the South Caucasus.

The main achievement of this project was the completion of the Baku-Tbilisi-Ceyhan oil pipeline in 2005 and of the Baku-Erzurum gas pipeline the following year. Both projects benefited from strong American support, which proceeded in spite of efforts by the Armenian diaspora to block the projects as they were considered to bypass Armenia. By contrast, objections by the Armenian diaspora succeeded in blocking not only American but also European support for the Baku-Tbilisi-Kars (BTK) railroad line. In fact, the railroad project was necessary because Turkey's closure of the Armenian border led to the closure of the Kars-Gyumri railroad. Armenian diaspora organizations successfully argued that the BTK project was designed only to bypass Armenia. This led to a long delay in the implementation of the project; but following the completion of the twin pipeline projects, BTK became part and parcel of a broader vision of an "Iron Silk Road" connecting Europe to China by rail, with the link between Turkey and Azerbaijan being one of two missing links, the other being the connection between the European railway grid and Turkey's Anatolian railroads. The Marmaray project connecting the European and Asian shores of Istanbul will resolve the latter link. Significantly, the BTK project proceeded without financial support from Western banks, because Azerbaijan's newly found oil wealth enabled it to provide favorable financing for the construction of Georgia's portion of the project.[10]

Nevertheless, Turkish-Azerbaijani relations have not been devoid of tensions. From the mid-2000s, new leaders took office in both capitals. Compared to their predecessors, Heydar Aliyev and Süleyman Demirel, Ilham Aliyev and Tayyip Erdoğan had much less in common. While Turkish officials implemented all projects that had been launched, it rapidly became clear that Turkish leaders were focused on other matters—at first, on relations with the EU, and later, Turkey's ambitions of leadership in the Middle East. Paradoxically, therefore, energy issues became a matter of discord. This related mostly to Turkey's aim to establish itself as an energy "hub" for Europe—one that would acquire energy at lower prices in the east, and sell it at higher prices in the West, in a manner reminiscent of Gazprom's operations in the late 1990s. This ambition, and the general lack of coordination of Turkish energy policy, was the main reason for long delays in the negotiation of a transit agreement for the second stage of the Shah Deniz field's natural gas.[11] Already in 2008, this lack of a transit agreement led to delays in the development of the field; only in late 2011 was a deal reached. This delay led to souring relations between the two governments, undoubtedly complicated by Turkey's shift in an increasingly Islamist direction, while Baku stuck to a staunchly secularist domestic policy.

THE TURKISH-ARMENIAN PROTOCOLS

When Ankara closed the border with Armenia in 1993, it made its reopening contingent on Armenia's withdrawal from Azerbaijani territories. While Turgut Özal's comments, quoted above, indicated this meant *all* occupied territories, including Nagorno-Karabakh itself, the Turkish position subsequently became more nuanced. Turkey has not been a major participant in negotiations, but it has indicated that it would be willing to use the potential of opening the border as an incentive, in a coordinated step-by-step resolution of the conflict. This became particularly relevant in 2002. Shortly before he died, President Heydar Aliyev made an attempt to introduce an economic incentive to Armenia, offering the restoration of economic linkages between Armenia and Azerbaijan in exchange for the Armenian withdrawal from the four occupied provinces south of Nagorno-Karabakh. In addition, Baku pledged that it would no longer object to the opening of the Turkish-Armenian border.[12] However, Armenia's leadership rejected the offer, ensuring the continuation of Turkey's established position.

While official relations remained deadlocked, there were subtle changes under the surface. With US and European funding, numerous track-two and civil society initiatives were launched to improve Turkish-Armenian relations. In 1997, the Turkish-Armenian Business Development Council was formed, with the aim of fostering economic ties between the two countries, and to function as a go-between for communications between the two governments.[13] Subsequently, in 2001, the initiative was taken to form the Turkish-Armenian Reconciliation Commission, a three-year initiative funded by several Western governments consisting of senior but unofficial figures from both countries.[14]

By 2008, efforts to bring about Turkish-Armenian reconciliation were beginning to bear fruit. A diplomatic effort was launched after Turkish President Abdullah Gül accepted an invitation to attend a Soccer World Cup qualifier game between the two countries in Yerevan in September 2008, followed by a reciprocal invitation to President Sargsyan to Turkey the next year. The effort, which culminated with the signing of diplomatic protocols in October 2009, expired the following year over disagreements on the ratification process. But the causes for this failure remain poorly understood.

In fact, the effort was launched not primarily for reasons relating to the Turkish-Armenian relationship itself: it was prompted by two external developments, the first being the regional shakeup of the Russian invasion of Georgia, and the second being the approaching election of Barack Obama as President of the United States. For the purposes of this chapter, it is crucial to observe that the entire effort was predicated on removing the linkage between the Turkish-Armenian relationship and the Armenian-Azerbaijani conflict. At least, this was the position of Western powers, Armenia, as well as the Turkish bureaucracy.[15]

By 2009, a number of developments seemed to warrant the major international effort that was launched to normalize Turkish-Armenian relations.

Firstly, Turkish and Armenian societies had evolved significantly. While a frank and open discussion of the fate of the Ottoman Armenians was virtually impossible in the Turkey of the 1990s, more than a decade on the situation had changed remarkably in conjunction with the broader liberalization of Turkish society. As for Armenia, the instinctive fear of and prejudices against Turks that were prevalent in the 1990s had also abated as increasing numbers of Armenians traveled to Turkey for work or vacation. Most of all, with the support of Western governments and NGOs, a number of projects on Turkish-Armenian dialogue had been implemented, which generated ripple effects in both societies.[16] Secondly, and to its credit, the AKP government in Turkey distanced itself from the defensive and suspicious thinking that had plagued much of republican Turkish foreign policy. Previously, Turkish officials had routinely accused Western powers of seeking to dismantle Turkey, much as they had sought to do in the 1920 Treaty of Sèvres, in which support for Armenian territorial claims played a key role. Instead, the AKP embarked on a policy of "zero-problems with neighbors"—one that would later turn out to be naïvely simplistic, but which provided a considerably more positive attitude to neighbors, whether Armenia and Syria or Iran and Iraqi Kurdistan. Thirdly, the Russian invasion of Georgia in 2008 also played a role, as it shook up the stalemate in the South Caucasus and forced Western powers, as well as Turkey, to "think outside the box" in order to ameliorate the regional situation. Fourth and perhaps most important, Barack Obama had been elected President of the United States. Indeed, while Turkish diplomats are quick to point out that the 2009 effort to normalize relations was conducted under Swiss mediation and at the request of the two countries, it cannot be understood in isolation from the Obama administration's considerable involvement. In fact, this can be termed the sole meaningful initiative of the Obama administration in the South Caucasus. As such, this involvement requires careful study.

During the 2008 presidential campaign, Obama promised, more ardently than previous Democratic candidates for the presidency, that if elected, he would support a resolution labeling the massacres of Armenians in 1915 as genocide. Only when he arrived in office was Obama forced to face the reality that such a move might mortally affect relations with one of America's oldest allies in the region, Turkey. This was all the more problematic because Obama also made Turkey a centerpiece in his effort to improve America's standing in the Muslim world. The US president was, so to speak, in a bind—especially as he had presented himself as a new brand of politician who would not simply ignore earlier promises. Thus, he resolved to insert himself (and, thereby, the USA) directly into the middle of this most infected historical wound. Obama now made Turkey the focal point of his first major foreign trip. In so doing, both in his public address to the Turkish parliament and especially in his private meetings with Turkish officials, he made the Armenian issue a priority. Indeed, the administration brought to bear the full force of its influence on the Turkish government, pressing it to normalize relations with Armenia and, most importantly, to open the Turkish-Armenian border.[17]

President Obama's decision to embark on this venture suggests that he sought to bring to the issue his unique personal history and self-described skills in building bridges, drawing on his combination of Christian and Muslim heritage. The president saw in the Turkish-Armenian issue an opportunity to accomplish an early foreign policy triumph—one that, moreover, would liberate him from his campaign promise to recognize the massacres as genocide which, given the role of Turkey in America's coalition, would have had serious negative repercussions on America's ability to extricate itself from the wars in Iraq and Afghanistan, as Obama had also promised.

This American involvement at the highest level—and run out of the White House rather than the State Department—to a large extent explains why the process went as far as it did. As Nigar Göksel has observed, "it remains puzzling that the Turkish and Armenian sides continued voicing contradictory interpretations ... how could the two capitals and the involved third parties such as Washington, not have foreseen the train wreck that would inevitably take place because of the discrepancy of positions?"[18] Indeed, a simple look at the facial expression of the Armenian and Turkish foreign ministers during the signing of the Protocols in Zürich suggests that they had more or less been dragged to the altar; both parties, as would soon become clear, had serious misgivings about the process.

The Obama administration's rosy scenario did not materialize. While Turkey and Armenia did sign protocols to establish diplomatic relations and to open their common border, neither the Turkish nor the Armenian parliament saw fit to ratify the accord, let alone implement it.

EXPLAINING FAILURE: FAULTY ASSUMPTIONS

If the Obama administration brought such pressure on the parties, and if the situation had indeed appeared ripe for a settlement, why then did it fail? In order to answer this question, it is instructive to study the assumptions underlying the Turkish-Armenian normalization process. Roughly rendered, the assumptions were as follows. First, the normalization process would help Turkey come to terms with its own history, and thus be beneficial for Turkish democracy. Second, in a deadlocked situation in the Caucasus, Turkish-Armenian normalization of relations would open one of the many closed borders in the region, and potentially help reduce Russia's domination of Armenia. Third, it would make Armenia feel more safe and secure, and it would therefore lead Yerevan to become more constructive on the Nagorno-Karabakh conflict. Thus, and fourth, it was concluded that it was not only feasible and possible to de-link the Turkish-Armenian relationship from the Armenian-Azerbaijani conflict; it was in everyone's interest—including Azerbaijan's— to do so.[19] But do these assumptions stand up to closer scrutiny?

The first assumption was essentially correct: the process of Turkish-Armenian normalization had a healthy effect on Turkish society, including Turkey's coming to terms with some of the darkest episodes of its history, and was therefore positive for Turkish democracy. However, there is a question of causality involved. Did the Turkish-Armenian normalization process contribute to the improvement of the internal Turkish debate? Or, alternatively, did the liberalization of Turkey's society make such a dialogue possible? While both processes clearly influenced one another, it seems clear that the Turkish-Armenian civil society dialogue had only a limited, albeit positive, effect on Turkish society. Rather, it was the improvement of the general environment in Turkey, and the growing willingness of both state and society to break with historical taboos, that made the dialogue possible in the first place.

As for the second assumption, the normalization of Turkish-Armenian relations could certainly be conceived to be a game changer in the South Caucasus—especially at a time when Russia had brutally reasserted its pre-eminence in the region by invading and dismembering Georgia. Thus, the opening of the border would break Armenia's economic dependence on Russia, as it would gradually integrate Armenia's small market with Turkey's large and booming economy. Moreover, it would break Armenia's strategic isolation, reorient it toward the West, and gradually reduce its strategic dependence on Russia. This argument makes sense in theory; and given Russia's vehement reaction to any Western plans to reduce its influence in its "near abroad," one could thus have expected Moscow to strongly oppose or seek to undermine the protocols. But in fact, the opposite was the case, at least on the surface: Russia eagerly sought to promote a process that Western pundits argued would reduce Moscow's dominance in the South Caucasus. Thus, Moscow must have interpreted the process differently. And indeed it did. Russian officials, to begin with, were obviously keenly aware both of the close security ties linking Moscow and Yerevan, including a large Russian military base at Gyumri, and of the fact that Russia owns key sectors of the Armenian economy—from the country's nuclear power plant to its gas distribution network. In other words, Moscow did not appear overly concerned at losing its sway in Armenia. But on the other hand, Moscow appeared to see a historic opportunity in the process: that of exploiting the growing Azerbaijani frustration with Ankara and Washington, and to break Azerbaijan's Western orientation once and for all.

Indeed, the normalization process did not occur in a vacuum: it took place a year after the war in Georgia, upon which President Dmitry Medvedev had publicly declared a "zone of privileged interests" in the former Soviet sphere. Moscow had followed up its military dismemberment of Georgia with nothing less than a proposal, only weeks after that event, of taking the lead in seeking a negotiated solution to the Armenian-Azerbaijani conflict. This effort engendered hope in the West that Moscow would help lift a potential stumbling block to the Turkish-Armenian normalization process. But in fact, the premise of that mediation effort was preposterous to begin with. Having invaded one country in the South Caucasus, Moscow's offer of taking the lead in mediating the conflict between the other two sent a clear signal across the region: Moscow was staking out the claim to being the sole arbiter of war or peace in the region. War, as everyone understood, had happened on Moscow's terms in

Georgia; peace would now happen on Moscow's terms between Armenia and Azerbaijan. Baku fully understood this to imply the imposition of a Russian military presence on the ground in the guise of "peacekeeping"—an unpalatable prospect given the experience of Georgia and Moldova, with Russia's approach to peacekeeping tantamount to keeping the pieces of the former Soviet empire. In parallel, Moscow sought to exploit the stalemate in Turkish-Azerbaijani negotiations regarding the transit of Azerbaijani gas to Europe by offering to buy all of Azerbaijan's natural gas at European prices. Simply put, Moscow appeared to be feigning support for the Turkish-Armenian normalization process, while making both Turkey and the West accomplices in its own gambit to veer Azerbaijan away from its Western orientation. And had Azerbaijan's top leadership not been unwavering in its determination to safeguard its political independence, that gambit might have worked: Azerbaijan had keenly observed the West's inability to prevent the dismemberment of Georgia; followed by what it perceived as a complete desertion by its key allies—the United States and Turkey—who both appeared to ignore Azerbaijan's single most important security consideration, the conflict with Armenia, as they detached the Turkish-Armenian normalization process from the conflict over Nagorno-Karabakh. Yet instead of reacting emotionally, Baku proved able to observe strategic patience and to bring to bear its influence on Turkish public opinion to contribute to halting the ratification of the protocols. And indeed, Turkish officials gradually came to understand that Moscow's rhetorical support for the process masked a deeper and different agenda. As a former Turkish parliamentarian involved in the process put it, Ankara "discovered that the Russians were not so helpful after all."[20] Thus, the premise of the second assumption underlying the process appears questionable at best.

Third and most importantly, both the US and Turkish governments appeared to have accepted the notion promoted by Western NGOs, particularly International Crisis Group, that a Turkish-Armenian deal would make Armenia more secure, and thereby more inclined to engage in the difficult compromises required to strike a negotiated agreement with Azerbaijan over the Nagorno-Karabakh conflict. In other words, so the argument went, the cause of peace between Armenia and Azerbaijan would be *promoted* by de-linking the two relationships from one another. And, since 15 years of maintaining the linkage had yielded no result, it was time to try something new.

This is arguably the most fundamentally flawed of the assumptions underlying the normalization process. First, the very assumption that the two relationships could be de-linked—even if that would be desirable—hardly stands up to closer scrutiny. The assumption ignores the very strong support that Azerbaijan's cause carries in Turkish public opinion. Put simply, it would require only a camera crew beaming a few interviews with Azerbaijani refugees back to Turkish living rooms to build a strong opinion in Turkey against the opening of the Armenian border. This is indeed what Turkish Prime Minister Tayyip Erdoğan discovered, and what led him to rapidly fly to Baku to reassure Azerbaijan, and to effectively kill the normalization process.

Furthermore, the assumption ignores that an Armenia which feels more secure—once its main strategic problem, the closed border with Turkey, is resolved—would essentially have two options: first, doubling down on that process of reconciliation and seeking to resolve its other outstanding issue, the conflict with Azerbaijan. Alternatively, it could conclude that this removes the major obstacle to safely holding on to what many Armenians regard the nation's first major military victory in a thousand years. In other words, since the conflict over Nagorno-Karabakh was now so obviously on the international backburner, why would Armenian leaders go the extra mile to accommodate Azerbaijan in a situation where Yerevan's regional and international position had greatly improved? It seems clear that the operational logic of the politics of the Caucasus would greatly favor the latter scenario. Especially given the certitude of powerful domestic and diaspora opposition to the protocols with Turkey, an Armenian leadership would spend rather than gain political capital by implementing the normalization process with Ankara, leaving it in a weaker position to offer any concessions to Azerbaijan, even if it should be so inclined. Indeed, President Serzh Sargsyan saw the defection of one of the coalition partners in his government over the issue.

The limited empirical record is instructive: as Turkey and Armenia grew closer and drafted protocols normalizing their relationship, Armenia's position in the negotiations with Azerbaijan hardened. Far from becoming more flexible and accommodating, Armenia rejected the basis for the negotiations over the occupied lands that had been agreed upon in 2008, known as the Madrid Principles. Clearly, the opening with Turkey either emboldened Armenia to increase its demands on Azerbaijan; or forced its leadership to be more nationalistic in the relationship with Azerbaijan because it had shown itself to be overly conciliatory in the relationship with Turkey. The latter interpretation is strengthened by the evolution of Armenia's relationship with Georgia during the same period. Indeed, in September 2009 Armenian President Serzh Sargsyan made an unprecedented statement announcing a heightened Armenian aspiration to advocate for the rights of Georgia's Armenians. In particular, Sargsyan "mentioned the protection of Armenian monuments, registration of the Armenian Church in Georgia and recognition of Armenian as a regional language in Javakheti as cornerstones for strengthening Armenia's friendship with Georgia."[21] This policy strongly departed from Armenia's prior policy of non-interference in Georgian affairs. Thus, the little empirical record that is available speaks directly against the assumption underlying the process: it suggests instead that the Turkish-Armenian rapprochement made Armenia less conciliatory not only toward Azerbaijan, but also toward Georgia.

DANGERS FOR REGIONAL SECURITY

The discussion above has made it clear that the assumptions underlying the Turkish-Armenian normalization process were fundamentally flawed. That does not mean that Turkish-Armenian normalization *per se* is undesirable. Quite to the contrary, it is a necessary condition for the transformation of the South Caucasus from a troubled and conflict-ridden region to a peaceful region living in harmony with its neighbors. The fundamental problem, viewed in a regional perspective, lies in the artificial isolation of the Turkish-Armenian relationship from its regional realities—more specifically, in the deliberate efforts to remove any linkage between that relationship and the Armenian-Azerbaijani conflict.

Indeed, the policy decision taken in 2009 to seek to remove such linkages did not occur in a vacuum: it occurred in the immediate aftermath of the first major military confrontation in the South Caucasus since 1994. And as discussed above, it was motivated (though to a limited extent) by an effort to change realities in the Caucasus following Russia's invasion of Georgia. But it represents a very unfortunate reading of the situation following that war. In fact, the major lesson of the war in Georgia was that the international community had fundamentally misunderstood the security situation in the South Caucasus. First, the international community—and especially the West—had come to understand the conflicts in the region as "frozen." This was valid as much for Georgia's conflicts as for that between Armenia and Azerbaijan. But as the war showed, the conflicts were not frozen—they were highly dynamic processes that risked re-erupting, the very antithesis of frozenness. Second, it had failed to understand that the region's conflicts had changed. Initially, these conflicts had been mainly intra-communal conflicts which featured the involvement of foreign powers. With the passage of time, they were absorbed by the geopolitics of the region; in a sense, they ceased being primarily intra-communal, and their fate instead became largely determined by the great power politics of the Caucasus, especially as a result of Russia's manipulation of the conflicts for its purposes of regional hegemony. And finally, in this light, the international community's mechanisms and efforts to seek a resolution to the conflicts were woefully inadequate.

Therefore, the main lesson to be drawn from the war in Georgia was that the West had failed to prevent the escalation of the conflict, and had gotten it wrong: the conflicts were not frozen, and they were not solely between Georgia on one hand and Abkhazia and South Ossetia on the other—but, rather, involved Russia as a direct party. Thus, the logical policy implication— once the West realized it had failed to thwart the escalation to war in Georgia— would have been to investigate whether similar risks of escalation to war existed in other controversies in the region. Among them, the Turkish-Armenian relationship, as bad as it was, posed little risk of war. The conflict between Moldova and Transnistria similarly was at no real risk of escalation. Only the Armenian-Azerbaijani conflict exhibited a clear and present risk of such.

Indeed, the conflict had begun to show dangerous signs that should have given policy-makers pause. At the most basic level, the dynamics between the parties had changed: while Armenia had won the war militarily, its position was increasingly problematic. Azerbaijan had been a failed state in 1993; but in 2009, powered by its oil exports, it was an emerging regional powerhouse, with an economy several times larger than Armenia's, and a defense budget larger than Armenia's entire state budget. Clearly, the situation was not frozen: the power balance between the protagonists had changed dramatically and rapidly, and the status quo appeared increasingly untenable. The OSCE Minsk Process, tasked with resolving the conflict, was increasingly moribund, and the conflict moving toward escalation rather than resolution. And given the amount of armaments that the two countries have acquired since 1994, a renewed conflict would profoundly affect regional security far beyond their borders, risking the involvement of Russia, Iran as well as Turkey. In this light, it would have been logical for the West to mobilize its resources to redouble efforts to resolve—or at least manage—the Armenian-Azerbaijani conflict. Reality has been exactly the opposite: while the Obama administration threw itself into the Turkish-Armenian rapprochement, Germany launched the Meseberg Process to bring about a solution to the Transnistrian conflict. In fact, the Armenian-Azerbaijani conflict is the only regional conflagration in which no serious Western effort has been initiated.

Not only has the West failed to take an initiative in the conflict, the policy decisions that Western leaders took actually made matters worse. First, the decision to lend legitimacy to Moscow's initiative to take the lead in resolving the conflict flew in the face of logic: having just invaded Georgia, Moscow lacked even rudimentary legitimacy in acting as an honest broker. Not only did the West show weakness in supporting this initiative, its support also implicitly undermined its opposition to Russia's actions in Georgia. If the West indeed opposed and sought to reverse Moscow's dismemberment of Georgia, then how could it sanction, let alone support, a heightened Russian role in any other conflict in the South Caucasus?

But much greater damage was done by the decision to prioritize the Turkish-Armenian rapprochement in a way that pushed the resolution of the Armenian-Azerbaijani conflict to the backburner. For that is essentially what happened: since the capacity and attention of the international community is limited, a decision to prioritize one issue is effectively a decision not to prioritize another. When that is coupled with a deliberate effort to remove an existing linkage between two political relationships, the signal is even louder. Read from Baku, the signal sent by the country's two chief international partners—Washington and Ankara—was crystal clear: Azerbaijan's top national priority was not only demoted on its partners' list of priorities, but these partners had instead prioritized an effort that had the direct effect of harming Azerbaijan's top national interest. The fact that neither partner properly consulted Baku or even kept it fully informed of developments only made matters worse. This situation provided Baku with a choice: it could either accept the demotion of its top priority on the international agenda, or it could try to do something to keep it there. The escalation of tensions in the conflict zone in part testify to the decision that Azerbaijan's chief partners forced it to take. Conversely, once the process had failed, Armenia's internally weakened government was pushed in a similarly confrontational direction as its subsequent policies suggest, not least the ill-advised decision to build an airport servicing Stepanakert in Khojaly, the site of the largest massacre of civilian Azerbaijanis during the war.

To sum up, the decision to prioritize the Turkish-Armenian rapprochement actually contributed to worsening the security situation in the South Caucasus, by dampening the prospects for a resolution to the Armenian-Azerbaijani conflict, and instead speeding up a process of escalation.

IMPLICATIONS FOR POLICY

Several policy implications flow from this discussion. First, the international community, but especially Western powers, need to reverse their willful neglect of the Armenian-Azerbaijani conflict. This neglect has only gotten worse: when the US co-chair of the Minsk Group, Robert Bradtke, completed his mission in December 2012, a successor was not named; instead, the US Ambassador to the OSCE was appointed to the position *ad interim*. Three months later, in March 2013, a State Department official announced that a replacement would be appointed "within a year."[22] No further comment is necessary to illustrate the lack of importance the US government assigns to the issue. To reverse this situation, it is important that a respected and high-profile official with deep experience of conflict resolution processes be appointed to the position; and that America then take the lead in seeking a resolution to the conflict, committing adequate diplomatic resources for this purpose. Moreover, since the resolution of the conflict will be inextricably linked to the Turkish-Armenian relationship, it will be important to involve Ankara in an organic way in the conflict resolution process. That may not mean a revision of the existing format—which Armenia and Russia are likely to oppose—but it will likely mean much deeper coordination between the negotiators and Turkish officials.

Second, if any link should be removed, it is the one between Turkish-Armenian diplomatic relations and the opening of the border. Since the issue of diplomatic relations had no linkage to the Armenian-Azerbaijani conflict, it would only be logical for Turkish officials, under the right conditions, to proceed with efforts to establish diplomatic relations with Armenia. Such a move could be useful not only in promoting the prospects for the bilateral relationship, but also for Turkey to play a constructive and supportive role in the Armenian-Azerbaijani conflict resolution process. This will nevertheless require Ankara to be extremely clear on the distinction between these issues. As for the question of the border, it is worth noting that Prime Minister Erdoğan went further than necessary in reassuring Azerbaijani officials in May 2009: he affirmed that "there will be no normalization [with Armenia] unless the occupation of Azerbaijani territory ends."[23] This goes further than Turkey's traditional position, which is that an opening of the border could take place at a point in the settlement process, but not necessarily at its end. As a renewed effort to resolve the conflict is undertaken, it would therefore be important to involve Turkish officials in discussions regarding when the most beneficial timing of a border opening would be for the conflict resolution process—most likely upon the Armenian withdrawal from some or all of the occupied territories outside Nagorno-Karabakh.[24]

The main lesson of the Turkish-Armenian normalization process is that whatever one may consider desirable, Turkish-Armenian relations cannot be disconnected from the regional realities, particularly the Armenian-Azerbaijani conflict. Efforts to artificially remove the linkage between the two relationships are bound not only to fail, but also to exacerbate an already critical situation. That said, the normalization of Turkish-Armenian relations remains an important part of the path to a solution to all regional problems, *if* linked tightly and positively to the process of a resolution to the Armenian-Azerbaijani conflict.

NOTES

1. Known in English as the Justice and Development Party.
2. For example, a January 2010 poll found that 70 percent of Turks approved of the opening of the Armenian border only on the condition that Armenia withdraw from Azerbaijani territory and abandon claims of genocide. Ankara University European Community Research Center, "Kamuoyu ve Türk Dış Politikası Anketi" [Public Opinion and Turkish Foreign Policy], January 2010, http://www.ataum.ankara.edu.tr/basinduyurusu.doc
3. Blaine Harden, "Turkish Premier Voices Worries over Pull of Ethnic Conflict in Caucasus," *Washington Post*, March 18, 1992, A17.
4. Mustafa Aydın, "Foucalt's Pendulum: Turkey in Central Asia and the Caucasus," *Turkish Studies* 5, no. 2, Summer (2004): 1–22.
5. Interview with Deputy Foreign Minister Armen Baibourtian, Yerevan, 1998.
6. Nigar Göksel, "Turkey and Armenia Post-Protocols: Back to Square One?," *TESEV Foreign Policy Bulletin*, October 2012, 12, http://www.tesev.org.tr/assets/publications/file/TurkeyArmenia.pdf
7. Armenian National Committee of America, "The Turkish-Armenian Protocols Explained," 2009, http://anca.org/assets/pdf/misc/protocols_explained.pdf
8. "Turk Says Russia is Tangled in Caucasus War," *New York Times*, April 14, 1993, A9.
9. Süha Bölükbasi, "Ankara's Baku-Centered Transcaucasia Policy: Has it Failed?," *Middle East Journal* 50, no. 1, Winter (1997): 80–94.
10. Taleh Ziyadov, "The Kars-Akhalkalaki Railroad: A Missing Link Between Europe and Asia," *Central Asia-Caucasus Analyst*, April 19, 2006, http://cacianalyst.org/publications/analytical-articles/item/10802
11. Svante Cornell, *Azerbaijan Since Independence* (Armonk: M.E. Sharpe, 2011), 380–384.
12. Gerard Libaridian, *Modern Armenia: People, Nation, State* (New Brunswick, NJ: Transaction, 2007), 262.

13. Burcu Gültekin Punsmann, "Addressing Controversy I: Public Diplomacy between Turkey and Armenia," in *Turkey's Public Diplomacy*, eds. B. Senem Çevik and Philip Seib (New York: Palgrave Macmillan, 2015).

14. David Philips, *Unsilencing the Past: Track-Two Diplomacy and Turkish-Armenian Reconciliation* (New York: Berghahn Books, 2005).

15. In March 2009, at an event in Washington D.C., the Deputy Undersecretary for Political Affairs in the Turkish Ministry of Foreign Affairs, Ünal Çeviköz, stated that "the relations between Turkey and Armenia are not linked to a third country." "Turkey, Russia, and the West in the Caucasus: a Turkish Perspective," Central Asia-Caucasus Institute Forum, Johns Hopkins University-SAIS, March 11, 2009.

16. Philips, *Unsilencing the Past*.

17. "Turkish Intellectuals Reflect on Obama's Visit, Armenian Issue," *Armenian Weekly*, April 8, 2009, http://armenianweekly.com/2009/04/08/turkish-intellectuals-reflect-on-obama%E2%80%99s-visit-armenian-issue/; "Turkey and Armenia Agree on Reconciliation Roadmap," *Deutsche Welle*, April 23, 2009, http://www.dw.com/en/turkey-and-armenia-agree-on-reconciliation-roadmap/a-4201193

18. Göksel, "Turkey and Armenia Post-Protocols: Back to Square One?," 11.

19. See e.g. International Crisis Group, "Turkey and Armenia: Opening Minds, Opening Borders," *Europe Report* No. 199, April 14, 2009, 7, http://www.crisisgroup.org/~/media/Files/europe/199_turkey_and_armenia___opening_minds_opening_borders_2.pdf

20. Interview with a former AKP Member of Parliament, Ankara, 2012.

21. Vahagn Muradyan, "Armenia and Georgia in the Context of Turkish-Armenian Rapprochement," *Central Asia-Caucasus Analyst*, March 17, 2010, http://old.cacianalyst.org/?q=node/5287/print

22. "U.S. to Appoint New OSCE Minsk Group Co-Chair within a Year," *news.am*, March 14, 2013, http://m.news.am/eng/news/144412.html

23. "Prime Minister Erdoğan Puts Baku's Armenia Concerns to Rest," *TurkishPress*, May 14, 2009.

24. It should be recalled that in 2002, former Azerbaijani President Heydar Aliyev offered Armenia the restoration of economic relations in exchange for the liberation of only the four southern of the seven occupied districts. This could presumably be a model for negotiations.

CHAPTER 6

The Islamic Republic of Iran's Policy Toward the Nagorno-Karabakh Conflict

Brenda Shaffer

Since the emergence of the Nagorno-Karabakh conflict in the late 1980s, the Islamic Republic of Iran's stances and policies toward the dispute and the two main actors—Azerbaijan and Armenia—played an important role in the developments of the conflict. Iran borders both Armenia and Azerbaijan and at times the battles waged close to Iran's borders. Thus, Iran's own national security is directly affected by the conflict. Iran's domestic stability is also potentially influenced by the conflict since over a third of the population of Iran is ethnic Azerbaijani; the regions of northwest Iran that are contiguous to the conflict zone are populated primarily by ethnic Azerbaijanis, many of whom share family ties with co-ethnics in the Republic of Azerbaijan, and Iranian Azerbaijanis have at times mobilized in support of Baku in this conflict, often in contrast to Tehran's policies.

Iran's relations with most of its neighbors are connected to domestic policy, since Iran is a multi-ethnic society with approximately half of its citizens of non-Persian origin. Most of the ethnic minorities are located primarily in Iran's periphery regions and share ethnic and family ties with co-ethnics in neighboring states. Apart from the Azerbaijanis who comprise the largest ethnic minority group, other significant minority groups include Kurds, Arabs, Baluch and Turkmen. The northwest provinces of Iran—East Azerbaijan, West Azerbaijan and Ardebil—which are contiguous with Azerbaijan, Armenia and the conflict zone, are populated primarily by ethnic Azerbaijanis. In the Republic of Azerbaijan, many refer to the area of northwest Iran as "South Azerbaijan." Consequently, Iran's policy toward the conflict, and the wider question of its

B. Shaffer (✉)
Washington, DC, USA

© The Author(s) 2017
S.E. Cornell (ed.), *The International Politics of the Armenian-Azerbaijani Conflict*, DOI 10.1057/978-1-137-60006-6_6

relations with Azerbaijan, is as much a question of domestic policy as foreign policy.

This chapter will examine the interests and policies of the Islamic Republic of Iran toward the Nagorno-Karabakh conflict since the dissolution of the Soviet Union in 1991. The chapter argues that Iran's policy toward the conflict and the two main protagonists, Azerbaijan and Armenia, is shaped chiefly by a number of factors: Iran's own security interests, including its threat perception of Azerbaijan; its desire to preempt ethnic mobilization of its domestic Azerbaijani minority; and Iran's relations with third parties, primarily Russia, Turkey and the United States. Iran has also to striven to gain a role as a sponsor of negotiations between Armenia and Azerbaijan in order to bolster its standing as a power.

The analysis to follow shows that Tehran's policy toward the Nagorno-Karabakh conflict is very pragmatic, based primarily on Iran's security interests—and not based on either ideology or considerations of shared identity. In contrast to its widely held image as a state where Islamic solidarity plays an important role in its foreign policy, Iran's policies toward the conflict display no special preference toward Azerbaijan despite their shared Shiite Muslim identity. In fact, for most of the post-Soviet period, Tehran has maintained better relations and more advanced cooperation with Armenia than its rival, Shiite-majority Azerbaijan.

This chapter proceeds with a short history of Iran's policies toward the Nagorno-Karabakh conflict during the period of the Soviet breakup and the open war between Azerbaijan and Armenia from 1992 to 1994. It will then analyze the interests that have shaped Iran's policies toward the conflict. The chapter will end with an analysis of the implications of Iran's policies for future developments in the conflict.

Iran's Policy During the Soviet Breakup and War over Nagorno-Karabakh

Despite the many changes that have occurred in Iran and the South Caucasus, the initial policy that Iran formed toward the conflict in the early post-Soviet period has continued to be valid for most of the last two decades. Based primarily on geopolitical interests, which are still applicable today, Tehran's policy has therefore not shifted considerably since its inception.

Tehran viewed the early stages of the conflict between Armenians and Azerbaijanis, beginning in the late 1980s, as an internal Soviet matter; and during this period most of its dealings with the region were conducted via Moscow. In June 1989, the Speaker of the Iranian Parliament Akbar Hashemi Rafsanjani made a landmark visit to the USSR, the first by a senior Iranian official to the Soviet Union in ten years, and Rafsanjani's first foreign visit following Ayatollah Khomeini's death. Tehran and Moscow signed a comprehensive cooperation agreement during the visit, as well as agreed to Soviet arms sales to Iran and—for the first time—cooperation in the field of nuclear energy.[1] Furthermore, Rafsanjani also visited Baku on the same trip, the capital of what was then Soviet Azerbaijan. While offering to lend support for Islamic religious studies and institutions in the region, Rafsanjani did not express support for or call for self-rule for the Azerbaijanis.

As Moscow's control over the republics waned during the late 1980s under Mikhail Gorbachev's rule, it was evident that Tehran was eager to maintain stability on its northern border with the USSR. Iran's concerns were fueled by the activities of the main opposition political force operating at the time in Soviet Azerbaijan—the Popular Front of Azerbaijan. The Popular Front of Azerbaijan was espousing an agenda of a "greater Azerbaijan," campaigning for language rights and even reunification with the Azerbaijanis of northeastern Iran. In addition, beginning in December 1989, large-scale protests of Azerbaijanis emerged in the border area between Iran and Soviet Azerbaijan. Activists from Baku, together with local villagers, held rallies in the border area, lit bonfires, and attempted to communicate with co-ethnics and family members in Iran. The Popular Front movement organized these events at the Soviet–Iranian border in the region of Nakhchivan. At times during the demonstrations, protestors called for "the unity of Northern and Southern Azerbaijan." Throughout December, the number of demonstrators swelled to several thousand and on December 31, the tone of the demonstrations changed as protestors burnt and tore down several border posts and sections of the fence that divided the border of Soviet Azerbaijan and Iran. At this point, a large number of Soviet Azerbaijanis illegally crossed the border into Iran. Azerbaijanis from both sides swam or took small boats across the Araxes River that separates the two states. In parallel to the intensifying activity in the border area, large demonstrations in support of opening the border with Iran took place in Baku.

Initially, Iranian authorities did not express open concern about the attempts to renew ties between Azerbaijanis from both sides of the border and coordinated with Moscow to set up an orderly process for these meetings. However, Tehran's policy and concerns about the instability on its border shifted over the course of 1990–91, with the steady increase in the number of Azerbaijanis from Iran and the Soviet Union attempting to meet, the surge in political activity in Baku calling for reunification of "Southern and Northern Azerbaijan," the successive breakdown in Soviet power and control over the South Caucasus, and the significant rise in violence between Azerbaijanis and Armenians related to control over Nagorno-Karabakh.

Consequently, Iran did not support the independence of the Soviet republics, including the Muslim populated ones, until after the demise of the USSR. In August 1991, the *Tehran Times* stated:

> The Islamic Republic of Iran [also has] very good relations with the central Soviet Government, and does not desire to witness any weakening of President Gorbachev's government ... From a general geopolitical point of view, Iran

believes that the disintegration of the Soviet Union will result in an undesirable wave of instability in the region, and for that reason Iran is against some of the extremist nationalistic movements of the republics of the Soviet Union.[2]

The Soviet breakup in December 1991 caught Iran somewhat by surprise. While Iran and Russia/the Soviet Union had a long history of conflict from the late eighteenth century until the Second World War and exchanged control of territories a number of times, the Soviet breakup created new strategic threats for Iran on its northern border. In contrast to the perception held by many analysts in the West at the time, Tehran did not view the Soviet breakup and the establishment of six new states populated by Muslim-majorities in Central Asia and Azerbaijan as an opportunity to expand its influence and "export the revolution." Rather, Tehran's position was defensive: the new states could be a source of threats to Iran. The official state-sponsored newspaper, the *Tehran Times*, wrote shortly after the collapse of the USSR that

> The first ground for concern from the point of view in Tehran is the lack of political stability in the newly independent republics. The unstable conditions in those republics could be serious causes of insecurity along the lengthy borders (over 2,000 kilometers) Iran shares with those countries. Already foreign hands can be felt at work in those republics, [e] specially in Azerbaijan and Turkmenistan republics, with the ultimate objective of brewing discord among the Iranian Azeris and Turkmen by instigating ethnic and nationalistic sentiments.[3]

In addition, following the independence of the Republic of Azerbaijan, Iran's hardline journal *Jomhuri-ye Islami* pointed out that while Azerbaijan was populated by Muslims, it had adopted a pro-Western and specifically pro-Turkish orientation, and thus its independence created limited opportunity for Iranian influence.[4] Consequently, after the Soviet breakup, Iran began to place limitations on direct ties between ethnic Azerbaijanis in Iran and in the new Republic of Azerbaijan.

As Baku stepped-up its articulation of desire for ties with Iran's Azerbaijanis, Tehran expanded its cooperation with Armenia. Azerbaijan's first elected president after independence, Abulfez Elchibey, raised the issue of language and cultural rights for the Azerbaijanis in Iran to the level of state policy. For instance, Elchibey appointed as his first Ambassador to Tehran professor Nasib Nasibli, whose academic work had focused on the issue of unification of North and South Azerbaijan. In addition, the newly independent Republic of Azerbaijan under Elchibey published its first new textbooks for elementary schools with a map on their cover of "Greater Azerbaijan" that included territories in present-day Iran. Iranian Azerbaijanis were also showing signs of growing ethnic-based awareness and political activity, adding to Tehran's concerns.

In the initial period after the independence of the new republics and throughout most of President Elchibey's tenure, Iranian officials and the mainstream media rarely criticized Armenia, generally calling for both sides to "peacefully resolve the conflict." Tehran also developed relations and trade with Armenia during the height of the battles between Azerbaijan and Armenia in 1992. Considering that the Armenians were the force changing the status quo in the borders between Armenia and Azerbaijan and occupied a significant amount of territory within the internationally recognized borders of Azerbaijan, the lack of Iranian criticism and the adoption of a "balanced" approach to the sides in actuality favored Armenia. In this period, official statements of the Iranian foreign ministry continued to reflect a balanced approach toward the two belligerents, even following a series of significant Armenian conquests in Azerbaijan and the creation of thousands of new Azerbaijani refugees:

> The Islamic Republic believes that the continuation of these clashes is not in the interest of either of the warring parties and will only inflict further losses and casualties on both nations and states ...The Islamic Republic, in accordance with its heartfelt desire to restore peace and tranquillity to the region, taking into account the interests of both Azerbaijan and Armenia, and in view of the formal request of the governments of these states for mediation, deems it a duty to continue its serious efforts to restore stability and tranquility to the region and to halt the war and bloodshed.[5]

Tehran's lack of action on behalf of Azerbaijan in this period was so pronounced that hard-liners in Iran voiced criticism of the official policy, stating that Iran's policy toward the conflict and its cooperation with Armenia was not a proper reflection of Iran's "religious and ideological responsibilities."[6] Even in forums with all Muslim-majority state membership, such as the Economic Cooperation Organization (ECO), Tehran in this period refrained from criticizing Armenia.[7] Iranian representatives and Iranian official media reserved any of its criticisms in the early 1990s for "colonial powers" and other external agents, such as Russia, Turkey, the United States and occasionally the "Zionists," and even blamed Azerbaijani President Elchibey for the conflict, while seldom pointing its finger at Yerevan.[8]

While on the rhetorical level, Tehran remained neutral in the conflict, in actual fact Tehran's actions contributed to sustaining the war between Armenia and Azerbaijan over Nagorno-Karabakh. Iran served as the main supply route for Armenia during the bulk of the war. In 1992 and 1993, supply routes from all of Armenia's neighbors except for Iran were closed or unreliable; the civil war in neighboring Georgia at the time hindered Russia from providing supplies by land to Yerevan. Thus, Armenia was only able to continue the war because of critical fuel and food supplies that reached it via Iran. For instance, in April 1992, at one of the most crucial points in the escalation of the conflict between Azerbaijan and Armenia, Iran agreed to supply fuel and improved transportation links with Armenia.[9] Moreover, fuel from Russia during the war was often delivered to Armenia by way of Iran, thus further contributing to

Yerevan's war effort after the ending of the Soviet-era trade routes that went through Azerbaijan.[10] In April 1992, two cargo planes of aid funded by ethnic Armenians in Iran arrived in Yerevan.[11] The planes were dispatched to Armenia through the Iranian Red Crescent. Iranian Armenians also reportedly contributed funds to the construction of a bridge linking Armenia and Iran, which was inaugurated in May 1992.[12]

Armenian officials thanked Iran a number of times for the supplies and for serving as a supply route during the war. For instance, pointing out Tehran's role in helping Armenia receive trade supplies during the war, Armenian Prime Minister and Vice President Gagik Arutyunyan remarked in 1992 at a ceremony commemorating the opening of the bridge over the Araxes that the bridge would contribute to stabilizing the economic situation in the republic by providing alternatives to transport routes blocked as a result of the war.[13] This bridge was opened just after Armenian forces had captured the pivotal city of Shusha at a time when Iran hosted the leaders of Armenia and Azerbaijan for peace negotiations. Despite the embarrassing timing of the fall of Shusha, Tehran offered no condemnation of Yerevan, and its reaction did not go beyond an expression of "concern over the recent developments in Karabakh."[14]

Iran's specific positions on various subsequent proposals during the negotiation process following the cease-fire between Azerbaijan and Armenia often appeared dictated by its internal Azerbaijani considerations. For instance, Tehran opposed an American proposition for the sides to trade corridors— Armenia obtaining a corridor to Karabakh, and Azerbaijan receiving one to Nakhchivan—since the endeavor could have resulted in a significant extension of the border between the Republic of Azerbaijan and Iran, while robbing Armenia of direct access to Iran.[15]

One of the best indications of Iran's conciliatory position toward Armenia was the fact that both Yerevan and the Karabakh Armenians repeatedly praised Iran's role in the negotiation process, expressed its preference for Tehran over many other foreign representatives,[16] and called for the deployment of Iranian observers at the border between Azerbaijan and Armenia and in the Nakhchivan area.[17] Armenia's President Levon Ter-Petrossian, stressing the importance of Iran's mediatory mission in settling the conflict, stated "the Iranians have proved their complete impartiality in this issue, respecting the rights of both sides and striving for a just solution, and therefore the sides trust Iran."[18] Moreover, in April 1992, the press center representing Nagorno-Karabakh Armenians released this statement:

> The Nagorno Karabagh Republic [NKR] leadership is currently discussing rejecting Russia's mediation role because the mediation conditions proposed by Iran are preferable. The Iranians are proposing that direct talks be held between the leaders of Azerbaijan and the NKR without the so-called participation of Nagorno Karabagh Republic's Azerbaijani community. Russia, on the other hand insists on the participation of the Azerbaijan community.[19]

In contrast, Azerbaijan's representatives voiced critical statements regarding Iran's role in the negotiations, illustrating their perception that Tehran was not promoting their interests. Abulfez Elchibey remarked,

> Unfortunately, there was no benefit from the activity of Iran's peacemaking mission, for example. Khodzhaly fell after their first visit to Karabagh, and Shusha fell after their second visit, and the fall of Lachin is the sequel to this.[20]

However, a shift emerged in Iran's position in spring 1993, as developments in the war began to threaten some additional vital Iranian security interests: namely, Armenia's territorial gains led to a significant increase in Azerbaijani refugees fleeing toward Iran, and Turkey openly voiced that it would potentially intervene in the conflict. Moreover, Iranian Azerbaijanis openly criticized Tehran's stance on the conflict. During the escalated fighting between the two sides, Armenia captured large parts of Azerbaijani territory located outside the Nagorno-Karabakh region and expanded the de facto border between Iran and the Armenian-held zone. Fleeing the conflict zone, many Azerbaijani refugees from the conflict sought protection in the area of the border with Iran and many requested to cross the border, seeking refuge among members of their extended families in Iran. To prevent their entry into Iran, Tehran established refugee camps within the Republic of Azerbaijan and reinforced the border through strengthening the presence of border guards and the Revolutionary Guards.

In parallel, Turkey issued a number of statements indicating willingness to intervene in the conflict. Iran explicitly stated that the escalation in the conflict increased the risk of Turkish intervention:

> the fighting has extended to areas near the borders of the Islamic Republic of Iran. The Turkish Government has reacted sharply and now there are implicit or explicit talks about Turkey's military intervention to end the offensives.[21]

Moreover, the Armenian successes on the battlefield and conquest of new territories were so expansive that the absence of Iranian condemnation was conspicuous, and somewhat politically embarrassing to Iran, evidently triggering domestic ramifications. In this period, Iranian Azerbaijani activists openly voiced condemnations and organized political activity calling for a change in Tehran's policy toward the conflict. This included the distribution of petitions, the holding of demonstrations, and even through the leadership of ethnic Iranian Azerbaijani members of parliament, the passing of resolutions in the Iranian Majles.

Thus in spring 1993, a subtle change took place in Iran's official rhetoric toward the conflict. However, no concrete changes of Iran's relationship with Armenia took place in 1993. Iran continued to allow supplies to reach Armenia and regularly conducted high-level and cordial exchanges with Armenian officials, and in July 1993 inaugurated direct flights between Tehran and Yerevan.[22]

Armenian President Levon Ter-Petrossian expressed understanding of the rhetorical change, dismissing the notion that it reflected any concrete change in the relations between the sides:

> The Armenian president informed the Iranian president that Armenia understands the sensitive approach of the Iranian public, press, and parliament toward developments in Azerbaijan and does not regard the occasional sharp reactions as a hostile disposition.[23]

A further shift in Iran's rhetoric toward the conflict emerged after the fall of President Elchibey's government from power in Azerbaijan in June 1993. With the removal of Elchibey's government and its cessation of the government-sponsored campaign for ethnic and language rights of Azerbaijanis in Iran, Tehran seemed to perceive less of a threat from the independence of the Republic of Azerbaijan and the capacity to balance its own varying security interests that were affected by the conflict. Under Elchibey's successor, Heydar Aliyev, and in turn under his successor, Ilham Aliyev, the government of Azerbaijan declined to officially champion the rights of ethnic Azerbaijanis in Iran and has proven very careful to signal to Tehran that it has no irredentist claims or desires to stir up ethnic sentiments in Iran.

Iran's Interests in the Conflict

Tehran possesses significant interests in the developments in the conflict between Armenia and Azerbaijan, particularly as Iran is a bordering state to both states and to the conflict zone. Developments in the conflict directly affect Iran's domestic stability, and the security of its borders. Indeed, Iran's policies toward bordering states are generally based on clear geopolitical interests; only in further-flung areas where there are few direct consequences for its own security, Iran tends to apply its ideological principles and rhetoric.

Iran's official media displays no special sentiments toward the Azerbaijani refugees from the war (over 800,000) or the loss of Azerbaijani lands, nor special identification or solidarity with Azerbaijan as Muslims or Shiites. For most of the early post-Soviet period, Iranian official and official media have been neutral on the conflict. The following quote is illustrative of such: "both Azerbaijan and Armenia claim the territory of Nagorno-Karabakh, which is mainly populated by Armenians, but located in Azerbaijan."[24] A small shift in the official Iranian messaging took place since around 2012: Iranian officials and official media now add that Iran supports the restoration of Azerbaijan's territorial integrity.

Despite this rhetorical shift, Armenian officials continue to praise Iran's stances on the conflict. For instance, following a meeting in Tehran with the Iranian foreign minister, Javad Zarif, in May 2015, Armenia's foreign minister, Eduard Nalbanian, praised Iran's position: "I appreciate Iran for its moderate and balanced stances on Armenia's dispute with Azerbaijan."[25]

Since the Soviet breakup and the emergence of the war between Azerbaijan and Armenia for control of Nagorno-Karabakh, Tehran's policies toward the conflict have been led by four main interests: Iran's promotion of its own security, including its threat perception of Azerbaijan; its desire to preempt ethnic mobilization of its domestic Azerbaijani minority; Iran's relations with third parties (primarily Russia, Turkey and the United States); and, to a lesser extent, its goal to serve as a sponsor of negotiations between Armenia and Azerbaijan.

Iran's Security and Threat Perception from Azerbaijan

Iran's utmost aim in its policy toward the Armenia-Azerbaijan conflict is protecting its own security, and especially that of its borders. Thus, Tehran aspires to prevent a flare-up of the conflict in the area adjacent to its border and any escalation to a level that could lead to foreign intervention or renewed refugee flows toward Iran. Iran also aims to prevent a settlement or cease-fire arrangement that would entail the deployment of foreign forces in the area, especially US or Turkish forces. As Iran's Ambassador to Armenia, Mohammad Reis, stated at a press conference in July 2014, "I am sure the deployment of foreign forces would jeopardize security in the region."[26]

In terms of power relations in the region, it is advantageous to Iran that the conflict and particularly Armenia's location inhibit Turkey's ability to trade with Azerbaijan and Central Asia, and prevent its security involvement in the region. Armenia is, in practice, a wedge dividing Turkey from the main part of Azerbaijan while also separating Baku from its non-contiguous region of Nakhichevan. Consequently, Baku is dependent on Iran for transiting energy and other supplies to Nakhichevan, thereby increasing Tehran's leverage over Baku.

The continued existence of the conflict in principle serves Tehran's interests, because it creates vulnerabilities that provide an opportunity for Iran to leverage. In its relations with the two main actors in the conflict—Armenia and Azerbaijan—Tehran views Armenia as an ally and Azerbaijan as an adversary. Yerevan maintains strong security cooperation with Iran and has not supported sanctions and other policies aimed at isolating Iran. In contrast, Baku conducts extensive security and military cooperation with the United States.

Azerbaijan also maintains strong security trade and cooperation with Israel. Observers have often quoted this factor as an explanation for the hostile relations between Azerbaijan and Iran. However, the adversarial relations between Tehran and Baku predated the security cooperation between Israel and Azerbaijan by over six years.[27] Rather, the cooperation between Baku and Tel Aviv, and hence Iran's disposition in regard to Azerbaijan, is based on the latter's strong security orientation toward the United States and Turkey since its inception, and more importantly, on Azerbaijan's potential influence on Iran's domestic ethnic Azerbaijani population. So while in the first decade of the twenty-first century Azerbaijan's cooperation with Israel reinforced Tehran's hostility toward Azerbaijan, it was not a core reason for Tehran's fundamental approach toward the state of Azerbaijan.

As part of its efforts to coerce Baku to change its strategic orientation toward the West and to constrain Azerbaijan's activities in the region, Tehran has provided funding and support for a variety of anti-government elements in Azerbaijan, with focus on domestic Islamic forces and Persian-speaking minorities. Iranian-supported Islamic groups in Azerbaijan have plotted a number of various terrorist acts, such as efforts to disrupt the 2012 Eurovision song competition hosted in Baku, or planned attacks on the US and Israeli Ambassadors to Azerbaijan, as well as on local Jewish community institutions in Baku.

In periods of heightened tension between Iran and Azerbaijan, such as when Baku believes Iran is involved in terrorist plots or supporting insurgencies in Azerbaijan, Baku tends to recall publically the Iranian support for Armenia during the war period. For instance, in response to the fall 2015 Nardaran riots, in which Baku believed Tehran had a hand among this highly religious population, Azerbaijani authorities publically launched criminal proceedings against the vice-president of the National Security and Foreign Policy Committee of Iran's parliament, General Mansour Haqiqatpour, for his alleged relaying of intelligence to Armenian military units during the war in 1993.[28]

The official Iranian-sponsored media is also in most periods very hostile to Azerbaijan President Ilham Aliyev. The *Voice of the Islamic Republic of Iran* radio station in Mashad stands out in this respect, as do official Iranian broadcasts in the Azerbaijani language.[29] Iran also reportedly sponsors a Talysh-language radio station located in Nagorno-Karabakh that promotes secessionism of this minority from Azerbaijan. The Talysh ethnic group speaks an Iranian language and lives primarily in regions of Azerbaijan that are close the border with Iran, and by and large, much more religious and socially conservative that the bulk of the population in Azerbaijan. Thus, members of this group are especially susceptible to cooperation with Iran.

Iran's trade with both Armenia and Azerbaijan is not extensive; however, it is meaningful to the Armenian economy in terms of its volume. In 2014, trade between Tehran and Baku stood at US$ 500 million, having experienced successive annual declines. By comparison, trade in 2014 between Armenia and Iran stood at US$ 300 million.[30]

Iran openly advocates for expansion of cooperation with Armenia, including in infrastructure projects that traverse the occupied territories. On a visit to Yerevan, the Iranian foreign minister, Javad Zarif, remarked "Iran is ready to cooperate with Armenia in different areas, including telecommunications, railway, energy, gas, electricity and the cleaning of the Aras River."[31] Iran is even involved in infrastructure projects located in the Azerbaijani territories occupied by Armenia. For instance, Iranian and Armenian company officials in 2010 inaugurated a hydroelectric dam on the Araxes River near the Khoda Afarin Bridge in an area that straddles Iran and the occupied territories.

Iran is connected to both Armenia and Azerbaijan in energy infrastructure and energy trade. Azerbaijan supplies Iran with natural gas in quantities approximately equivalent to Iranian gas supplies to the exclave of Nakhchivan. Iran also supplies natural gas to Armenia, while Armenia supplies Iran with electricity through two power lines from its nuclear power plant. The sides aim to establish a third electricity line and thus to expand the amount of electricity supplied from Armenia to Iran.

Iran's Domestic Azerbaijani Concern

Tehran's concerns regarding the potential impact of the independence of the Republic of Azerbaijan on its domestic ethnic Azerbaijani minority was one of the most significant factors influencing its policies toward the Nagorno-Karabakh conflict. Indeed, during the war period Iran's deputy foreign minister, Mahmud Va'ezi, pointed to internal considerations as one of Iran's major factors in its policy toward the Karabakh conflict.[32] Evidently, Azerbaijan's embroilment in a conflict is viewed as useful in preempting irredentist policies from Baku. The change in Azerbaijan's policies toward the ethnic Azerbaijani minority in Iran following the fall of Elchibey from power in 1993, lessened the impact of this factor, but it remains pertinent. In fact, since the independence of the Republic of Azerbaijan, Iran uses support for domestic insurgencies in Azerbaijan as a perceived payback for domestic Azerbaijani activity. The levers used most frequently by Tehran have been the activation of Islamic cells in the city of Nardaran near Baku, the Islamic Party of Azerbaijan and members of the Talysh minority. For instance, following riots in Azerbaijani-populated cities in northern Iran in late fall 2015, Iran evidently supported violent activity in Nardaran. Iran operates in this way despite the fact that since the summer of 1993, the government in Baku has rarely encouraged Azerbaijanis in Iran to take action against the government in Iran or foment trouble on an ethnic basis, and actually in the current period has little leverage or influence over this community. Iran, however, does not appear to accept this, and appears to act on the premise that Baku still tries to incite its domestic Azerbaijani community.

In actual fact, it is not clear if Iran has grounds to be concerned about the identity trends of its own Azerbaijani minority. There is a great diversity of opinion on the collective identity among Azerbaijanis in Iran. Some of Iran's ethnic Azerbaijanis, such as the Supreme Leader Ali Khamenei himself, are an integral part of the ruling elite of Iran. Others view themselves as primarily Iranians, but support Iran granting language and cultural rights to the Azerbaijanis and take offense at the strongly engrained element of public Iranian culture that is derogatory toward the Turkic and especially Azerbaijani minorities. Yet others, especially those that live in the Azerbaijani-populated provinces and not in multi-ethnic cities like Tehran, tend to view their ethnic Azerbaijani identity as their primary collective identity, and many residents of the provinces are not even fluent in Persian. For most Azerbaijanis on different parts of the identity spectrum, the establishment of an independent Republic of Azerbaijan challenged and spurred exploration of their self-identity.[33]

In the early 1990s, there was a significant rise in expressions of Azerbaijani ethnic identity and ethnic related political activity among Azerbaijanis in Iran, evidently motivated in response to an independent Azerbaijani state. However, this upsurge in Azerbaijani ethnic awareness generated few calls for the Azerbaijani provinces to secede from Iran and join the new republic, but did lead to demands for increased cultural and language use rights within Iran.

In addition, following the independence of the Republic of Azerbaijan, there emerged open, coordinated political activities and the founding of organizations that brought together Azerbaijanis from all over Iran. Majles members of Azerbaijani origin, for example, formed a caucus to promote Azerbaijani interests in the parliament, while some student groups sought change in the government's policy toward the country's ethnic minorities.

Following the fall of the Soviet Union, indeed fundamental changes took place in the opportunities for direct contact between Azerbaijanis on both sides of the border. Inter-marriage between these communities was very frequent in the early 1990s. Improvements also took place in communications and transportation links between the Azerbaijani provinces in Iran and the Republic of Azerbaijan, including direct flights between Tabriz, the major ethnic Azerbaijani-populated city in Iran, and Baku. In addition, regular daily bus services were established between the various cities in the Azerbaijani-populated provinces in Iran and the Republic of Azerbaijan.

In the early 1990s, open and direct cooperation and interchange between the local government of the Azerbaijani provinces in Iran and the Republic of Azerbaijan was inaugurated. Delegations from all three Azerbaijani provinces visited Baku and established formal direct cooperation in many fields, including trade, education and scientific research. For instance, representatives of the Iranian Azerbaijani provinces and the republic signed protocols and agreements for direct bilateral technical and economic cooperation.[34]

The exposure to Azerbaijani and Turkish television broadcasts and the renewed interaction with Azerbaijanis in the Republic of Azerbaijan, including visits and exchanges, seemed to contribute to a heightened ethnic awareness and pride among Azerbaijanis in Iran. The introduction of wide-scale viewing of television from Turkey in 1992 was especially significant, as Turkic-speaking Azerbaijanis became exposed to a positive image of Turks as presented in the broadcasts, which contrasted with their low-class image in the Iranian media and mainstream Iranian culture.[35]

In contrast to the past, Azerbaijanis now began to express opposition to the widespread derogatory manner that the Iranian media and mainstream culture relate to the Turkic culture and Azerbaijani minority in Iran. Comedians and other cultural figures that commonly made jokes about the *Turki-khar* (Turkish donkey) reference to Azerbaijanis in the 1990s began to encounter nearly violent responses from ethnic Azerbaijanis, in contrast to their past complacency. In the open "Letter of the Azerbaijani Students Studying in the Tehran Universities to the Azerbaijani Deputies of the Iranian Majles," the authors declared a feeling of humiliation in Iran as ethnic Azerbaijanis. The authors of the letter described the Iranian media's policy as one designed to "mimic and defame the culture and language of the Azerbaijan Shi'a," and asked, "When will it be possible to give an effective answer to all these humiliation and mockeries?"[36]

In the last decade, large-scale political mobilization of ethnic Azerbaijanis has continued to occur in response to ethnic slurs appearing in the official Iranian media. For instance, in response to a cartoon depicting a cockroach as an ethnic Azerbaijani published in the Iranian newspaper *Iran* in May 2006, large-scale demonstrations took place in the Iranian cities of Meshkin Shahr, Ardebil, Zanjan, Tabriz, Urmiya and other Azerbaijani-populated cities. The crackdown on the demonstrations caused at least four deaths and led to thousands of arrests and some lengthy prison sentences for the reported organizers of the demonstrations. In addition, in November 2015, large demonstrations took place in Iran centered in Tabriz, Urmia and Zanjan following the broadcast of the *Fitilehha* TV show on official Iranian TV children's programming that depicted an ethnic Azerbaijani–Iranian child using a toilet brush to brush his teeth. Following the large-scale response, the show was pulled from Iranian television. The massive and seemingly disproportionate responses to these various incidents seem to indicate a larger underlying sense of discrimination and degradation of the ethnic minorities in Iran.

In the last two decades, Iranian soccer matches have also become a venue for frequent expression of ethnic sentiments among Azerbaijani fans of Tabriz's main soccer team—Traktor Tabrizi—and of ethnic Azerbaijanis in Tehran and national teams. In parallel, ethnic-based slurs are commonly voiced at matches from supporters of rival teams playing Traktor Tabrizi. Teams and their fans from Persian-majority centers often hurl Armenian flags at games in attempt to incite the ethnic Azerbaijani players and thus to commit fouls.

Iranian Azerbaijani Mobilization in the Nagorno-Karabakh Conflict

Iranian Azerbaijanis have frequently mobilized in support of Baku in this conflict, in contrast to Tehran's policies. Iranian Azerbaijanis organized political activity aimed to exert pressure on Tehran to change its position toward the conflict and to adopt a more pro-Azerbaijani stance, and this internal activity may have been a factor in the shift in Iranian official rhetoric toward the conflict in spring 1993. Moreover, the gap between Tehran's position and that of many of the Azerbaijanis in Iran on the Nagorno-Karabakh conflict may have added an additional element of tension in the relationship between members of this ethnic group and the regime in Iran.

Among the clerics, Ayatollah Musavi-Ardebeli, an ethnic Azerbaijani, often mentioned the Nagorno-Karabakh conflict in his Friday sermons and frequently expressed solidarity with the plight of the Azerbaijani side. Iranian Majles deputies from the Azerbaijani provinces led campaigns aimed at impelling Tehran to minimize its relations with Armenia and they have issued protests against Yerevan. In the Majles, Azerbaijani delegates openly called for

Tehran's assistance to Azerbaijan,[37] and the ethnic Azerbaijani Majles delegates have participated in demonstrations against Armenia.[38] Ethnic Azerbaijani Majles members distributed petitions and succeeded in attaining the signatures of the majority of the Majles members in a call for a change in Tehran's stance on the conflict. In April 1993, Kamel Abedinzadeh, Azerbaijani deputy from Kho'i, even spoke in the Azerbaijani language in the Majles when he condemned Armenian actions against Azerbaijan. He also issued press releases for publication in *Hamshahri* and other journals on this issue.[39]

In addition, on the grassroots level, many Iranian Azerbaijanis expressed their solidarity with the Republic of Azerbaijan in its struggle with Armenia and criticized the Iranian government's support for Armenia in the conflict. In May 1992, 200 students demonstrating at Tabriz University chanted "Death to Armenia" and, alluding to Tehran, described the "silence of the Muslims," in the face of the Armenian "criminal activities" as "treason to the Quran."[40] According to the Iranian newspaper *Salam*, the Azerbaijani demonstrators in Tabriz urged Tehran to support the Republic of Azerbaijan in this struggle during a march that was marked by "nationalist fervor and slogans." *Salam* reported that the demonstration was held "despite the opposition of the authorities."[41] The next year, Tehran University students held a demonstration in front of the Armenian Embassy to show their support for Azerbaijan in the conflict.[42] During the demonstration, the embassy was stoned, and subsequently the Iranian ambassador in Yerevan was summoned by the Armenian foreign minister to present an explanation of the incident.[43]

Iran allows the publication of a limited number of literary journals in the languages of its ethnic minorities. *Varliq* is a bilingual Azerbaijani–Persian publication produced in Tehran,[44] and it is the only Azerbaijani journal that has been published since the revolution in 1979. This publication has frequently published articles on the Nagorno-Karabakh conflict, which often expressed solidarity with the plight of the Azerbaijanis in this conflict. In the spring of 1994, the journal editor, Javad Heyat, addressed an article to then Turkish President Suleyman Demirel, calling on Turkey to come to Azerbaijan's aid in the conflict.[45] *Varliq* frequently carried articles about the Azerbaijani victims of this conflict, as well as poems written in memory of the fallen Azerbaijani soldiers.[46]

In addition, Azerbaijanis in Iran have been involved in providing aid to their co-ethnics in the Republic of Azerbaijan. In 1992–93, much of the humanitarian and refugee assistance from Iran to the Republic of Azerbaijan was organized directly from the Azerbaijani provinces.[47] Commencing in the summer of 1992, many Azerbaijanis wounded in the war with Armenia were treated in Tabriz hospitals. Throughout 1992–93, and initially organized by Azerbaijani representatives from the Iranian provinces, convoys of supplies and other aid were sent directly from these provinces to the needy and refugees in the republic.[48] For instance, a delegation from Urmia in June 1992 set up a refugee center in Nakhchivan and the East Azerbaijan Province opened a refugee camp within the territory of the Republic of Azerbaijan in September 1993.[49]

Relations with Third Parties

Iran's relations with third party actors—chiefly Turkey and Russia, and to a lesser extent the United States and Europe—influence its policies toward the Nagorno-Karabakh conflict. As stated, Tehran aims to prevent the military intervention or deployment of foreign forces, even as peacekeepers, in the conflict zone, due to its proximity to Iran. Despite the friendly rhetoric, Iran would not like to see Russian or Turkish forces deployed close to the border with Iran or engaged in fighting in the conflict zone.

While Tehran strives to prevent the deployment of additional foreign forces, including Russian ones, close to its border, it does share some common interests with Russia in relation to the conflict. Both Moscow and Tehran share an interest in a no-war, no-peace status of the conflict. This leaves Baku and Yerevan more vulnerable to dictates from Moscow and Tehran.

Iran has also aimed to sponsor peace talks between the leaders of Armenia and Azerbaijan, especially during the period of the war in 1992–94 and in response to renewal of fighting between Armenia and Azerbaijan in April 2016. It seems that Tehran is especially interested in sponsoring peace talks in order to illustrate its importance and role as a regional power broker. At times, Tehran has sought cooperation with the Organization for Security and Co-operation in Europe (OSCE) Minsk Group that is tasked with promoting Nagorno-Karabakh conflict resolution, as a means to help circumvent its political isolation.

IMPLICATIONS FOR DEVELOPMENTS IN THE CONFLICT AND ITS RESOLUTION

While Iran has strong interests in developments of the conflict, its posture is relatively defensive. Iran chiefly aims to prevent any spillover of the conflict, mobilization of its own Azerbaijani ethnic minority or the deployment of foreign forces. Tehran benefits from the continuation of the conflict, but in contrast to Russia, does not take steps to intensify the conflict, aspiring for a situation of no-war, no-peace between Armenia and Azerbaijan.

Thus, Iran is not likely to block most conflict resolution initiatives, unless they would entail an exchange of territories that would lengthen its border with Azerbaijan or include the deployment of foreign forces. At the same time, Iran's cooperation with Armenia and its tacit support in the conflict strengthens Yerevan's actual and perceived power and consequently reduces its willingness to compromise and sense of urgency to resolve the conflict. Conversely, Iran's antagonism toward Azerbaijan creates an additional constraint on Baku's activity and its calculations on whether to renew the war effort to retake its territories occupied by Armenia.

The July 2015 Joint Comprehensive Plan of Action agreement between Iran and the United States, Europe, Russia and China and the subsequent removal of sanctions on Iran creates greater opportunity for Iran's activity in the South

Caucasus. The end of Iran's economic and political isolation has strengthened Iran's confidence in its dealings with its neighbors to the north. The Nagorno-Karabakh Conflict has also entered a new stage, where open direct fighting between Armenia and Azerbaijan is no longer exceptional and can easily escalate to full-scale battles, as was evident in April 2016. The combination of escalation of the conflict together with Iranian reintegration in global politics and trade creates new opportunity for Iranian activity toward the conflict and its neighbors. Tehran's policies will most likely continue to be driven by considerations of its own national security, and not ideology. Precisely because Iran's policies are driven by practical considerations, Tehran may act to take advantage of the meaningful changes in the conflict and the region.

NOTES

1. Interview with Viktor Mikhailov in *Priroda* (Russian), August 1995, no. 8, pp. 3–11 (FBIS-SOV-95-245-S); *Tehran Times,* May 9, 1995, p. 1.
2. *Tehran Times,* August 18, 1991, p. 2.
3. *Tehran Times,* December 30, 1991, p. 2.
4. *Jomhuri-ye Islami,* March 4, 1992, p. 4.
5. Tehran Voice of the Islamic Republic of Iran First Program Network, March 10, 1992 (FBIS-NES-92-107).
6. *Jomhuri-ye Islami,* March 2, 1992, p. 2.
7. For example, the communiqué issued at the end of the first ECO summit in Tehran (February 16–17, 1992) does not even mention the Nagorno-Karabakh conflict. In contrast, it makes a clear statement supporting the "restoration of the inalienable rights" of the Palestinian people and respecting the rights of the people of Kashmir. See, IRNA (in English), February 17, 1992.
8. For an example of ascribing the blame to "foreign powers" and the Popular Front of Azerbaijan leadership, see IRNA in English, August 19, 1992.
9. Interfax (in English), April 15, 1992.
10. SNARK (Yerevan), January 29, 1993.
11. Yerevan Armenia's Radio International Service in Armenian, April 25, 1992 (FBIS-SOV-92-081).
12. Interfax (in English), May 7, 1992.
13. Interfax, May 7, 1992.
14. IRNA in English, May 13, 1992.
15. Based on author's interview with source involved in the negotiations during the 1990s. Interview took place winter 2000.
16. See, for instance, TASS, February 28, 1992 (FBIS-SOV-92-040).
17. Moscow Programma Radio Odin, May 31, 1992 (FBIS-SOV-92-105); Yerevan Armenia's Radio First Program, May 20, 1992 (FBIS-SOV-92-099).

18. ITAR-TASS, May 1, 1992 (FBIS-SOV-92-086).
19. Armenia's First Program Network, April 22, 1992 (FBIS-SOV-92-079).
20. *Komsomolskaya Pravda*, May 20, 1992, p. 1.
21. Voice of the Islamic Republic of Iran First Program Network, April 7, 1993 (FBIS-NES-93-065).
22. See, for instance, Yerevan Armenia's Radio First Program Network, December 23, 1993 (FBIS-SOV-93-246) on contacts on the agreement for construction of a gas pipeline between Iran and Armenia. On coal deliveries from Iran to Armenia, see ITAR-TASS, October 23, 1993 (FBIS-SOV-93-204).
23. Armenpres International Service, September 8, 1993 (FBIS-SOV-93-173).
24. "Iran ready to help resolve Nagorno-Karabakh issue diplomatically," Mehr News Agency, March 12, 2013.
25. "Armenian minister praises Iran's 'balanced' stance on Nagorno-Karabakh dispute," Fars News Agency (Tehran, English), May 5, 2014.
26. Trend News (Baku, English), 18 July 2014.
27. Brenda Shaffer, "Azerbaijan's Cooperation with Israel Goes Beyond Iran Tensions," *POLICYWATCH* 2067, Washington Institute for Near East Policy, 16 April 16, 2013, http://www.washingtoninstitute.org/policy-analysis/view/azerbaijans-cooperation-with-israel-goes-beyond-iran-tensions
28. "Azerbaijan initiates criminal case against Iranian General Haqiqatpour," APA (Baku), December 17, 2015.
29. See for example, *Voice of the Islamic Republic of Iran* (Mashad, Persian), April 16, 2013.
30. Fars News Agency, October 6, 2015; Tasnim News Agency, November 25, 2014.
31. As reported by Thai News Service Group, August 13, 2015.
32. Mahmud Va'ezi in Interfax (in English), March 25, 1992 (FBIS-SOV-92-059). See, also, *Tehran Times*, March 10, 1992, p. 2 for reference to the internal Azerbaijan and Armenian factor as affecting its suitability to mediate in the conflict.
33. For more on the question of the impact of the independence of the Republic of Azerbaijani on the collective identity of Azerbaijanis in Iran, see Brenda Shaffer, *Borders and Brethren: Iran and the Challenge of Azerbaijani Identity* (Cambridge, MA: MIT Press, 2002).
34. See, for instance, IRNA in English, February 22, 1993.
35. Based on author's interviews with Iranian Azerbaijanis conducted in 1998 (East Turkey).
36. "Letter of the Azerbaijani Students Studying in Tehran Universities to the Azerbaijani Deputies of the Iranian Majles" (unpublished document gathered by author).
37. *Resalat*, April 19, 1993, p. 5.

38. IRNA in English, April 13, 1993.
39. *Resalat*, April 14, 1993, p. 5.
40. *Salam*, quoted by Reuters, May 25, 1992.
41. *Salam*, as quoted by Agence France Presse, May 25, 1992.
42. IRNA, April 13, 1993.
43. Armenia's Radio First Program, April 14, 1993 (FBIS-SOV-93-071).
44. Varliq means in Azerbaijani "existence" and was so named to symbolize that the Azerbaijani ethnic group exists in Iran.
45. Javad Heyat, *Varliq* (April-June 1994), pp. 25–30.
46. "Khujali," *Varliq* (April-June 1992), pp. 31–33; "Shahidlar," *Varliq* (January–May, 1995), pp. 135–136.
47. See, for instance, IRNA in English, August 31, 1993.
48. Tehran Voice of the Islamic Republic of Iran First Program Network in Persian, June 11, 1992 (FBIS-NES-92-114), and IRNA in English, April 22, 1993.
49. IRNA in English, September 7, 1993.

CHAPTER 7

Missing in Action: US Policy

Stephen Blank

Since 2010, there have been many disturbing signs that the supposedly frozen conflict in Nagorno-Karabakh might soon reignite.[1] Unprecedented violations of the cease-fire concluded in 1994 have taken place since 2014; and during 2015, there were many large-scale incidents, including cross-border shelling, leading to heavy casualties on both sides.[2] In April 2016, four days of fighting led to small but symbolically important changes in territorial control on the ground. In September 2015, Russia lent money to Armenia to buy weapons from it, thus continuing its practice of selling weapons to both sides and stoking the conflict for its own purposes of regional domination.[3] Turkey, too, sells weapons to Azerbaijan and is very closely tied to it on energy issues, as it serves as the export corridor for Azerbaijan's oil and gas. Meanwhile, Iran's connections with Armenia and checkered history of relations with Azerbaijan are also well known, as described in Brenda Shaffer's contribution to this volume. Accordingly, any intensification of the Armenia–Azerbaijan conflict could easily escalate to become a major international crisis involving Russia, Turkey and/or Iran. Moreover, any such conflict would involve not only Europe but also the United States. The latter is one of the guarantors of the Minsk Process that is tasked with resolving the conflict, while security in the South Caucasus cannot be separated from that of Europe.

Any reoccurrence of war would mark both a strategic and humanitarian disaster in a region that can ill afford to suffer such a catastrophe. Adding to

---

This chapters draws from and expands on the article "US Policy, Azerbaijan and the Nagorno-Karabakh Conflict," which appeared in *Mediterranean Quarterly* 26, no. 2, June (2015): 99–114.

S. Blank (✉)
Washington, DC, USA

© The Author(s) 2017
S.E. Cornell (ed.), *The International Politics of the Armenian-Azerbaijani Conflict*, DOI 10.1057/978-1-137-60006-6_7

the sense of a ticking time bomb, both Armenia and Azerbaijan continue to indulge in violent, threatening rhetoric. Armenian President Serzh Sargsyan's recent speeches and statements display a worrying bellicosity, in which he has talked about the necessity of new preemptive and/or asymmetrical measures against Azerbaijan, including preemptive strikes. In January 2015, Armenian Defense Minister Seyran Ohanyan explicitly gave commanders the freedom to act preemptively to restrain "subversive infiltration." He also stated that the recent escalation along the Line of control (LOC) did not require the involvement of the Collective Security Treaty Organization (CSTO). By such logic, therefore, Armenia could act alone, even preemptively, if it chose to do so.[4]

Despite the self-evident dangers throughout the Caucasus and in this conflict, US policy in recent years has been conspicuous by its incoherence and detachment, if not America's virtual absence from the region. That disengagement has been the defining policy characteristic of the Obama administration since 2009. Indeed, it is difficult to discern any coherent or consistent US policy in the South Caucasus, except mounting indignation driven by human rights activists at Azerbaijan's growing repressiveness, a policy trend that overlooks Armenia's equally authoritarian governance and that cannot substitute for a consideration of US strategic interests. Accordingly, US policy in the South Caucasus is striking for its absence and continues to remain "missing in action."[5]

Yet it is not that American policy is simply passive and disengaged. Since 2011, US relations with Azerbaijan in particular have steadily worsened. Indicating the extent of the deterioration in ties between Washington and Baku, on February 4, 2015, a high-level Azerbaijani presidential advisor told an interviewer that the United States backs the separatists in Nagorno-Karabakh by rendering direct financial assistance to them.[6] He also claimed that Russia and Azerbaijan had "complementary" energy projects, an implicit threat that Azerbaijan was not dependent on the West.[7] In December 2014, a high Azerbaijani official published a 13,000-word diatribe that blamed the United States for orchestrating regime change in the post-Soviet space, and called Azerbaijan's human rights activists a "fifth column" of the United States.[8]

In the United States, a similarly harsh tone prevailed. The *Washington Post* found Azerbaijan important enough to pen no less than eight editorials on its human rights record in 2014–15.[9] Former US ambassadors and senior NGO leaders endorsed sanctions on Azerbaijan, while President Obama himself singled out Azerbaijan's poor human rights record in a 2014 speech.[10]

Since late 2015, US–Azerbaijani relations have nevertheless improved considerably, as the US Government changed its approach, largely quitting the practice of public shaming of Azerbaijan in favor of a more discreet approach, and by showing greater interest for regional security issues. Baku reciprocated by ending its anti-American rhetoric, and by releasing numbers of political prisoners.

Despite the unmistakably heightened tensions throughout the entire post-Soviet space, US policy remains unfocused and inattentive, with virtually the entire discussion in US policymaking circles on the region centering on democratization and human rights. The fact that much attention is focused on the latter is not the problem per se; rather, the point is that there is very little interest in any of the other issues affecting this region, whether security, trade, or energy. Meanwhile, both South Caucasian and Central Asian diplomats, as well as US and foreign analysts, regularly complain that these areas do not receive substantive attention in the US government.[11]

Consequently, should any violent conflict escalate in the South Caucasus, it is likely that while Washington will issue warnings to the belligerents, if not to Moscow, the administration will likely quickly conclude that there is nothing it can do there, thereby demonstrating to all interested audiences that what happens in these countries is ultimately not a priority for the Obama administration. Whether the next administration will adopt a different approach remains to be seen. This long-standing neglect has occurred even though the strategic importance of the Caucasus as a whole has risen by an order of magnitude since 2010. If anything, the Russian invasion of Ukraine and Vladimir Putin's subsequent moves to incorporate Abkhazia and South Ossetia into Russia—as well as his implicit threats to countries like Kazakhstan, and Moscow's encroachments upon Kyrgyzstan and Armenia—suggest an extremely ambitious and expansive long-term Russian program in the former Soviet Union. Given that expansive program and Moscow's long-term strategic prioritization of the former Soviet space, the Caucasus necessarily grows in importance, and in particular, so does Azerbaijan as an independent, pro-Western, Muslim-majority state that provides an alternative energy source to the West. Prominent thinkers have long acknowledged Azerbaijan's importance. For example, Zbigniew Brzezinski stated in 1997 that

> Azerbaijan can be described as the vitally important 'cork' controlling access to the 'bottle' that contains the riches of the Caspian Sea basin and Central Asia. An independent, Turkic-speaking Azerbaijan, with pipelines running from it to the ethnically related and politically supportive Turkey, would prevent Russia from exercising a monopoly on access to the region and would thus also deprive Russia of decisive political leverage over the policies of the new Central Asian states.[12]

Elsewhere, Brzezinski described Azerbaijan as the "geographical pivot" of the entire Caspian region and that it deserved America's "strongest geopolitical support."[13] Similarly, Vladimir Socor has written that "Azerbaijan is the irreplaceable country as a gas producer for...the [Southern Gas] Corridor's first stage. Azerbaijan will again be irreplaceable as a transit country for Central Asian gas in those projects' follow-up stages."[14] Accordingly, Azerbaijan is a crucial, if not *the* crucial, lynchpin of any future Southern Gas Corridor (SGC) that will bring Caspian gas to Europe while bypassing Russia and (at least for now) Iran. Indeed, the US interest in ensuring that Russia does not monopolize Eurasian energy supplies to Europe originated during the Clinton administration. The objectives of strengthening the Caspian providers (among them Azerbaijan) and reducing Russia's ability to monopolize their supplies are crucial geopolitical goals because they ensure the economic and political interests of America's European allies and partners, prevent a recrudescence of Russian imperial designs, reduce Moscow's ability to deflect these states from democratization, and create more favorable conditions for the independence and ultimate movement of supplier states toward a more democratizing trajectory.[15]

In addition, pending the potential opening up of the Caspian Sea to unimpeded international maritime and energy trade, Azerbaijan's strategic location offers Central Asian energy producers and littoral states an excellent alternative to dependence on Moscow. Furthermore, Azerbaijan (like the entire Caucasus) could serve as a platform for the projection of US and European influence and values into Central Asia.[16] It should be obvious to all observers that Moscow's threat to all of the post-Soviet states and to the post-Cold War order enhance the strategic importance of these states' sovereignty, integrity and energy resources. Indeed, President Obama himself has acknowledged that Russia's invasion of Ukraine represents a threat to global order.[17]

Beyond these abiding considerations, Azerbaijan has also shown its growing ability to provide a significant alternative to Russia in provisioning Southeastern Europe with gas, particularly as the Trans-Anatolian pipeline through Turkey that links up to the Trans-Adriatic Pipeline (TANAP-TAP) continues to move forward.[18] It has continued to gather momentum among Balkan governments, especially as Russia's South Stream gas pipeline project is now a visible long-term casualty of the decision to invade Ukraine.

Therefore, it is hardly surprising that Russia's proposed Turkish Stream project essentially represented an effort to deflect Turkey away from the southern corridor and quash any realistic hopes for an independent Azerbaijani pipeline to Europe, certainly one carrying Central Asian gas as well. Indeed, Russia's threats to Europe and virtual ultimatum to support the Turkish Stream project typified the harsh tactics that have come to characterize Russian energy and foreign policies.[19] That project was shelved after the growing crisis in Turkish–Russian relations over Syria in late 2015, but it indicates that Russia's policies in ongoing conflicts are clearly connected with its energy policy. Moscow continues to encroach upon the security and sovereignty of South Caucasian countries—its latest move being a barefaced effort to annex Abkhazia and South Ossetia into Russia through systematic integration of these territories with Russia—and it continues to manipulate the conflict between Armenia and Azerbaijan.

Moreover, the demise of the Russian South Stream project places Azerbaijan's energy relevance to Europe on a higher plane, forcing the Balkan states to think seriously about expanding their sources of energy. This creates an opening for Azerbaijan to enlarge upon its preexisting Balkan ties due to the TANAP pipeline project that will link up with the TANAP-TAP.[20] The potential for an expanded Azerbaijani energy presence in Europe is also clearly on Moscow's mind as it is seeking to increase its ties with SOCAR, Azerbaijan's state energy company, even as it tries to limit Azerbaijan's energy exposure to Europe. In classic Russian and Soviet form, Moscow simultaneously wields both the stick and the carrot to deflect Azerbaijan from the West.

At the same time, there appears to be little happening in US–Armenian relations.[21] Armenia's previous policy of "complementarity" that strove, as like many post-Soviet states, to foster a balance in its relations between Moscow and the West was the primary casualty of the decision to repudiate entry into an Association Agreement with the European Union (EU) in 2013.[22] Although Azerbaijan's diplomats in Washington often ascribe power to the Armenian lobby, which registered several "victories" back in the 1990s (such as Section 907 of the Freedom Support Act of 1992 preventing aid to Azerbaijan), in fact there is no real sign of energy in these relations other than meetings on Nagorno-Karabakh.[23] As such, this lobby, whatever its real power, has not been able to help Yerevan or Washington overcome Moscow's coerced abridgement of Armenia's sovereignty.

This lack of dynamism in bilateral Armenian–American relations diminishes Washington's ability to act strongly regarding the Armenian-Azerbaijani conflict. It reflects the broader disengagement mentioned above, and contributes to it by inclining policy, as in any bureaucracy, toward the path of least resistance. Armenia, in any case, is probably in no position to launch any kind of major initiative toward the West or the United States in particular. Thus, in the absence of pressure for anyone to act in Washington, and the lack of means and danger that Yerevan risks if it tries to make a major move toward the West, it is quite unlikely in the foreseeable future that there will be any major change in US–Armenian relations.

The Obama Administration and the Caucasus

Under the Obama administration, US policy from the outset approached the Caucasus on the basis of policies that, however well intended, were shot through with strategic incomprehension of both local realities and Russia's objectives. This characterized both the "reset" policy with Russia and the early efforts in 2009–10 to engender normalization in Turkish–Armenian relations, as discussed in Chap. 5 of this volume. Administration officials admit that the objective of the reset policy was to restore some formula for integrating Russia with the West.[24] However, they never seemed to grasp that Russia, even during Dmitry Medvedev's presidency, was not interested in any such integration. Instead, it seeks and demands a perceived equal status with the United States commensurate with its standing in the Cold War—a status that entailed a free hand in the former Soviet space, not least the Caucasus.[25]

Unfortunately, the reset policy and its authors apparently never grasped these facts and came up with a solution that ultimately proved counter-productive. Dmitri Trenin, Director of the Carnegie Center in Moscow, has written that

The opinion that has predominated in our country to this day that the 'reset' is above all Washington's apology for the mistakes of the earlier Bush Administration and their rectification certainly does not correspond to the idea of the current team in the White House. For example, in our country the concept of the 'reset' is understood as almost the willingness in current conditions to accept the Russian point of view of the situation in the Near Abroad, which essentially is wishful thinking.[26]

Lilia Shevtsova, at the time also at the Carnegie Moscow Center, observed that "the Russian elite interpreted the reset as weakness on the part of the Obama Administration and as an invitation to be more assertive in the post-Soviet space and beyond."[27] Similarly, Russia's then-Ambassador to North Atlantic Treaty Organization (NATO), Dmitri Rogozin, said in March 2009 that "any new relationship with NATO would be on Moscow's terms."[28] Due to such a glaring misreading of Russian policy, the reset policy had already failed by 2012—well before the current war in Ukraine.

Obama's initial efforts to reconcile Armenia with Turkey were equally misconceived and ill-fated. Both the US and Turkish initiatives to undertake such a reconciliation were direct results of Russia's war against Georgia in 2008, which propelled Turkey to rethink its Caucasus policies and the United States to seek a breakthrough in the region. But neither party seemed to grasp that without addressing the Nagorno-Karabakh conflict, Azerbaijan would be left out and resent what it perceived as the legitimization in practice of Armenian conquests of its territory. Although both domestic pressure and a vociferous Azerbaijani campaign against the reconciliation process forced Ankara to insist on progress toward resolving Nagorno-Karabakh as a precondition of accepting the protocols of this agreement, the United States never seemed to understand that the normalization of Turkish–Armenian relations could not be achieved by ignoring the Armenia–Azerbaijan conflict. As a result, despite the fact that there were "unofficial" statements that the protocols could lead to progress on Nagorno-Karabakh, and organizations like the International Crisis Group recommended intensifying the Organization for Security and Co-operation in Europe (OSCE) Minsk process on Nagorno-Karabakh, Washington fumbled the chance to upgrade its commitment either to the Minsk Process or to an independent effort to resolve this conflict.[29] Secretary of State Hillary Clinton and the administration opposed the linkage between Turkish–Armenian relations and the conflict then, and the United States continues to oppose it today[30]—despite having previously been tacitly acknowledged by successive US administrations. Given this set of circumstances, Armenia refused to sign the protocols based on Turkey's revised conditions that pertained to the conflict, and the process fell apart to where it still languishes today. Yet even so, Washington's incomprehension of the need to coordinate progress on Turkish–Armenian normalization with conflict resolution between Armenia and Azerbaijan remains.

Senior officials as well as supporters of the Obama administration blame Azerbaijan for its campaign in opposition to the protocols, which allegedly led

Turkey to reconsider its position.[31] Yet domestic Turkish opposition was no less of a factor in the policy's demise. Moreover, it is elementary logic to grasp that trying to reconcile Yerevan and Ankara *without* an ironclad understanding that this would foster a conflict resolution of Nagorno-Karabakh made no strategic sense, especially given Armenian and Azerbaijani domestic politics. Ending the Turkish embargo of Armenia without regard to the resolution of the conflict would only have the effect of discouraging any kind of settlement. That still remains the case today. It appears, however, that this logic is lost on the current administration. At his confirmation hearing in 2014 Richard Mills, the US Ambassador to Armenia, stated that

> Important to reducing Armenia's isolation and bolstering its economy is timely progress toward reconciliation with neighboring Turkey. This year marks the fifth anniversary of Armenia's and Turkey's signing of the Protocol on Establishment of Diplomatic Relations and the Protocol on the Development of Bilateral Relations. We continue to emphasize the importance of proceeding with final approval of these Protocols, without pre-conditions or linkage to other issues, and have been clear that responsibility for moving forward lies with the Turkish Government.[32]

UKRAINE AND THE ABSENCE OF US STRATEGIC THINKING

While it was expected that the Ukraine crisis would lead to a return of strategic thinking regarding Eurasia in the United States, this does not appear to have occurred. To a certain extent, this is related to the Obama administration's broader thinking in terms of the promotion of US interests. There appears to be a widespread belief that any US foreign intervention essentially, if not exclusively, is fated to mean large-scale military operations as distinct from other approaches, whether diplomatic or indirect approaches like providing weapons or using force to display resolve and deter conflicts, as on the Korean Peninsula and elsewhere.[33] Moreover, leading thinkers in the administration and outside appear to consider any US intervention to be inherently futile, a maxim that consigns the United States to self-denying rationalizations, while precluding strategy and effective policymaking.[34] In other words, when it comes to Eurasia, the United States has not only abdicated policy but also abdicated strategy as well as a belief in the use of all the instruments of power, including non-military ones. This means, as Edward Lucas has observed, that there is a prevalent belief that "American engagement in Europe is increasingly irrelevant. Or counter-productive. Or expensive. Or useless."[35] The same wording could be applied to Eurasia, and increasingly the Middle East. But the costs of this strategic abdication are rapidly becoming obvious. Indeed, the current Ukrainian and Syrian crises show what this neglect of alliance management can lead to.

Unfortunately, the strategic torpor that has characterized this administration regarding Central Asia, the Caucasus, and Eastern Europe in general (and

Ukraine in particular) goes far to validate this observation of America missing in action.[36] Writing about the Ukrainian crisis in its early phase, Walter Russell Mead observed that

> Looking at Russia through fuzzy, unicorn-hunting spectacles, the Obama Administration sees a potential strategic partner in the Kremlin to be won over by sweet talk and concessions. As post-historical as any Brussels-based EU paper pusher, the Obama Administration appears to have written off Eastern Europe as a significant political theater.[37]

Mead's assessment applies equally to the Caucasus and Central Asia. As the present author has observed elsewhere, the United States appears to identify little or no interest in either of those regions and has no policy to meet already existing, not to mention impending, security challenges in the Caucasus or Central Asia.[38]

Worryingly, this appears to be the conventional wisdom of the foreign policy establishment. A Council of Foreign Relations' assessment of potential trouble spots for 2014 and the likelihood of their "eruption" into major violence omitted Ukraine. Furthermore, it concluded that the Armenia-Azerbaijan conflict is a "third-tier" conflict, that is, one that has a low preventive priority for US policymakers.[39] Thus, not only did the most prestigious institution in the US foreign policy establishment consider an outbreak of violence unlikely but it also judged that even if it occurred, it would have little impact on US interests. Not surprisingly, this reinforces the conclusion, also evident in Georgia's unresolved conflicts in Abkhazia and South Ossetia, that conflict resolution plays no real part in US policy in the Caucasus.[40] But we know from the Russo-Georgian war of 2008 that if these crises remain in a state of suspended animation, the more likely it is that they will one day unfreeze with profound, widespread and considerable strategic consequences for the United States and its allies and partners. Indeed, it should come as no surprise that there has not been a discernible reaction by the United States to Moscow's recent encroachments upon Georgian sovereignty, and indeed its territory, nor was there an immediate response when fighting flared up along the frontline between Armenian and Azerbaijani forces in April 2016.

The view that the United States should renounce an active role in conflict resolution in particular and the Eurasian region in general is pervasive among officials, and colors policy toward all of Eurasia. Former high-ranking officials have confirmed that not only does the United States have no real policy for Central Asia, but also it even lacks the capability of formulating or implementing one given official's poor understanding of the region. Nikolas Gvosdev of the US Navy War College wrote in connection with the Ukrainian crisis that

> The unspoken reality is that the post-Cold War generation now rising in prominence in the U.S. national security apparatus is no longer enthralled by the geopolitical assessments of Halford Mackinder and Nicholas Spykman, who posited

that Eurasia is the world's strategic axis and that an active effort to impact the balance of political forces in this part of the world is vital to the security and survival of the Western world. As the Obama administration is forced to balance between sustaining the U.S. presence in the Middle East while laying the foundation for the pivot to Asia—the two parts of the world seen as most important for America's future—the fate of the non-Russian Eurasian republics has dropped from a matter of vital interest to a preference. If Ukraine, Georgia or any other of those countries could be brought into the Western orbit cheaply and without too much trouble, fine—but once a substantial price tag is attached, one that could then take away from other, more pressing priorities, enthusiasm diminishes. The strategic calculation at the end of the day in both Brussels and Washington is that even if Russia succeeds in binding the other states of the region into a closer economic and political entity, a Moscow-led Eurasian Union, while it may not be welcomed by a large number of Ukrainians themselves, would still not pose a significant threat to the vital interests of the Euro-Atlantic world.[41]

The waning US attention to these areas as a whole despite this broad acknowledgment of the area's criticality for US interests lends credence to the belief that the Obama administration's policy reflected an outlook of selective commitment whereby Washington could reduce its presence and interest in certain regions and choose carefully what its priorities are.[42] Thus, as Gvosdev writes, "Washington is not really strengthening its presence in the area in a way that one might expect."[43]

Evidently, the war in Afghanistan and the Obama reset policy have interacted to diminish the importance in US considerations of Eurasia as a whole and regional conflict resolution in the Caucasus in particular. Widespread disillusionment with failed interventions, financial constraints, domestic gridlock and slow recovery from the global financial crisis all contribute to this disengagement from Eurasia.[44] But Gvosdev and Mead both rightly argue that there is no strategic will or vision in which Eurasia, or its supposedly "frozen conflicts," merit sustained US intervention or action.

Consequently, America has essentially adopted a self-denying ordnance with regard to Eurasia and its conflicts whether real, potential, or frozen. But past experience teaches that the refusal to address the issues at stake in so-called "frozen conflicts" all but ensures that they will unfreeze and turn violent with profound international repercussions. This happened in regard to the Georgian conflicts with Abkhazia and South Ossetia, where Western abstention from conflict resolution allowed Russia, as President Putin himself subsequently admitted, to plan a war from 2006 on, when Moscow began training local separatist forces.[45] The international ramifications of the Russo-Georgian war were plainly far-flung and foreboded the subsequent conflict in Ukraine. Thus, what ultimately is at stake in Ukraine and in the many unresolved conflicts in the Caucasus, including Nagorno-Karabakh, is the overall structure of security in Eurasia and thus Europe as a whole. For as was already apparent in the 1990s, the security of the South Caucasus and that of Europe are ultimately indivisible.[46]

Unfortunately, the appreciation of the enhanced strategic importance of the South Caucasus has not penetrated the walls of the White House. Instead, over several years there was a White House-led campaign to attack and discredit Azerbaijan largely due to its worsening human rights record.[47] This campaign intensified with President Obama's September 2014 speech to the UN explicitly decrying Azerbaijan's record and in subsequent media attacks on Azerbaijan and its defenders.[48] While poor human rights records have not precluded US cooperation with Uzbekistan, Saudi Arabia and Vietnam, among other countries—some of which have considerably worse records than Azerbaijan—the animus against Azerbaijan was remarkable, and showed that the administration lacked the strategic understanding that permeates US ties with other countries with dubious human rights records.

The problem is compounded by the fact that US policymaking circles seem to be strikingly uninformed of critical realities in the area. For example, former Secretary of Defense Robert Gates called Baku "a typical Central Asian city." And there has been little said by the administration on the urgency of support for a trans-Caspian gas or oil pipeline to present alternatives to Russian domination or against Moscow's recent efforts to close the Caspian Sea to foreign influence.[49] Indeed, recently an important administration official observed that Washington places more importance on the so-called TAPI pipeline (Turkmenistan–Afghanistan–Pakistan–India) than on a Trans-Caspian Pipeline (TCP).

The problem is that justified critiques of Baku's bad human rights record will have little or no effect on Baku as long as Washington does not seriously engage with it on the region's most pressing security issues, such as the conflict over Nagorno-Karabakh, as well as challenges emanating from Russia or Iran. Even if, as this author believes, Azerbaijan ultimately undermines its own domestic security by its crackdown on human rights, absent such engagement Baku has no incentive to listen to Washington. Instead, to advance a mutually beneficial agenda that addresses both hard and soft security issues—including human rights—it is necessary for both governments to listen seriously to the other and act on each other's concerns. Indeed, one of the reasons for Baku's intensified though cautious pursuit of improved relations with Moscow and Tehran is Baku's growing awareness that Washington does not seem to take it at all seriously.

On the other hand, as noted above, Washington began seeking a re-engagement with Baku in late 2015. Three high-ranking US delegations traveled to Baku in late 2015, clearly signifying renewed interest in dialogue. The subjects of their discussion, as revealed in the press, tend to corroborate that impression. In November 2015, Secretary of the Navy Ray Mabus arrived in Baku to talk about military and defense cooperation and specifically invoked cooperation with the US Navy and Marines. The published accounts of his meetings clearly suggest an emphasis on Azerbaijan's defense with regard to the Caspian Sea. Subsequently, a major delegation of officials and US businesses under the auspices of the US Department of Commerce traveled to Baku to discuss improved economic, trade and investment ties. Subsequent to this, newly appointed Deputy Assistant Secretary of State for European and Eurasian Affairs Bridget Brink held talks across virtually all of the non-military areas of the relationship. Her visit led a member of the opposition National Council's Coordination Center, Gultekin Hacibeyli, to note a direct link between this visit, President Aliyev's attendance at the G-20 summit in Turkey, and improving ties between Baku and Washington. It may also be that the release of Azerbaijani political prisoners Arif and Leyla Yunus served as a signal to the West in this context.[50] In April 2016, President Aliyev was invited to the Nuclear Security Summit in Washington, and held constructive meetings with Secretary of State John F. Kerry and Vice President Joe Biden.

US POLICY ON NAGORNO-KARABAKH

The United States took on the role as a co-chair of the Minsk Group in 1997, and for several years, the United States worked actively to promote a peaceful solution under both Democrat and Republican presidents. In 1999, Deputy Secretary of State Strobe Talbott took the lead in an American-led mediation effort that operated rather independently of the Minsk Group. It effectively faltered, however, with the murder of Armenia's Prime Minister and Speaker of Parliament Vazgen Sargsyan on October 27, 1999, only hours after Talbott had left the country. In April 2001, Secretary of State Colin Powell hosted a summit in Key West, Florida, to resolve the conflict—which failed in spite of several days of high-level negotiations. Since that failure, the United States has effectively taken a back seat in the negotiations. France took a leading position ahead of the 2006 Rambouillet conference; and in 2008, Moscow took the lead immediately after its invasion of Georgia. Both efforts failed.

In 2014 Ambassador James Warlick, the US co-chair of the Minsk Group, gave a series of speeches and interviews outlining US policy on the conflict. In these public appearances, Warlick outlined US support for the six principles that he claimed had been agreed to by all parties, and concluded that the main obstacle to resolving the conflict lay in the failure hitherto of both the Armenian and Azerbaijani governments to make the hard decision for peace over domestic opposition.[51] Warlick also claimed that the United States still regards the Minsk Process led by Washington, Paris and Moscow as the most suitable forum for negotiations, and that Washington and Moscow saw "eye-to-eye" on the conflict and the need to highlight the Minsk process as the primary instrument for conflict resolution.[52] Warlick's six points are as follows:

> First, in light of Nagorno-Karabakh's complex history, the sides should commit to determining its final legal status through a mutually agreed and legally binding expression of will in the future. This is not optional. Interim status will be temporary.

Second, the area within the boundaries of the former Nagorno-Karabakh Autonomous Region that is not controlled by Baku should be granted an interim status that, at a minimum, provides guarantees for security and self-governance.

Third, the occupied territories surrounding Nagorno-Karabakh should be returned to Azerbaijani control. There can be no settlement without respect for Azerbaijan's sovereignty, and the recognition that its sovereignty over these territories must be restored.

Fourth, there should be a corridor linking Armenia to Nagorno-Karabakh. It must be wide enough to provide secure passage, but it cannot encompass the whole of Lachin district.

Fifth, an enduring settlement will have to recognize the right of all IDPs and refugees to return to their former places of residence.

Sixth and finally, a settlement must include international security guarantees that would include a peacekeeping operation. There is no scenario in which peace can be assured without a well-designed peacekeeping operation that enjoys the confidence of all sides.[53]

While these points are all essential to a settlement, they do not resolve the fundamental issues of the conflict. Moreover, as noted above, they have been agreed to for years. Finally, the Minsk Process has long since proven itself to be a failure, while Moscow has exploited and incited tensions in the region for its own ends. Indeed, Moscow's malignant role confirms that the internationalization of the conflict complicates the situation and creates more risks of renewed violence.

Meanwhile, the US position means that the most critical issue to Azerbaijan, and one that has immense repercussions beyond the immediate conflict zone, is of little strategic importance to the United States. On this basis, it is not surprising that US–Azerbaijani relations have sharply deteriorated in the last several years regardless of Baku's human rights record—roughly beginning with the Obama administration's support for the Turkish-Armenian protocols. Not surprisingly, this assessment reinforces the conclusion, also evident in Georgia's unresolved conflicts, that conflict resolution plays no real part in US policy in the Caucasus.[54]

The belief that the United States sees eye-to-eye with Moscow, which by extension is allegedly playing a constructive role, is dubious. Warlick's remarks clearly reflect the administration's ongoing failure to grasp what is at stake in the Caucasus or to take conflict resolution there sufficiently seriously. Therefore, it is difficult not to agree with the complaint from Baku, which came soon after Warlick's speeches in Washington, that these statements did nothing to advance the cause of conflict resolution. Indeed, these statements came after the Ukraine crisis, after further Russian arms sales to both Armenia and Azerbaijan, as well as after Moscow's successful coercion of Armenia to desist from European Integration. For Washington to claim that it and Moscow concur as to what should be done regarding the conflict reflects, at best, a surprising degree of wishful thinking.

Finally, the argument that the leaders of Armenia and Azerbaijan have to make hard decisions is true but incomplete. While the decisions both these governments must make concerning a peace settlement are admittedly difficult, it is also the case that the scale of devastation in the conflict zone means that the costs of reconstruction are enormous and growing with the continuing delay in settling the conflict. This further entails that the material costs each side must incur are such as to suggest the need for large-scale assistance up front to make a peace deal possible.[55] Given the urgency of resolving this conflict—particularly after Moscow demonstrated its violent and imperial proclivities in Ukraine, and as a result of the heightened strategic urgency of ensuring that Azerbaijani energy flows unmolested to Europe—Washington needs to devise initiatives to help these governments commit to a solution and stand up to domestic opposition, much as it did in the Camp David agreement of 1978 between Egypt and Israel. But instead, Washington prefers lecturing to both governments on their approaches to the conflict as well as on human rights issues, and simultaneously refuses to devise or offer concrete initiatives. That underscores America's inability and unwillingness to come to grips with either the urgency of resolving the conflict or the realities of the Minsk Process. Moreover, Washington's posturing begs the question of why these governments should take risks for peace when Washington offers them no support for doing so. Finally, it should be obvious that it is impossible to convince either Armenia or Azerbaijan to improve their authoritarian domestic policies without taking a serious interest in their primary security challenge, and materially helping them to make peace.

AMERICA'S ABSENCE AND RUSSIA'S GEOPOLITICAL PUSH IN THE CASPIAN

The large-scale American misapprehension of the strategic importance of the Caucasus has left a vacuum to be filled. France partly tried to fill it by convening a meeting in October 2014 of Presidents Sargsyan and Aliyev and the Minsk Process ambassadors in Paris.[56] While France probably lacks the leverage to bring about a settlement, its moves clearly signify its sense that America has taken a passive role. In any case, France is hardly the only player. Evidently aware of the growing US–Azerbaijani disengagement, Moscow has consistently made serious moves to bring Baku back into its sphere of influence, despite long-held Azerbaijani suspicions concerning Russian goals and tactics, and Baku's determination to pursue an independent foreign policy course.[57] Russia's recent tactics consist of a classic Russian mixture of both blandishments and threats to move Azerbaijan into its corner. On the one hand, Russian Defense Minister Sergei Shoigu traveled to Baku in October 2014 to arrange joint Russo-Azerbaijani naval exercises and naval arms sales for next year and to propose a collective defense system in the Caspian Sea.[58] Yet, on the other hand, Azerbaijani experts see Moscow as attempting to exert leverage to facilitate Azerbaijan's entrance into the Russian-led Eurasian Economic Union.[59]

In August 2014, President Putin resolved to invite the two presidents for talks in Sochi. Shortly following this announcement, the most significant fighting along the cease-fire line since 1994 took place. While it is possible that Azerbaijan initiated the fighting, the Armenian counter-offensive was considerably stronger than customary in such situations. While the two presidents traveled to Sochi, no concrete results emerged from the meeting. The timing of the violence, and Russia's effort to organize the meeting outside of the Minsk Group's format, also led to suspicions that Russia had played a part in triggering the fighting.[60]

These pressures, and Moscow's diplomacy in the Nagorno-Karabakh conflict, are part and parcel of a broader Russian policy that prominently features the manipulation of ethnic tensions and conflicts, and the politicization of energy projects.

Russia has consistently sought to undermine the integrity and sovereignty of the South Caucasian states. In 2008 Vafa Guluzade, former national security advisor for Azerbaijan, observed that President Medvedev's visit to Azerbaijan was preceded by deliberate Russian incitement of the Lezgin and Avar ethnic minorities there to induce Azerbaijan to accept Russia's gas proposals.[61] The same was true in 2013, ahead of a visit by Vladimir Putin and six Russian cabinet members.[62] More recently, Russian officials apparently began to deploy the Talysh minority, by allowing the organization of events in Moscow in support of Talysh rights, while it ensured trolls in the Russian media spread the notion that Talysh had never been part of medieval Azerbaijan.[63] Articles in the Russian press have advocated government action to protect Azerbaijan's minorities as Russian "citizens" to punish Azerbaijan for flirting with NATO.[64] Equally, Moscow proved its stranglehold over Armenia in 2013 by coercing the country to give up an Association Agreement with the EU for membership in the Eurasian Union. In defending the move, President Sargsyan cited national security reasons—a euphemism, no doubt, for Russian threats to alter its policy of support for Armenia on Nagorno-Karabakh. This type of policies appears to be systematic on Russia's part. Aside from dismembering Georgia, Moscow has intermittently encouraged separatist movements among the Armenian Javakhetian minority in Georgia and taken control of the Crimea and the Donbass to undermine Ukraine's viability as a state.[65]

Russian efforts to play the ethnic card against post-Soviet successor states are not limited to the Caucasus. Russian threats against the Baltic States are well known; Russian officials have also habitually reminded Kazakhstan's government that there is a large Russian minority in Kazakhstan and that Moscow has the power and means to incite them against the government if it diverges too far from Russian demands.[66] Putin also announced in 2014 that Kazakhstan had never been a state before 1991, provoking a significant Kazakh response.[67] In 2014, Russia also gave evidence of its capability and ever-present intention of exploiting Karakalpak nationalism against Uzbekistan, a state that has pursued a notably independent policy in Central Asia and aligned periodically with Washington and Beijing against Russia.[68]

Thus, in both word and deed, Moscow has shown that war in Eurasia is neither inconceivable nor impossible. And European governments know full well that revitalized Russian imperial designs represent a fundamental threat to European security as such. Russian law permits the president to dispatch troops abroad to defend the "honor and dignity" of other Russians—a group that can be easily fabricated by means of Russia's preexisting "passportization" policy, which entails the distribution of Russian passports to target populations in other countries without any parliamentary debate or accountability.[69]

The words of prominent Russian analyst Alexei Fenenko sum up Russia's strategy. He wrote that to force America into dialogue with Russia on equal terms, Moscow has periodically had to give demonstrations of power, namely using force against neighboring states. Specifically, he writes that "such tasks require from Moscow periodic doses of force in the post-Soviet space. In each instance, the Kremlin has sought to achieve three objectives: to compel Washington to compromise, to maintain a buffer zone of neutral countries between Russia and NATO, and to create the conditions to replace the most overtly anti-Russian regimes."[70]

Meanwhile, Moscow is keeping its pressure up on the energy sector, knowing that it forms the key to the economic independence of several of the region's states. Thus, Russia has been trying to induce Azerbaijan to sign an agreement on the Caspian that would bar all foreign military presence from the area. Furthermore, as Vladimir Socor has detailed, Russian analysts and officials have long threatened that if Turkmenistan adheres to the EU's planned Southern Corridor for energy trans-shipments to Europe through Azerbaijan that bypass Russia, Moscow would have no choice but to do to Turkmenistan and Azerbaijan what it did to Georgia in 2008.[71] Turkmenistan's Ministry of Foreign Affairs in 2011 blasted Russia's politicized objections to it participating in a TCP, stating that such a pipeline was an objective vital economic interest of Turkmenistan, rebuked Moscow for "distorting the essence and gist of Turkmenistan's energy policy," and announced that the discussions with Europe would continue.[72] Moscow's reply followed soon thereafter. On November 15, 2011, Valery Yazev, Deputy Speaker of the Russian Duma and head of the Russian Gas Society, openly threatened Turkmenistan with the Russian incitement of an "Arab Spring" if it did not renounce its "neutrality" and independent sovereign foreign policy, including its desire to align with the EU's Southern Corridor. Yazev said that,

> Given the instructive experience with UN resolutions on Libya and the political consequences of their being 'shielded from the air' by NATO forces, Turkmenistan will soon understand that only the principled positions of Russia and China in the UN Security Council and its involvement in regional interna-

tional organizations—such as the SCO (Shanghai Cooperation Organization), CSTO (Collective Security Treaty Organization), Eurasian Economic Union—can protect it from similar resolutions.[73]

Mikhail Aleksandrov, Director of the Caucasus division at the state-sponsored CiS Research Institute, stated that in order to stop a TCP, "Russia would have to act in the manner of its operation to compel Georgia to peace"; he also opined that NATO's 2011 Libya operation gave Moscow the right to use force in the Caspian Basin.[74] These are by no means the only threats directed at Azerbaijan or Turkmenistan, or indirectly to their interests and potential partners.[75]

In October 2014, Russian media claimed that the Caspian summit held in September that year in Astrakhan had agreed to prohibit foreign soldiers, that is, those from non-littoral states, from being present in the region. Russian analysts warned that Washington was trying to obtain a NATO base in Azerbaijan and that this was against Baku's interests and needs. Given that no such plans were even remotely in existence, this can be interpreted as a clear threat targeted at Baku.[76]

At the same time, the Russian defense minister, Sergey Shoigu, proclaimed that Moscow espouses a collective security system for the Caspian Sea, and wants Azerbaijan to step up naval cooperation with it toward this end. While joint drills have been held and Baku is interested in buying Russian Bal-E coastal missile systems, Azerbaijan sidestepped Shoigu's proposals and pushed back saying that it had not agreed to bar foreign forces and that such talk reflected both Moscow's paranoia and search for pretexts for smothering Azerbaijan.[77] Moscow is pressing to exclude any Western presence, including that of the EU in the Caspian. Thus, it opposes any EU "interference" in the issue of a TCP, or the Southern Corridor that would relieve Europe from some of the threats associated with Russian energy dominance.[78]

CONCLUSIONS

The situation described above suggests a profound American interest in engaging the states of the South Caucasus, primarily on the crucial issues of security and unresolved conflicts. The first geopolitical reason for engaging all three states of the South Caucasus is to uphold the principles of territorial integrity, sovereignty and the borders of the 1989–91 Eurasian settlement in the region where they are most challenged. The predicament of Ukraine epitomizes what not responding to such threats can effectively lead to. Thus by engaging, the United States would also be strengthening the similarly challenged situations of other countries.

Unless and until the states of the South Caucasus can find partners with sufficient leverage, they are perpetually vulnerable to Russian pressure using a variety of instruments. In particular, the greatest vulnerability of both Armenia and Azerbaijan is tied to the festering conflict in Nagorno-Karabakh, which undermines both states' sovereignty but especially that of Armenia; paradoxically, maintaining its territorial acquisitions from its war with Azerbaijan have robbed it of its sovereignty vis-à-vis Russia.

Of course, a greater US engagement on issues of security and conflict in the region would not occur in isolation. The diversification of energy flows from the Caspian and Central Asia remains a vital Western interest in terms of both the West's own needs and the producer states' objective of ensuring their independence and freedom to act as independent sovereign actors in their foreign and economic policies. Further, it has long been a paramount Western goal to uphold the principles of the sovereignty and territorial integrity of the post-Soviet states of the Caucasus, Ukraine and Central Asia. The West's failure to uphold its own commitments in Ukraine, shameful as they might be, does not invalidate that overriding strategic objective. If anything, it makes the need for curtailing Russian threats all the more urgent—especially as Russia's imperial drive can only be maintained by war or the threat of it, and the perpetuation of frozen conflicts in Eurasia, particularly Nagorno-Karabakh.

Finally, from the humanitarian viewpoint, the United States has a moral duty, even more strongly reinforced by its strategic benefit to the West, of trying to bring peace to the peoples of this region. A policy that combines what is in practice strategic disengagement with moralistic lecturing and sanctions may find appeal, but it neither brings peace nor advances human rights. Leaving Azerbaijan and Armenia to Moscow's tender mercies may represent strategic wisdom to some misguided policymakers. But in reality, it actually represents, and will be seen in those countries and be exploited by Russia, as another strategic abdication of responsibility by Washington, with potentially ominous results.

NOTES

1. David M. Herszenhorn, "Clashes Intensify Between Armenia and Azerbaijan Over Disputed Land," *New York Times*, January 31, 2015, http://www.nytimes.com/2015/02/01/world/asia/clashes-intensify-between-armenia-and-azerbaijan-over-disputed-land.html?_r=0
2. Alexander Skakov, "Nagorno-Karabakh Conflict: March Madness," *Russian International Affairs Council*, April 29, 2015, http://russian-council.ru/en/inner/?id_4=5802#top-content
3. Giorgi Lomsadze, "Russia to Loan Armenia $200m for Guns," *Eurasianet.org*, September 8, 2015, http://www.eurasianet.org/node/74981
4. "Armenia: Official Statements Suggest New Tactics Against Azerbaijan," *Open Source Center, Foreign Broadcast Information Service, Central Eurasia*, February 2, 2015, henceforth *FBIS SOV*, February 4, 2015.
5. Stephen Blank, "US Policy, Azerbaijan, and the Nagorno-Karabakh conflict."

6. Baku, *1News.az*, in Russian, February 4, 2015, *FBIS SOV*, February 4, 2015.

7. Ibid.

8. Joshua Kucera, "Azerbaijan Snubs the West," *New York Times*, January 8, 2015, http://www.nytimes.com/2015/01/09/opinion/azerbaijan-snubs-the-west.html

9. See the following articles in *The Washington Post*: "Azerbaijan prosecutes a prominent human rights defender on absurd charges," August 13, 2014, https://www.washingtonpost.com/opinions/azerbaijan-prosecutes-a-prominent-human-rights-defender-on-absurd-charges/2014/08/13/2971c430-2254-11e4-958c-268a320a60ce_story.html; "Jailed without Trial in Azerbaijan," March 1, 2015, https://www.washingtonpost.com/opinions/jailed-without-trial-in-azerbaijan/2015/03/01/34a1d342-bea1-11e4-bdfa-b8e8f594e6ee_story.html; "The Country that Diminishes the Olympic Flame," April 15, 2015, https://www.washingtonpost.com/opinions/the-country-that-diminishes-the-olympic-flame/2015/04/15/25b37c24-e2d1-11e4-b510-962fcfabc310_story.html; "Lady Gaga and members of Congress accept the paychecks of a tyrant," August 7, 2015, https://www.washingtonpost.com/opinions/blinders-in-azerbaijan/2015/08/07/7fd77636-3d19-11e5-8e98-115a3cf7d7ae_story.html; "Azerbaijan's Injustice," August 16, 2015, https://www.washingtonpost.com/opinions/azerbaijans-injustice/2015/08/16/ea72941e-42bc-11e5-846d-02792f854297_story.html; "Azerbaijani reporter sentenced to more than 7 years after a farcical trial," September 2, 2015, https://www.washingtonpost.com/opinions/azerbaijani-reporter-sentenced-to-more-than-7-years-after-a-farcical--trial/2015/09/02/93c6480a-5193-11e5-8c19-0b6825aa4a3a_story.html; "No, this is the Truth about Azerbaijan's Repression," September 25, 2015, https://www.washingtonpost.com/opinions/no-this-is-the-truth-about-azerbaijan/2015/09/25/d68a6fd0-608f-11e5-b38e-06883aacba64_story.html; "Azerbaijan's Continuing Mistreatment of Rights Activists," November 21, 2015, https://www.washingtonpost.com/opinions/azerbaijans-continuing-mistreatment-of-rights-activists/2015/11/21/7059b820-897e-11e5-9a07-453018f9a0ec_story.html

10. The White House, Office of the Press Secretary, "Remarks by the President at Clinton Global Initiative," September 23, 2014, https://www.whitehouse.gov/the-press-office/2014/09/23/remarks-president-clinton-global-initiative

11. Conversations with Azerbaijani, Georgian and Uzbek diplomats as well as US officials and analysts, Washington, D.C., 2013–2015.

12. Amir Veliev, "The Israel-Turkey-Azerbaijan Triangle: Present and Future," *Central Asia and Caucasus Journal*, no. 8, 2000, http://www.ca-c.org/journal/eng-02-2000/08.veliev.shtml

13. Zbigniew Brzezinski, *The Grand Chessboard: American Primacy and Its Geostrategic Imperatives* (New York: Basic Books, 1998), 179.

14. Vladimir Socor, "Southern Corridor, White Stream: the Strategic Rationale," *Eurasia Daily Monitor*, October 30, 2009, http://www.jamestown.org/regions/turkey/single/?no_cache=1&tx_ttnews%5Bpointer%5D=4&tx_ttnews%5Btt_news%5D=35676&tx_ttnews%5BbackPid%5D=645&cHash=efd1cd665044ba69de7a4c6833138b0e#.VrxlP9srLcs

15. See Ilya Levine, "US Interests in Central Asia Under George W. Bush: Democracy, the War on Terror, and Energy," a doctoral dissertation submitted to the Asia Institute and School of Social and Political Sciences, University of Melbourne, 2012, 39–43, which outlines the many expert and official sources that all subscribed to this outlook; Committee on Foreign Relations, the United States Senate, Testimony of Leon Fuerth on "Oil, Oligarchs, and Opportunity: Energy from Central Asia to Europe," June 12, 2008, http://www.foreign.senate.gov/imo/media/doc/FuerthTestimony080612p.pdf

16. Richard Giragosian, "US National Interests and Engagement Strategies in the South Caucasus," in *South Caucasus: 20 Years of Independence* (Berlin: Friedrich Ebert Stiftung, 2011), 246.

17. Mark Landler, "Obama Rebukes Russia Over Its Actions in Ukraine," *New York Times*, November 16, 2014, http://www.nytimes.com/2014/11/17/world/asia/obama-close-to-calling-russian--action-in-ukraine-an-invasion.html

18. Stephen Blank, *Azerbaijan's Security and U.S. Interests: Time for a Reassessment* (Stockholm and Washington D.C.: Central Asia-Caucasus Institute & Silk Road Studies Program, 2013), http://www.isdp.eu/images/stories/isdp-main-pdf/2013-blank-azerbaijans-security-and--us-interests.pdf

19. Stephen Blank, "Russia Gives EU, Turkey and Azerbaijan an Ultimatum on 'Turk Stream,'" *Eurasia Daily Monitor*, January 22, 2015, http://www.jamestown.org/programs/edm/single/?tx_ttnews%5Btt_news%5D=43431&cHash=2cab7dd2a05a409c987e29be629f97e2#.VrxlHNsrLcs

20. Blank, "Russia Gives EU, Turkey and Azerbaijan an Ultimatum on 'Turk Stream.'"

21. U.S. Department of State, Bureau of European and Eurasian Affairs, "U.S. Relations with Armenia," March 20, 2015, http://www.state.gov/r/pa/ei/bgn/5275.htm

22. Vladimir Socor, "The End of 'Complementarity' in Armenian Foreign Policy," *Eurasia Daily Monitor*, September 18, 2013, http://www.jamestown.org/programs/edm/single/?tx_ttnews[tt_news]=41374&tx_ttnews[backPid]=685&no_cache=1#.VrKOsvGA2UY; Khatchik DerGhougassian, "Farewell to Complementarity: Armenia's Foreign Policy at a Crossroad," *The Armenian Weekly*, April 1, 2014.

23. Author's conversations with Azeri diplomats in Washington, D.C.
24. Conversations with US officials, Washington, D.C., 2014–2015.
25. Stephen Blank, "The Sacred Monster: Russia as a Foreign Policy Actor," in *Perspectives on Russian Foreign Policy*, ed. Stephen Blank (Carlisle Barracks, PA: Strategic Studies Institute, U.S. Army War College, 2012), 25–194.
26. Trenin is quoted in Sergei Strokan and Dmitry Sidorov, "In the World: and Now the Rest," Moscow, *Kommersant Online,* in Russian, July 27, 2009, *FBIS SOV,* July 27, 2009.
27. Lilia Shevtsova, "A Second Act for U.S. Foreign Policy," *The American Interest,* April 8, 2014, http://www.the-american-interest.com/2014/04/08/a-second-act-for-u-s-foreign-policy/
28. House of Commons Defence Committee, *Russia: A New Confrontation? Team Report of Session 2008-09* (London: The Stationery House for the House of Commons, 2009), 56, http://www.publications.parliament.uk/pa/cm200809/cmselect/cmdfence/276/276.pdf
29. International Crisis Group, "Turkey and Armenia: Opening Minds, Opening Borders," *Europe Report* No. 199, 2009, 17, http://www.crisisgroup.org/~/media/Files/europe/199_turkey_and_armenia___opening_minds_opening_borders_2.pdf; Alexander Iskandaryan and Sergey Minasyan, *Pragmatic Policies Vs. Historical Constraints: Analyzing Armenia-Turkey Relations* (Yerevan: Caucasus Institute Research Papers, No. 1, 2010), http://c-i.am/research/paper%201_eng.pdf
30. Statement of Richard Mills Ambassador-Designate to Armenia Before the Senate Foreign Relations Committee, September 17, 2014, http://www.foreign.senate.gov/imo/media/doc/Mills_Testimony.pdf
31. Conversations with US as well as Azerbaijani officials, Washington, D.C., 2014–2015.
32. Ibid.
33. See for example John Mearsheimer, "America Unhinged," *The National Interest,* No. 129, January-February 2014, 9–30, http://nationalinterest.org/files/digital-edition/1388435556/129%20Digital%20Edition.pdf
34. The most vivid account is David Samuels, "The Aspiring Novelist Who Became Obama's Foreign-Policy Guru", *New York Times Magazine,* May 5, 2016. (http://www.nytimes.com/2016/05/08/magazine/the-aspiring-novelist-who-became-obamas-foreign-policy-guru.html?_r=1)
35. Edward Lucas, "Getting It Right on Ukraine: Realpolitik vs. Wishful Thinking," *Center for European Policy Analysis,* January 28, 2014, http://www.cepa.org/content/getting-it-right-ukraine-realpolitik-vs-wishful-thinking-1
36. Blank, *Azerbaijan's Security and U.S. Interests: Time for a Reassessment;* Blank, "AWOL: US Policy in Central Asia," *Central Asia Caucasus*

Analyst, October 30, 2013, http://www.cacianalyst.org/publications/analytical-articles/item/12848-awol-us-policy-in-central-asia.html

37. Walter Russell Mead, "Via Meadia, The Great Ukrainian Knife Fight," *The American Interest,* December 3, 2013, http://www.the-american-interest.com/2013/12/03/the-great-ukrainian-knife-fight-2/

38. Blank, *Azerbaijan's Security and U.S. Interests: Time for a Reassessment;* Idem: "AWOL: US Policy in Central Asia."

39. Council on Foreign Relations, Center for Preventive Action, *Preventive Priorities Survey, 2014,* December 2013, http://www.cfr.org/peace-conflict-and-human-rights/preventive-priorities-survey-2014/p32072

40. Samuel Charap and Cory Welt, *A More Proactive U.S. Approach to the Georgia Conflicts* (Washington, D.C.: Center for American Progress, 2011), https://www.americanprogress.org/issues/security/report/2011/02/15/9108/a-more-proactive-u-s-approach-to-the-georgia-conflicts/

41. Nikolas Gvosdev, "For U.S., Keeping Ukraine on Side No Longer a Vital Interest," *World Politics Review,* December 13, 2013, http://www.worldpoliticsreview.com/articles/13440/the-realist-prism-for-u-s-keeping-ukraine-on-side-no-longer-a-vital-interest

42. Volodymyr Dubovyk, "Kyiv and Tbilisi: No Longer Washington's Favorites?," *Eurasia Policy Memo,* no. 93, 2010, Program on New Approaches to Russian Security, http://www.ponarseurasia.org/sites/default/files/policy-memos-pdf/pepm_093.pdf

43. Gvosdev, "For U.S., Keeping Ukraine on Side No Longer a Vital Interest."

44. Ibid.

45. President of Russia, "Press statements and answers to journalists' questions following a meeting with President of Armenia Serzh Sargsyan," August 10, 2012, http://en.kremlin.ru/events/president/transcripts/16180

46. Stephen Blank, "Russia and Europe in the Caucasus," *European Security* 4, no. 4, Winter (1995), 622–645; Robert Legvold, "Introduction: Outlining the Challenge," in *Statehood and Security: Georgia After the Rose Revolution,* eds. Bruno Coppieters and Robert Legvold (Cambridge, MA and London: MIT Press, 2005), 29.

47. "Obama Criticizes Crackdown on NGOs in Azerbaijan," *YouTube,* https://www.youtube.com/watch?v=V-on4wkWqCs

48. Ibid.

49. Joshua Kucera, "After Foreign Navies 'Banned' From Caspian, U.S. and Azerbaijan Push Back," *Eurasianet.org,* October 2, 2014, http://www.eurasianet.org/node/70276; Anton Mardasov, "Astrakhan Calibration—Why European Union Found Itself Overboard at Caspian Summit," *Svobodnaya Pressa,* in Russian, September 29, 2014, *FBIS SOV,* September 29, 2014.

50. Stephen Blank, "Is Washington Re-Engaging Baku?," *Central Asia Caucasus Analyst*, January 19, 2016, http://www.cacianalyst.org/publications/analytical-articles/item/13322-is-washington-re-engaging-baku?.html

51. Embassy of the United States to Armenia, "Ambassador James Warlick Nagorno-Karabakh: The Keys to a Settlement," May 7, 2014, http://armenia.usembassy.gov/news050714.html

52. Stephen Blank, "Washington Misses the Point on Nagorno-Karabakh," *Central Asia Caucasus Analyst*, June 18, 2014, http://www.cacianalyst.org/publications/analytical-articles/item/12998-washington-misses-the-point-on-nagorno-karabakh.html

53. "Warlick Nagorno-Karabakh: The Keys to a Settlement."

54. Charap and Welt, *A More Proactive U.S. Approach to the Georgia Conflicts*.

55. Nazim Muzaffarli and Eldar Ismailov, *Basic Principles for the Rehabilitation of Azerbaijan's Post-Conflict Territories* (CA & CC Press, 2010), passim.

56. Paris, *AFP* (North European Service). In English, October 22, 2014, *FBIS SOV*, October 22, 2014.

57. On Azerbaijan's foreign policy course, see Alexandra Jarosieiwcz, "Azerbaijan—a Growing Problem for the West," *OSW Commentary*, Centre for Eastern Studies, September 15, 2014, http://www.osw.waw.pl/en/publikacje/osw-commentary/2014-09-15/azerbaijan-a-growing-problem-west

58. Joshua Kucera, "In Azerbaijan, Russian DefMin Proposes 'Collective Security' On Caspian," *Eurasianet.org*, October 14, 2014, http://www.eurasianet.org/node/70431

59. Baku, *Yeni Musavat*, in Azeri, October 2, 2014, *FBIS SOV*, October 2, 2014.

60. Brenda Shaffer, "Moscow's Next Land Grab," *New York Times*, September 9, 2014, http://www.nytimes.com/2014/09/10/opinion/russias-next-land-grab.html

61. *Kavkazskiy Uzel* in Russian, June 19, 2008, *FBIS SOV*, June 19, 2008.

62. Svante E. Cornell, "Azerbaijan: Going it Alone," in *Putin's Grand Strategy: the Eurasian Union and Its Discontents*, eds. S. Frederick Starr and Svante E. Cornell (Stockholm and Washington, D.C.: Central Asia-Caucasus Institute and Silk Road Studies Program, 2014), 153, http://www.silkroadstudies.org/resources/1409GrandStrategy.pdf

63. Paul Goble, "Is Moscow Putting the Talysh in Play Against Azerbaijan?," *Eurasia Daily Monitor*, February 3, 2015, http://www.jamestown.org/programs/edm/single/?tx_ttnews%5Btt_news%5D=43490&cHash=7bf56406812e1cc67ea3df6a2fd1a234#.Vrx4ktsrLcs

64. Moscow, *Interfax*, in English, February 13, 2011, *FBIS SOV*, February 13, 2011; Makhachkala, *Novoye Delo*, in Russian, August 29, 2008, *FBIS SOV*, August 29, 2008.

65. Maciej Falkowski, *Russia's Policy in the Southern Caucasus and Central Asia* (Warsaw: Centre for Eastern Studies, OSW, 2006), 56. http://www.osw.waw.pl/sites/default/files/prace_23_1.pdf;   William Varretoni, "Sweetness of the Status Quo: Strategic Patience and the Technology of Russia's Capture of Crimea," Paper Presented to the Annual Convention of the Association for the Study of Nationalities, Columbia University, New York, April 15, 2010; Lada Roslycky, "The Soft Side of Dark Power: a Study in Soft Power, National Security and the Political-Criminal Nexus With a Special Focus on the Post-Soviet Political-Criminal Nexus, the Russian Black Sea Fleet and Separatism in the Autonomous Republic of Crimea," Doctoral Dissertation, University of Groningen, 2011.
66. Author's conversations with US analysts, Washington, D.C., 2010.
67. Farangis Najibullah, "Putin Downplays Kazakh Independence, Sparks Angry Reaction," *Radio Free Europe Radio Liberty*, September 3, 2014, http://www.rferl.org/content/kazakhstan-putin-history-reaction-nation/26565141.html
68. Paul Goble, "Moscow Set to Use Karakalpak Separatism Against a Pro-Western Tashkent," *Eurasia Daily Monitor*, August 12, 2004, http://www.jamestown.org/single/?tx_ttnews[tt_news]=42744&no_cache=1#.Vrx6o1Jzujs; Paul Goble, "Window on Eurasia: Moscow Again Focusing on Karakalpak Separatism as Leverage against Tashkent," *Window on Eurasia,* November 4, 2014, http://windowoneurasia2.blogspot.se/2014/11/window-on-eurasia-moscow-again-focusing.html
69. Yuri E. Fedorov, "Medvedev's Amendments to the Law on Defence: The Consequences For Europe," *Briefing Paper* No. 47 (Finnish Institute of International Affairs, November 2009), www.fiia.fi/assets/publications/UPI_Briefing_Paper_47_2009.pdf
70. Alexei Fenenko, "After Ukraine: The Potential for conflict Between Russia and NATO," *Russia Direct*, February 3, 2015, http://www.russia-direct.org/analysis/after-ukraine-potential-conflict-between-russia-and-nato
71. Vladimir Socor, "Bluff in Substance, Brutal in Form: Moscow Warns Against Trans-Caspian Project," *Eurasia Daily Monitor*, November 30, 2011, http://www.jamestown.org/single/?tx_ttnews%5Btt_news%5D=38723&no_cache=1#.Vrx2s9srLcs
72. Moscow, *Interfax*, in English, October 19, 2011, *FBIS SOV*, November 19, 2011.
73. "Senior MP Advises Turkmenistan to Stick with Russia to Avoid Libya' Fate," Moscow, *Interfax*, November 15, 2011, also available from *BBC Monitoring*.
74. Socor, "Bluff in Substance, Brutal in Form."
75. Ibid.

76. Mardasov, "Astrakhan Calibration –Why European Union found Itself Overboard at Caspian Summit."
77. Ibid.; Kucera, "After Foreign Navies 'Banned'"; Kucera, "In Azerbaijan, Russian Defmin Proposes 'Collective Security' On Caspian;" "Azerbaijani, Russian Navy to Hold First Ever Joint Drills in Caspian Sea," *Azeri-Press Agency*, May 22, 2015, http://en.apa.az/xeber_azerbaijani__russian_navy_to_hold_first__227436.html
78. Moscow, *Interfax*, in English, October 20, 2014, *FBIS SOV*, October 20, 2014.

CHAPTER 8

The European Union and the Armenian–Azerbaijani Conflict: Lessons Not Learned

Svante E. Cornell

The role of the European Union (EU) in Eastern Europe and the South Caucasus has grown steadily over the past decade. That engagement has included the creation of the Eastern Partnership, as well as a growing European role in the management of conflicts in its Eastern neighbors—including in Georgia, Moldova and most recently Ukraine. Yet thus far, the Armenia–Azerbaijan conflict has been the exception to that rule. While a trove of EU documents note the importance of regional conflicts to European security and to the EU, the EU has remained mainly a passive bystander to this the most significant of these conflicts. This passivity appeared rooted in a failure to resolve the different priorities of the EU, and thus in the failure of strategic leadership. On one hand, the EU has sought a greater profile in security affairs of the region; but on the other, the conflict involves two independent states with which the EU seeks closer engagement, and which led the EU to seek a position of neutrality. In turn, the EU has tended to square the circle by promoting different principles in its relations with the two countries, emphasizing territorial integrity in its relations with Azerbaijan and self-determination in those with Armenia. This has proven a recipe for confusion that has not helped the EU to gain a role in influencing the course of the conflict.

S.E. Cornell (✉)
Nacka, Sweden

S.E. Cornell (ed.), *The International Politics of the Armenian-Azerbaijani Conflict*, DOI 10.1057/978-1-137-60006-6_8

EUROPEAN INSTITUTIONS AND THE ARMENIA–AZERBAIJAN CONFLICT

The European character of the Armenian–Azerbaijani conflict was confirmed as early as the spring of 1992, when the Conference for Security and Cooperation in Europe created the Minsk process to achieve a resolution to the conflict. Prior to this, regional powers including Turkey and Iran had begun to take on a mediating role, but were gradually elbowed out of the process. Whereas the conflict over Abkhazia came under the purview of the United Nations (UN), the Armenian–Azerbaijani conflict was delegated specifically to the Organization for Security and Cooperation in Europe (OSCE), which major powers at the time sought to promote as a Europe-wide security organization. This had the advantage of assigning the conflict to an organization where Russia and Western states were members, but where Iran was not.

Of course, this took place at a time when there was no EU: the Maastricht Treaty had been signed in February 1992, but would only enter into force in November 1993. In other words, the negotiation mechanism that remains in place for the conflict is one that was designed in a time where there were great hopes for the OSCE as a provider of security in Europe. But by the time of the Balkan wars of the mid-1990s, such prospects turned out to be a pipe dream, and the role of security provider has remained in the hands of North Atlantic Treaty Organization (NATO) and, increasingly, the EU.

As a result, the Armenian–Azerbaijani conflict has institutionally remained outside the purview of the EU—and there has to date been no major event that has forced a reassessment of that state of affairs. It is the only unresolved conflict of Eurasia where the EU has no seat at the table. This contrasts with the situation in Moldova, where the EU has been a member of the 5+2 format since 2005[1]; in Georgia's conflicts, the EU obtained a formal status following the 2008 war. Until that time, the peacekeeping and negotiation formats had comprised no Western presence whatsoever. But since 2008, the "Geneva International Discussions" co-chaired by the EU, OSCE and UN are the formal international mechanism charged with the conflicts. Moreover, the EU deployed a Border Assistance Mission to Moldova in 2005 as well as a Monitoring Mission to Georgia in 2008 that provides the EU with a presence on the ground in both conflicts. Yet in the Armenian–Azerbaijani case, the EU's only instrument is the EU Special Representative to the South Caucasus, who has no formal role in peace talks, but a mandate to "contribute to" the settlement of conflicts.[2]

The OSCE Minsk Group, created in 1992 to find a resolution to the conflict, included a number of European states in individual capacities.[3] The most consequential of these were Sweden and Finland, who chaired the Minsk Group from 1994 to 1997. Yet although Russia was a party to the Minsk Group, it pursued a parallel mediation effort, and while the cease-fire achieved in May 1994 was to a great extent the result of the Minsk Group's work, the unilateral Russian mediation hijacked the process at the last minute—with

Russia refusing to invite Minsk Group Chairman Jan Eliasson to the signing.[4] In its December 1994 Budapest Summit, the CSCE acknowledged this reality by making Russia a co-chair of the Minsk Group. This created a lopsided situation, as a permanent Russian co-chair existed alongside a rotating European co-chair, who stood no chance of playing an active role in Russia's shadow. At the end of 1996, the OSCE chose France to replace Finland as co-chair, leading to protests in Azerbaijan given the prevailing perception of France as a pro-Armenian country, given the large Armenian diaspora in France. The impasse was resolved by the addition of a third co-chair, the United States. While France's co-chairmanship was in principle a rotating one, the negotiations mechanism has remained intact in the 19 years since.

THE EU AND THE SOUTH CAUCASUS: A SLOW START

For the first decade after the collapse of the Soviet Union, the Caucasus did not take an important place in Europe's foreign relations. During the conflicts in the South Caucasus in the early 1990s, European states and the EU as a whole remained wary of involvement. European states gradually become important donor countries to the South Caucasus in terms of development cooperation, primarily assisting Georgia and Armenia; the EU launched its visionary project of TRACECA (Transport Corridor Europe-Caucasus-Asia), which nevertheless was allowed to slip into oblivion.[5]

Europe's approach remained cautious and tentative, as the EU was beset by much more urgent and nearby crises, primarily the Balkan wars, and by the absence of a common European Foreign and Security Policy. The Balkan experience is indicative of the difficulties for European states to act rapidly and in unison to manage serious crises in their own neighborhood. But the central problem was that Europe did not feel that it had important interests at stake in the South Caucasus, and therefore remained largely aloof from the region. Some projects with regional importance developed, chief among which was the INOGATE (Interstate Oil and Gas Transport to Europe) project, which was launched in the mid-1990s and worked for the integration of oil and gas pipeline routes to Europe to increase the security of supply.

A decade later, this situation began to change. Europe itself had changed, with an ambition to act more cohesively in the external arena. In parallel, the need for a more visible presence in the Caucasus had come to be recognized.[6] The second Chechen war was raging, European corporate interests had become involved in Caspian energy development, and European states put increasing emphasis on democratization and good governance in their neighborhood. Georgia joined the Council of Europe in 1999, and Armenia and Azerbaijan followed suit in 2001. The military operations in Afghanistan from late 2001 onward also increased Europe's understanding of the strategic value of the Caucasus corridor to Central Asia.

During the 2001 Swedish Presidency of the EU, the EU troika led by Anna Lindh made its first ever visit to the three countries of the South Caucasus. As such, the Caucasus slowly became an issue on the European agenda. Successive EU presidencies groped for a way to deal with the conflict-ridden region, yet never managed to accord the Caucasus a priority position within their limited six-month timeframes. It became clear that the Caucasus lacked a constituency within the Union: there were no important member state sponsors who could elevate the region to a prominent position on the EU agenda. This was exacerbated by the diverging perspective of the three states of the South Caucasus concerning Euro-Atlantic integration. Georgia has consistently been the most ambitious, desiring both NATO and EU membership; Azerbaijan has been more low-key, expressing a fading interest in NATO membership and none in EU membership; while Armenia's wishes for EU integration have been limited by its dependence on Russia, a fact vividly illustrated in 2013, when Russian pressure forced Armenia to forego an Association Agreement with the EU.

In March 2003, the EU launched its European Neighborhood Policy (ENP), but the states of the South Caucasus were literally reduced to a footnote in the document. This was the case in spite of the inclusion of countries like Libya and Syria in the ENP—who unlike the states of the South Caucasus were not members of Euro-Atlantic institutions such as the Council of Europe or NATO's Partnership for Peace program, and whose foreign policies had no European vocation. This decision caused consternation in the region, and came rapidly to be understood as a mistake even in Brussels. A series of circumstances since then contributed to make the South Caucasus distinctly more present in European thinking, making the EU revise its decision and incorporate the South Caucasus into the ENP in 2004. In July 2003, the EU appointed a Special Representative to the South Caucasus, Finnish Ambassador Heikki Talvitie. However, Talvitie was based in Helsinki and not in Brussels, financed by Finnish rather than EU funds, and had a relatively circumspect mandate. This solution showed the ad hoc evolution of European intent, but betrayed the lack of institutional readiness on the part of the EU to seriously take a role in the region.

An EU Role Emerges: From the ENP to the Creation of the Eastern Partnership

Between 2003 and 2006, this changed. A first factor was the Rose Revolution of 2003 in Georgia, which increased the Caucasus's prominence in the European debate. Perhaps more importantly, the EU expanded to include a number of post-socialist countries in Central and Eastern Europe, who quickly came to form a constituency of states with an interest in and understanding of the region. When Swedish diplomat Peter Semneby was appointed to succeed Heikki Talvitie in 2006, he took up an office in Brussels and his mandate and resources were expanded to enable a more active EU role in the Caucasus. With regard to the unresolved conflicts, his mandate was amended to include a reference to "contributing to" rather than "assisting in" the settlement of conflicts.[7] During this period, however, the efforts of the EU Special Representative were focused largely on Georgia, because of the escalation of Russian–Georgian tensions that led, ultimately, to the Russian invasion of Georgia in August 2008. Meanwhile, France had taken the lead in the Minsk Group in 2006, and convened a summit at Rambouillet to flesh out a deal between the Armenian and Azerbaijani leaders. At that point, the EU also announced its readiness to contribute to a post-conflict peace support operation. Reportedly, the EU Council "launched a round of informal discussion on the planning of a possible EU peacekeeping contribution."[8] But the talks failed, rendering this prospect moot.

Prior to the war in Georgia, both the EU and individual EU states had taken on a growing role in the Caucasus. This included several Central and East European states as well as Sweden, whose foreign minister, Carl Bildt, frequently traveled to Georgia; and Germany, whose foreign minister Frank-Walter Steinmeier sought to launch an initiative to de-escalate the tensions over Abkhazia in spring 2008. Yet these efforts failed, and the Russian invasion of Georgia took much of Europe by surprise. The Bush administration indicated clearly that it believed America should not take a direct role in the negotiations, as that could exacerbate the conflict. As a result, Europe found itself unable to rely on American backup to resolve a raging war in Europe. Since France held the rotating presidency of the EU at the time, French President Nicolas Sarkozy had a mandate to intervene, which suited both France's ambitions to a great power role and his personal leadership style. Through energetic diplomacy, Sarkozy achieved a cease-fire—though his inexperience led to severe flaws in the cease-fire, the terms of which Russia has still not complied with.[9] The EU deployed a Monitoring Mission to observe the cease-fire, though that mission was not allowed into the Russian-occupied areas of Georgia, which Moscow had recognized as independent states. In addition, the EU and United States pledged an international aid package totaling $4.5 billion for Georgia over three years.

The lessons of that conflict were several. The first was that Europe cannot ignore a conflict erupting in the South Caucasus. The second was that preventing an outbreak of war is preferable to, and cheaper than, intervening once one has already emerged. And third, the responsibility for addressing such a conflict lands, by default, in the lap of the EU. NATO and the OSCE are unlikely to address the conflict because leaving aside its relationship with Russia, NATO is a mainly military organization that does not engage in conflict resolution, while the OSCE lacks political power to act, and has become a disappointment in terms of its expected role as a security provider. A third European organization, the Council of Europe, is not involved in security matters; and the presence of the United States and Russia in the UN Security Council means that the UN would be deadlocked in any conflict involving Russia. This leaves the EU as the only European institution with a capacity to intervene and address conflicts in the region.

The war had multiple implications for European security writ large. Russia's unilateral use of force to alter internationally recognized borders had challenged the very basis for European security in the post-cold war order to its core. These lessons were only poorly internalized in the years that followed. The war helped secure the creation of a greater European role in the region through the Eastern Partnership, but the broader security implications were largely ignored until the conflict in Ukraine exploded six years later. The war in Georgia was not seen in its broader regional context, and certainly, the implications for the Armenian–Azerbaijani conflict were not thoroughly understood.

In June 2008, Poland and Sweden had proposed to ramp up the ENP in Eastern Europe by creating an "Eastern Partnership." The reception was initially lukewarm, and without the Georgia war, it is unlikely that the proposal would have been implemented. But the war prompted a Europe-wide understanding that the EU had to take some step to deepen its relations with the six states along its eastern border, including those of the South Caucasus—and the Eastern Partnership was officially launched in May 2009 at a summit in Prague.

The Eastern Partnership lacked serious financial muscle, and its mandate remained relatively timid. Most importantly, it largely shies away from addressing the security questions that dominate the region—the unresolved conflicts and Russia's ambitions to forcibly reintegrate the region. That lacuna would significantly contribute to the Ukraine crisis of 2013–14. But it should be recognized that the EU is primarily a soft power: it has no security muscle, and mainly operates on the power of attraction provided by its large single market, democratic institutions, rule of law, and assistance in the transformation of states into liberal democracies. Considering the conditions at the time of its creation, it is a wonder that the Eastern Partnership was created at all: Europe was deeply hit by the global financial crisis, which shook the EU monetary union, forcing all the EU's energies to be mobilized to handle the internal crisis. Very little was left for strategic thinking regarding the wider neighborhood.

In this sense, given its inherent limitations, the Eastern Partnership must be termed a success. First, it included the South Caucasus on an equal footing with Ukraine and Moldova, countries considered much more "European" in many EU states. In other words, the EU did not repeat the 2003 mistake of leaving the South Caucasus out. Secondly, it managed to strike a delicate balance regarding the hot potato of potential membership by simply ignoring the issue. It did not offer membership to the Eastern neighbors—but did not rule it out either. The intentions were clear, however. At the core of the Eastern Partnership lies the opportunity to conclude Deep and Comprehensive Free Trade Agreements (DCFTA), which if implemented would amount to the implementation of over 85 percent of the EU *acquis communautaire*. Thus, if the countries of the Eastern Partnership implement the Association Agreements, they will gradually become *eligible* for EU membership whenever that would be politically feasible. The great power of attraction of the EU became apparent in 2013, when an Association Agreement with the EU came to symbolize the aspirations of Ukrainians to live in a "normal country," and the Yanukovich government's failure to sign the agreement led to the second Ukrainian revolution in less than a decade.

In the South Caucasus, the Eastern Partnership faced a serious challenge. The three countries approached it very differently. Georgia was the most enthusiastic partner, committed to the rapid signing and implementation of the agreement. Armenia, despite its dependence on Russia and to the surprise of many, also negotiated an Association Agreement from 2010 to 2013. The Armenian leadership sought to keep this matter under the radar; and it is unclear whether Armenia hoped, somehow, to sign the agreement in spite of what it knew were Russian objections; or whether a more elaborate strategy was at play, in which relations with Europe served the purpose of improving Armenia's negotiating position vis-à-vis Russia. As for Azerbaijan, it has clearly indicated that it was not interested in the DCFTA, but in a separate, strategic partnership with the EU.

The Vain Quest for Neutrality: Finessing Armenia and Azerbaijan

While the EU bolstered its engagement in the region through the Eastern Partnership, including the upgrading of the Commission Delegations in Baku and Yerevan to full EU delegations, the EU did not alter its policies toward the Armenian–Azerbaijani conflict. For a brief period following the 2008 war in Georgia, there were discussions and debates in Brussels about a more direct EU role in the conflict, possibly through an expansion or alteration of the Minsk Group format to include the EU. Such a move made sense, as the conflict was now the only unresolved conflict in Europe in which the EU did not have a seat at the table.[10] Advocates of such a step have operated on the assumption that a more forceful Western role was needed in the conflict resolution process, and that the EU would be able to make its considerable resources available, and would add needed capacity to provide post-conflict assistance and organize peacekeeping and policing operations in the event of a negotiated solution. As Thomas de Waal has noted,

> The most glaring absence from the Karabakh peace process in this regard is the European Union. The EU has vast resources and expertise it could bring to bear, as demonstrated by its successful stabilisation and reconstruction efforts in the Balkans. The EU has expressed interest in devoting more resources to Nagorno-Karabakh, and EU Special Representative for the South Caucasus Peter Semneby has tried to secure a greater role for Brussels in the peace process...Yet to date it has not found a useful role in this conflict on its borders.[11]

In 2012, the European Parliament's Committee on Foreign Relations actually voted for an effort to include the EU in the Minsk Group.[12] But such proposals have fallen on deaf ears, for what appears to be three major reasons: French opposition, Russian opposition and Armenian opposition. Paris's membership in the Minsk Group puts France on a par with the United States and Russia, and European diplomats report in private that any suggestions of a change in the format are met with stiff resistance by French diplomats. Thus, French policy appears to be motivated as much by its own prestige as by the aim of achieving a resolution of the conflict, a fact commonly observed by European diplomats.[13]

Secondly, even before the war in Georgia, Russia had made it a priority to oppose any change of format in the unresolved conflicts of Eurasia. This was most visible in 2004–08, when the Georgian government actively sought to alter the highly skewed peacekeeping formats that provided Russia with a mediating and peacekeeping role in Abkhazia and South Ossetia, even though Russia was clearly, by then, exerting direct control over the secessionist authorities in the two territories. But in all diplomatic fora, Russian diplomats raised the importance of maintaining existing formats for negotiations and peacekeeping.[14] Similarly, Russia rejects any change to the negotiating format over the Armenian–Azerbaijani conflict which would reduce Russia's dominant role in the region.

Finally, Armenia also prefers French mediation to EU mediation, given the strong Armenian diaspora in France. Armenian media in 2012 referred to suggestions of replacing France with the EU as resulting from "pressure from the Azeri lobby."[15] Moreover, the United States has never voiced support for a change in the format of the Minsk Group, preferring instead to work within the framework of the existing format. As a result, facing opposition from Armenia, France, and Russia, and lacking US support, those forces in the EU that see the logic of changing the existing format have not been in a position to make their case, and EU leaders have not found the conflict an important enough concern to risk alienating either Russia or one of its own member states.

While the EU does not have a seat at the table, its policies toward the Armenian–Azerbaijani conflict have been characterized by deep contradictions. On one hand, the EU has clearly identified the conflict as a leading risk to peace and security in its neighborhood. But on the other, it has studiously avoided direct involvement in the issue, and has instead deferred to the OSCE and assiduously sought to maintain neutrality between the two countries. Predictably, this effort at finessing the conflict has failed to promote a resolution, and done little to improve the EU's standing in the region.

The 2003 European Security Strategy clearly reflects an understanding of the importance of the region's conflicts. It mentions the South Caucasian conflicts in second place, after the Balkans but before the Arab–Israeli conflict, observing that the EU needs "to extend the benefits of economic and political cooperation to our neighbors in the East while tackling political problems there. We should now take a stronger and more active interest in the problems of the Southern Caucasus."[16] Similarly, the May 2004 Strategy Paper of the EU Commission on its ENP identified as one of its highest priorities "to reinforce the EU's contribution to promoting the settlement of regional conflicts."[17] And in a speech on the South Caucasus in 2006, EU Commissioner for External Affairs Benita Ferrero-Waldner stated that "uppermost in my mind in thinking about the South Caucasus today is the ENP's potential to help support conflict resolution."[18]

In other words, from 2003 to 2006, a major shift occurred in the EU approach to the region and its conflicts—which seemed to usher in a considerably increased role in conflict resolution. As Nicu Popescu has observed, these developments were a "turning point for increased EU involvement in the conflicts in Georgia and Moldova."[19] In the conflict in Transnistria in particular, the EU became heavily involved in the deployment of the EU Border Assistance Mission to Moldova and Ukraine (EUBAM), which effectively introduced a monitoring system for the 470-kilometer portion of the Moldova–Ukraine border that is outside Chisinau's control—a game-changer in the political economy of the conflict. Not staying at this, the EU twice— in 2003 and 2006—got involved in efforts to alter the Russian-dominated peacekeeping structures in the conflict, although it eventually failed to achieve progress.[20] Regarding the conflicts in Georgia, the EU actively sought ways to get involved in the peacekeeping and negotiation formats in 2005–08, most notably in the period immediately preceding the 2008 war. Following that conflict, the EU not only was instrumental in the cease-fire agreement but also deployed the EU Monitoring Mission along the administrative boundary lines and became a co-chair of the Geneva discussions.[21]

However, nothing similar happened in the Armenian–Azerbaijani conflict. It could be argued, as one scholar has, that the Armenia–Azerbaijan conflict does not "lend itself to the kinds of activities that the EU does best—confidence building measures, post-conflict management, and addressing soft security issues."[22] In particular, the adamant opposition of Azerbaijan to external activities in the occupied territories has made such bottom-up efforts difficult to implement. But as Popescu has helpfully summarized the situation, in all other three conflicts in the Eastern Partnership, the EU has been involved in negotiations, deployed missions on the ground, disbursed funds for the rehabilitation of conflict zones, and worked to strengthen the metropolitan states. In the case of Armenia–Azerbaijan, the only instrument available to the EU is the EU Special Representative in the capacity of assisting in conflict resolution.[23]

The EU's approach rested essentially on deferring to and verbally encouraging the OSCE Minsk Group. Thus, standard EU phrases are that the Special Representative is "working closely with," or "supporting" the co-chairs of the OSCE Minsk Group. What that means in practice is anyone's guess.[24] There is one exception to the EU's passivity. In 2006, coinciding with the expectations of a rapid resolution to the conflict ahead of the 2006 Rambouillet talks, the EU stated its readiness to contribute to the process *after* a negotiated settlement had been found. The EU's strategy paper for Azerbaijan, produced in 2006, states a readiness "if the Nagorno-Karabakh conflict is settled...to provide further specific assistance to help consolidate the settlement," going on to list various areas in which the EU could be active.[25] But when Rambouillet fell through, these plans were retired and the EU returned to its wait-and-see policy—instead of continuing to concretize its possible role in post-conflict reconstruction and stabilization, which would have been a factor to encourage peace talks.[26]

In the decade that has passed since, the EU has remained far from this level of attention to the conflict. The war in Georgia did not lead to a visible momentum to accord greater attention and resources to the conflict, in spite of efforts by some analysts to raise the issue in Brussels in the aftermath of the war. Such ideas were quickly overtaken by enthusiasm for the Turkish–Armenian protocols, pushed by the Obama administration—and which appeared much more likely to succeed than any effort to address the Armenia–Azerbaijan conflict. While that gambit also failed, the EU profile in the region gradually refocused to the Association Agreements and DCFTAs that Armenia and Georgia began to negotiate in 2010, with the conflicts being relegated, once again, to the backburner.

But as Tabib Huseynov has argued, the EU's manifest "wait-and-see" approach is a self-defeating strategy: "While the EU recognizes that a solution to the Karabakh conflict is the key to the stabilization of the whole South Caucasus region, it tacitly admits it is not prepared to assume a more active role in the Karabakh peace process unless a political agreement is reached."[27] And given that the current setup has failed to advance a political agreement for a quarter of a century, the EU position becomes a catch-22: the Union is willing to support an agreement, but not to do anything to actually change the status quo surrounding the conflict and thereby improve the likelihood that such an agreement will ever be reached. In the meantime, the EU is not only paying the opportunity cost of the unresolved conflicts as regard its broader strategic interests in the South Caucasus but it has also appeared to play the role of a bystander to the escalation of the conflict since 2010.

However, upon closer look, the EU has not been just a bystander: in fact, it has been worse than passive, because its attempts to pursue Action Plans with both countries under the ENP actively sowed confusion through efforts to dodge the apparent contradiction between the basic international principles underlying the conflict.

When the EU signed Partnership and Cooperation Agreements (PCA) with Armenia and Azerbaijan in 1999, these documents included the following identical language in the respective preamble:

> Recognizing in that context that support for the independence, sovereignty and territorial integrity of the Republic of [Armenia/Azerbaijan] will contribute to the safeguarding of peace and stability in Europe.[28]

This language was standard procedure, included also in agreements signed with other partner countries.[29] Yet when the EU embarked on the process of developing Action Plans under the ENP for the countries of the Eastern Neighborhood in 2005, it no longer applied the same language across the board. On the one hand, the EU appeared to differentiate Armenia and Azerbaijan from Moldova and Georgia; and on the other, it applied different language to Action Plans with Armenia and Azerbaijan.

All Action Plans state in their introduction that the ENP "sets ambitious objectives based on mutual commitments of the EU and its Member States and [country name] to common values [and] effective implementation of political, economic and institutional reforms." But only the Action Plans for Armenia and Azerbaijan include language on "compliance to international and European norms and principles," which do not exist in the documents for Georgia and Moldova. The differences do not end there. The Action Plans all list areas of priority, but conflict resolution is ranked remarkably differently among the countries. It is priority no. 1 in the Action Plan for Azerbaijan, no. 6 for Georgia, and no. 7 for Armenia. The Action Plan for Moldova is structured differently and does not rank priorities by number, but mentions the Transnistria conflict first among "Priorities for Action."[30]

More importantly, the language used in describing EU attention to the conflict differs considerably.[31] Thus, the Georgia Action Plan lists Priority area number six under the heading "Promote peaceful resolution of internal conflicts." There, the EU commits to "contribute to conflict settlement ... based on respect of the sovereignty and territorial integrity of Georgia within its internationally recognised borders."[32] The Moldova Action Plan is equally unequivocal, discussing "sustained efforts toward a settlement of the Transnistria conflict, respecting the sovereignty and territorial integrity of the Republic of Moldova within its internationally recognised borders."[33] But in the Action Plans on Azerbaijan and Armenia, the EU does not commit to a direct role, only to "increase political support to OSCE Minsk Group conflict settlement efforts..."

More surprisingly, the language on EU efforts regarding the conflict is identical for the Armenia and Azerbaijan Action Plans, with one crucial exception: the very principles on which the EU commits to base its efforts. The Azerbaijan document includes a clause in the introduction to the Action Plan noting that the common values underlying the relationship include "the respect of and support for the sovereignty, territorial integrity and inviolability of internationally recognised borders." But unlike the Action Plans for Georgia and Moldova, this principle is not mentioned in the specific section on conflict resolution. That section only refers vaguely to "UN Security Council resolutions and OSCE documents and principles." The Armenia Action Plan, for its part, *specifically* refers to "the principle of self-determination of peoples," a principle included in no other Action Plan (Table 8.1).

This approach to conflict resolution is not serious. The fact that the EU uses the same exact paragraphs, with interchangeable principles on which it bases its efforts, implies that the EU in reality does not operate on the basis of any principles whatsoever. Moreover, the inclusion of the principle of self-determination *without* reference to the principle of territorial integrity is highly unusual diplomatic practice—whereas the opposite is commonplace. As

Table 8.1 Formulations on Nagorno-Karabakh conflict in EU actions plans with Armenia and Azerbaijan

EU Action Plan, Armenia	EU Action Plan, Azerbaijan

Contribute to a peaceful solution of the Nagorno-Karabakh conflict;
Specific actions:
  Increase diplomatic efforts, including through the EUSR, and continue to support a peaceful solution of the Nagorno-Karabakh conflict;
  Increase political support to the OSCE Minsk Group conflict settlement efforts *on the basis of international norms and principles, including the principle of self-determination of peoples;*
  Encourage people-to-people contacts;
  Intensify the EU dialogue with the parties concerned with a view to the acceleration of the negotiations toward a political settlement
	Contribute to a peaceful solution of the Nagorno-Karabakh conflict
	Specific actions:
	  Increase diplomatic efforts, including through the EUSR, and continue to support a peaceful solution of the Nagorno-Karabakh conflict;
	  Increase political support to OSCE Minsk Group conflict settlement efforts *on the basis of the relevant UN Security Council resolutions and OSCE documents and decisions;*
	  Encourage people-to-people contacts;
	  Intensify the EU dialogue with the states concerned with a view to the acceleration of the negotiations toward a political settlement

Source: European Union, 'EU/Armenia Action Plan,' 2006, p. 7, https://eeas.europa.eu/enp/pdf/pdf/action_plans/armenia_enp_ap_final_en.pdf; European Union, 'EU/Azerbaijan Action Plan, 2006, p. 3, http://eeas.europa.eu/enp/pdf/pdf/action_plans/azerbaijan_enp_ap_final_en.pdf'

discussed in detail in Johanna Popjanevski's contribution to this volume, the principle of self-determination can in no way be understood as negating the principle of territorial integrity, which remains a cornerstone of the international system.

The inclusion of the principle of self-determination in only one of the EU's Action Plans appears impossible to justify in any principled manner. Indeed, if the EU were to think seriously about the "self-determination of peoples," it would need to apply the recognized international definitions of what consists an "indigenous people" and what consists a "national minority." Under these definitions, as contentious as they may be, the only secessionist party in the region that could lay claim to being defined as an "indigenous people" is the Abkhaz. There is no other territory or motherland for the Abkhaz than Abkhazia; but Transnistria's population is a mixture of Moldovans, Ukrainians and Russians. In the case of South Ossetia, there is a North Ossetian Republic in the North Caucasus which had a higher status in the Soviet hierarchy precisely because it was considered the homeland of the Ossetians. As for Nagorno-Karabakh, unless a way is found to define the Karabakh Armenians as a people separate from the Armenians of Armenia, they are, in terms of international law, a national minority. And since two of the highest leaders of the self-proclaimed Nagorno-Karabakh Republic have gone on to hold the office of President of Armenia; any argument that Nagorno-Karabakh constitutes a separate people scarcely holds water. In other words, in the context of the unresolved conflicts in the post-Soviet space, there is no justification for the EU to apply the principle of self-determination of peoples selectively to the Nagorno-Karabakh issue.

Why, then, this differentiated treatment of conflict zones? The reasons are obviously political. The differentiation between Georgia and Moldova on the one hand, and the Armenia–Azerbaijan conflict on the other, is often explained by the main difference between the conflicts: the EU viewed conflicts in Georgia and Moldova as internal conflicts. Since the secessionist entities were not partners to the EU, Brussels had few qualms about stating unambiguously its support for sovereignty and territorial integrity. But since it viewed the Armenia–Azerbaijan conflict as an inter-state conflict involving two partner countries to the EU, that fact put the EU in the position of seeking neutrality between them. Put otherwise, precisely *because* Azerbaijan's territory is under occupation by a neighbor, the EU is less willing to stand up for the principle of territorial integrity.

Yet this approach contradicts the very nature of the EU, which is supposedly that of a normative, rules-based organization. The Cyprus analogy is particularly poignant: the same logic would lead the EU to downplay Greek Cypriot claims of territorial integrity, and withhold judgment until a solution is found. Instead, the EU backed Greek Cyprus's claims to the entire island, resulting in a situation where the EU effectively embargoes a territory, Northern Cyprus, which is formally considered part of the EU itself. Even leaving the Cyprus case aside, the only serious approach to the Armenia–Azerbaijan conflict would have been to include identical language reflecting the two supposedly contradictory principles of international law in *both* Action Plans. Given that official EU Commission documents themselves state that "portions of Azerbaijan's territory remain under Armenian occupation," the refusal to acknowledge the principle of territorial integrity casts a shadow over the EU's claim to uphold the principles of international law.[34]

This attitude on the part of the EU position has not been limited to just the Action Plans. In the aftermath of the 2008 war in Georgia, Ferrero-Waldner noted that "Ukraine, Georgia and Moldova can count on the EU's support for their territorial integrity and sovereignty."[35] Thus, five years before Russia's annexation of Crimea, high EU officials had the foresight to include Ukraine, whose territorial integrity was not yet under attack—but pointedly left out Azerbaijan from the list.

The same difference has been observable in the EU's response to elections being organized in the secessionist territories. As Paruyr Hovhannisyan has observed, the EU has been explicit in stating its support for the territorial integrity of Georgia in such conditions—but less so in the case of Azerbaijan.[36] In 2009, the EU Presidency responded to the presidential election in Abkhazia by noting that the "EU does not recognize the constitutional and legal framework within which these elections have taken place ... The EU continues to support Georgia's territorial integrity and sovereignty, as recognized by international law."[37] Later that year, a statement on elections in South Ossetia went further: "The EU does not accept the legality of the 'elections' ... the holding of such elections is illegitimate and represents a setback," and added that "the EU reiterates its firm support for the sovereignty and territorial integrity of Georgia within its internationally recognized borders."[38] The latter phrasing appears in countless EU documents, including EU statements on the Geneva discussions, as well as in the EU statement in response to the signature of a Treaty of alliance and integration between Moscow and South Ossetia in March 2015.[39] Regarding Transnistria, the story is the same: for example, the EU reacted to a 2006 referendum in Transnistria on the territory's status by noting that the referendum "contradicts the internationally recognized sovereignty and territorial integrity of the Republic of Moldova ... The European Union fully supports Moldova's territorial integrity."[40]

In the case of Azerbaijan, such statements were once commonplace, but gradually became increasingly rare. In the 1990s, they were most vividly illustrated by the 1996 Lisbon Summit of the OSCE. At that summit, all participating states except Armenia supported the inclusion of three principles for the resolution of the conflict. These were

1. Territorial integrity of the Republic of Armenia and the Azerbaijan Republic;
2. Legal status of Nagorno-Karabakh defined in an agreement based on self-determination which confers on Nagorno-Karabakh the highest degree of self-rule within Azerbaijan; and
3. Guaranteed security for Nagorno-Karabakh and its whole population, including mutual obligations to ensure compliance by all the Parties with the provisions of the settlement.[41]

Since Armenia vetoed the inclusion of this language, the OSCE Chairman-in-Office put the text in an annex to the document, noting explicitly that "I regret that one participating State could not accept this. These principles have the support of all other participating States."[42] Six years later, a 2002 EU declaration ahead of scheduled "presidential elections" in Nagorno-Karabakh similarly noted that "the European Union confirms its support for the territorial integrity of Azerbaijan, and recalls that it does not recognise the independence of Nagorno-Karabakh."[43]

But subsequently, the EU language changed. In 2010, High Representative for Foreign Affairs and Security Policy Catherine Ashton's statement on parliamentary elections held in the breakaway territory only noted that the EU "does not recognize the constitutional and legal framework within which the 'parliamentary elections' in Nagorno-Karabakh will be held." But the statement only added that "this event should not prejudice the peaceful settlement of the Nagorno-Karabakh conflict."[44]

Thus, there was a clear but subtle shift in EU policy on Azerbaijan's territorial integrity over time. In the 1990s and early 2000s, the EU tended to treat the post-Soviet conflicts alike, and it was uncontroversial to include statements of support for Azerbaijan's territorial integrity. But following the launch of the ENP and the pursuit of Action Plans and subsequently Association Agreements with the countries of the Eastern Partnership, the EU continued to support the territorial integrity of Georgia and Moldova, while it moved to a position of neutrality on this key subject of negotiations regarding the Armenia–Azerbaijan conflict.

It should be noted, however, that the Russian annexation of Crimea has led to a reversal of this trend. In July 2015, EU President Donald Tusk unequivocally stated that the EU "recognizes Azerbaijan's territorial integrity, sovereignty and independence. Neither the EU nor its member states recognize Nagorno-Karabakh."[45] Similarly, during Latvia's 2015 presidency of the EU, Latvian diplomats began systematically including Azerbaijan alongside Georgia, Moldova and Ukraine in the listing of countries whose territorial integrity the EU supports.[46]

The conflict in Ukraine raises the broader question of the EU's handling of the matter of sovereignty and territorial integrity. It appears that EU attitudes toward the Armenia–Azerbaijan conflict have been affected considerably by matters external to the conflict, from Kosovo to Crimea.

From Kosovo to Crimea: The EU and Territorial Integrity

The EU's wavering on principles of international law has not taken place in isolation. While the EU handling of the issue appears in part to be the result of a lack of leadership and strategic thinking, it has also been a function of the EU position on major political developments in Europe. Indeed, the subtle EU downgrading of the importance of territorial integrity in favor of self-determination in the mid-2000s coincided with its inclination to recognize Kosovo, while the shift in the opposite direction in the past two years coincides with the Crimea issue.

In retrospect, the Western powers hardly excelled themselves during their handling of the Kosovo question. When the UN Interim Administration Mission in Kosovo was created in 1999, it was deployed under UN Security Council resolution 1244, which reaffirmed the "sovereignty and territorial integrity" of the Federal Republic of Yugoslavia. This was important, because the NATO intervention in Kosovo had been launched in order to stop Belgrade's policies of ethnic cleansing of Kosovo Albanians. Even after that conflict—which some legal scholars would argue voided Yugoslavia's right to maintain its territorial integrity—the international presence in the territory was deployed under a special regime that *maintained* Yugoslavia's territorial integrity *de jure*. In other words, Kosovo was what legal scholar Ralph Wilde calls a "Protected State Territory," which involved a deployment of international bodies that in effect administered the territory, a fact that explicitly did not prejudice Yugoslavia's legal title to the territory.[47] But following a period of escalating tensions, and the inability of Kosovar and Serbian leaders to reach a negotiated solution, Kosovo declared independence in 2008. The United States and a majority of EU members then recognized that declaration, in spite of their recognition constituting a direct breach of resolution 1244. The legal reasoning behind that decision was contorted; as discussed in detail in Johanna Popjanevski's contribution to this volume, neither Kosovo's declaration of independence nor Western recognition thereof was undertaken citing a right to self-determination, but took place on the basis of the "non-consensual breakup" of Yugoslavia, with the reasons cited being decidedly political rather than legal. UN Special Envoy Martti Ahtisaari recommended independence only because it was "the only viable option."[48] Upon recognizing Kosovo, Western powers went out of their way to declare it a case *sui generis*, which was an exception to international law and did not create a precedent. The EU Council conclusions on Kosovo reiterated

> the EU's adherence to the principles of the UN Charter and the Helsinki Final Act, inter alia the principles of sovereignty and territorial integrity and all UN Security Council resolutions. It underlines its conviction that in view of the conflict of the 1990s and the extended period of international administration under SCR 1244, Kosovo constitutes a sui generis case which does not call into question these principles and resolutions.[49]

Of course, this rationale was highly questionable. There was a considerable international presence in Kosovo, and both Serbia and Kosovo had a perspective of eventual EU membership. It remains unclear why the EU proved unable to devise a solution that would guide both territories toward EU membership in the long term, in which case the question of status could be resolved—or even made obsolete—through EU membership. In the end, the EU itself was divided on the question of recognition, and five EU members—Cyprus, Greece, Romania, Slovakia and Spain—continue to refuse to recognize the independence of Kosovo. That, in turn, left the EU in the convoluted situation where as an organization operating under the principle of consensus, it does not recognize Kosovo. All EU documents guiding its relationship with the territory simply call it "Kosovo," with an asterisk explaining that "this designation is without prejudice to positions on status, and is in line with UNSCR 1244 and the ICJ Opinion on the Kosovo Declaration of Independence."[50] In sum, the EU navigated itself into a position where it in practice treats Kosovo as an independent state, while basing its relations with the territory on a statement that explicitly acknowledges the territorial integrity of Serbia.

The West's recognition of Kosovo was an important factor in the escalation to war in Georgia, and particularly in Russia's retaliatory decision to recognize Abkhazia and South Ossetia as independent states. If the West could create its own exceptions to international law, reasoned Moscow, so could Russia. Of course, Western leaders rightly dismissed Russia's analogy between the two situations. The NATO-led intervention in Kosovo had been undertaken to stop ethnic cleansing; Russia's intervention in Abkhazia and South Ossetia *confirmed* the results of the ethnic cleansing in the early 1990s, while it created new waves of displaced Georgians from South Ossetia. Western intervention in Kosovo had been multilateral and transparent; Russia's had been unilateral, and patently planned in advance as well as based on motives that had nothing to do with the defense of human rights. But in terms of international law, the conclusion is inescapable that *both* of these 2008 episodes weakened the international legal regime centered on territorial integrity and the inviolability of borders.

For a variety of reasons, the West did not process the implications of the war in Georgia. The onset of the financial crisis turned the attention of Western leaders to urgent matters closer to home, and the Obama administration's "reset" with Russia buried the crucial issues of principle that had been raised by the war. It was left to diplomats and politicians in the South Caucasus to deal with the consequences—which left Armenia coming out in a more favorable position than Azerbaijan. Armenians could, and did, point out that if the West supported two Albanian state entities in the Balkans, then why not two Armenian states in the Caucasus? Of course, the analogy is false: the majority of victims of ethnic cleansing were Azerbaijanis and not Armenians, a fact that makes the parallel to Kosovo very hollow. However, such questions easily disappeared from view, and it is difficult to escape the conclusion that the EU's willingness to fudge the issues of territorial integrity and self-determination between roughly 2006 and 2013 were related to the Kosovo phenomenon.

That all changed with the Russian annexation of Crimea. Indeed, that event led many leaders in the West to draw exactly those conclusions which the war in Georgia should have led five years earlier. Most ironic was the indignation expressed by Frank-Walter Steinmeier, German foreign minister and the architect of Germany's "embrace" of Russia. Speaking at the UN in September 2014, he stated that

> some may see this as a limited conflict in Eastern Europe – but this conflict affects us all. Not just any state! A permanent member of the Security Council, Russia, has unilaterally changed borders in Europe with its annexation of Crimea, and thus violated international law.[51]

Of course, Russia had done exactly that in Georgia in 2008, with little in terms of a German reaction. Russia's moves in Georgia had led the EU to step up its rhetoric in defense of the territorial integrity of Georgia, but that did not translate into any effect on EU positions elsewhere, particularly regarding the Armenia–Azerbaijan conflict. But the Ukraine crisis was different. Russia's moves in Crimea led first of all to a reassessment of the political relationship with Russia, and to a much more durable sanctions regime targeting Russia. And while it also led to a strong defense of Ukraine's territorial integrity, this time it appeared to have had broader repercussions.

Indeed, EU language in Ukraine has been very direct. The first EU Council conclusions on Ukraine, in March 2014, set the tone by stating that the EU "strongly condemns the clear violation of Ukrainian sovereignty and territorial integrity by acts of aggression by the Russian armed forces..."[52] More importantly, the EU targeted sanctions imposed on Russia and on Russian leaders are justified explicitly as "targeted sanctions for actions undermining Ukraine's territorial integrity, sovereignty and independence."[53] Indeed, the official EU account of its policy on Ukraine mentions the term "territorial integrity" on 11 occasions in a 3000-word document, and going further: it underlines the EU's "unwavering support for the sovereignty, territorial integrity, unity and independence of Ukraine," thus including the concept of the country's "unity," which the EU does not employ for any other conflicts.

This EU policy inescapably had implications for the Armenia–Azerbaijan conflict, given the very visible parallels between the occurrences in Nagorno-Karabakh and Crimea. There are, of course, important differences between the conflicts. A first is the fact that Russia officially annexed Crimea, while Armenia maintains a fig leaf of distance from the issue, claiming that Nagorno-Karabakh is a separate entity, (in spite of the Armenian parliament's December 1989 resolution on the annexation of Nagorno-Karabakh into Armenia suggesting otherwise). Secondly, the invasion of Crimea was not preceded by any conflict or controversy—Russia's justification for it was entirely manufactured, whereas in the case of Nagorno-Karabakh, there was a real conflict with very real grievances. But still, the parallels are very obvious: one European country's armed force occupies the territory of another European country, where its ethnic kin have declared independence. And whereas Crimea continues to have an ethnic Ukrainian and Crimean Tatar population, the Armenian occupation of Azerbaijani territories was accompanied by a systematic campaign of ethnic cleansing.

EU officials are, of course, aware of these glaring similarities. It is therefore no surprise that slowly, these realities have gradually turned the tables in the conflict, and the EU has been at a loss to counter Azerbaijani accusations of double standards in the differentiated treatment of Crimea and Nagorno-Karabakh. High-level EU diplomats privately acknowledge as much, agreeing that their efforts to dodge the issue and cite their support for the Minsk Group as justification is decidedly unsatisfying. And in fact, this helps explain why EU officials including the President of the European Council have lately returned to a policy of expressing support for Azerbaijan's territorial integrity. In sum, it appears that the EU is slowly coming to the realization that, to quote Amanda Paul, "the EU cannot pick and choose when it comes to the territorial integrity of its partner states."[54] Whether this will lead to a more consistent application of the principles of international law, however, remains to be seen.

CONCLUSIONS

Little has changed on the ground in the 20 years since a cease-fire was concluded between Armenia and Azerbaijan. Armenia continues to occupy the territory and large areas of western Azerbaijan; Azerbaijan continues to harbor hundreds of thousands of displaced persons from these territories. Armenia continues to demand self-determination for Nagorno-Karabakh; while Azerbaijan continues to call for the restoration of its territorial integrity.

But in substance, a lot has changed. Armenia is increasingly isolated in the region, and has been bypassed by the large infrastructural projects connecting the region to Europe. It has sunk ever deeper into a military and security dependence on Russia, which has acquired a veto right over Armenian foreign policy, which includes the ability to stop Armenia's European integration. Azerbaijan has seen considerable economic growth as a result of its oil and gas resources, and while that growth is currently challenged by low oil prices, Azerbaijan sports an economy several times larger than Armenia's. With economic growth and ample financial resources, revanchist feelings have grown in Azerbaijan; but the deep Russian support for Armenia for the time being prevents a resurgence of violence greater than what took place in April 2016.

At the same time, the South Caucasus has increasingly clearly become a part of Europe, and the EU has evolved into the primary institution in foreign and security policy on the continent. It is thus an anomaly that the EU has no seat at the table in one of the most serious conflicts affecting the continent, and which furthermore is gradually escalating, presenting a clear and present danger of return to war, which it did not a decade ago. The EU has failed to directly affect the conflict, but its inability to take a principled and consistent stance on territorial conflicts in Europe over the past decade has hurt the EU's standing in the region. While there is growing realization that this situation must be addressed, the forces supporting the status quo remain formidable. It is, unfortunately, likely that only a major eruption of the conflict would drive home to European leaders the danger that the conflict presents to European security.

NOTES

1. EU External Action Service, "EU-Moldova Relations," http://eeas. europa.eu/moldova/pdf/internal_political_economic_en.pdf
2. This mandate is stated as follows: "to contribute to the peaceful settlement of conflicts in accordance with the principles of international law and to facilitate the implementation of such settlement in close coordination with the United Nations, the OSCE and its Minsk Group." See "COUNCIL DECISION 2012/326/CFSP, June 25, 2012 extending the mandate of the European Union Special Representative for the South Caucasus and the crisis in Georgia," http://eur-lex.europa.eu/ LexUriServ/LexUriServ.do?uri=OJ:L:2012:165:0053:0055:EN:PDF

3. More information on the Minsk Group's composition is available at http://www.osce.org/item/52558

4. Svante E. Cornell, *Small Nations and Great Powers: A Study of Ethnopolitical Conflict in the Caucasus* (Richmond: Curzon Press, 2001), 113.

5. See S. Frederick Starr, Svante E. Cornell, and Nicklas Norling, *The EU, Central Asia, and the Development of Continental Transport and Trade* (Washington/Stockholm: Central Asia-Caucasus Institute & Silk Road Studies Program Joint Center, December 2015), http://silkroadstudies.org/resources/2015-starr-cornell-norling-eu-central-asia-continental-transport-and-trade.pdf

6. See Dov Lynch, "The EU: Toward A Strategy," in *The South Caucasus: A Challenge for the EU,* Chaillot Paper no. 65, ed. Dov Lynch (Paris: EU Institute for Security Studies, December 2003), for a description of the evolution of EU thinking on the Caucasus.

7. "South Caucasus: EU Special Representative 'Hopeful' on Karabakh," *RFE/RL,* June 9, 2006, http://www.rferl.org/content/article/1069032.html

8. Nicu Popescu, *EU Foreign Policy and Post-Soviet Conflicts: Stealth Intervention* (London and New York: Routledge, 2011), 110.

9. Stephen Blank, "From Neglect to Duress: The West and the Georgian Crisis Before the 2008 War," in *The Guns of August 2008: Russia's War in Georgia,* eds. Svante E. Cornell and S. Frederick Starr (Armonk: ME Sharpe), 112.

10. Tabib Huseynov, "The EU and Azerbaijan: Destination Unclear," *The European Union and the South Caucasus,* Bertelsmann Europe in Dialogue, 2009, 78, http://www.isn.ethz.ch/Digital-Library/Publications/Detail/?id=104885

11. Thomas de Waal, "Remaking the Nagorno-Karabakh Peace Process," *Survival* 52, no. 4, (2010), http://carnegieendowment.org/2010/08/01/remaking-nagorno-karabakh-peace-process/3ldh

12. "EU to Replace France in OSCE MG?," *Yerkir Media,* March 23, 2012, http://www.yerkirmedia.am/?act=news&lan=en&id=5968

13. Interviews with European diplomats, 2011–2013.

14. Interviews with EU diplomats, 2006–2007.

15. Gayane Abrahamyan, "Negotiation Concerns: Removal of France from Minsk Group troubling to some," *ArmeniaNow,* March 24, 2012, http://www.armenianow.com/karabakh/36768/osce_minsk_group_france_mandate_eu

16. Council of the European Union, "A Secure Europe in a Better World: European Security Strategy," 8, https://www.consilium.europa.eu/uedocs/cmsUpload/78367.pdf

17. Commission of the European Communities, *European Neighborhood Policy – Strategy Paper,* Brussels, May 12, 2004, http://eur-lex.europa.eu/legal-content/EN/TXT/PDF/?uri=CELEX:52004DC0373&from=en

18. Benita Ferrero-Waldner, "Political Reform and Sustainable Development in the South Caucasus: the EU's Approach," *Speech at the Bled Strategic Forum*, August 28, 2006, http://europa.eu/rapid/press-release_SPEECH-06-477_en.htm?locale=en

19. Popescu, *EU Foreign Policy and Post-Soviet Conflicts: Stealth Intervention*, 101.

20. See a detailed treatment of the EU's role in the conflict in Moldova in Nicu Popescu, *Stealth Intervention: The EU and Post-Soviet Conflicts*, Phd Thesis, Central European University, 2009, 134–163, http://sar.org.ro/wp-content/uploads/2012/12/Stealth-intervention-the-EU-and-post-soviet-conflicts.pdf

21. Richard Whitman and Stefan Wolff, "The EU as Conflict Manager? The Case of Georgia and Its Implications," *International Affairs* 86, no. 1 (2010): 87–107.

22. Donnacha O Beachain, "The Role of the EU and the OSCE in Promoting Security and Cooperation in the South Caucasus and Moldova," in *Security and Cross-Border Cooperation in the EU, Black Sea Region and the Southern Caucasus*, eds. Ayça Ergün and Hamlet Isaxanli, NATO Science for Peace and Security Series no. 107 (Amsterdam: IOS Press, 2013), 46.

23. Popescu, *Stealth Intervention: The EU and Post-Soviet Conflicts*, 256.

24. See, for example, the contribution of former EUSR to the South Caucasus Peter Semneby, "Conflict and Security in Nagorno-Karabakh: What Contribution from the EU?," in *Europe's Next Avoidable War*, eds. Michael Kambeck and Sargis Ghazaryan (Basingstoke: Palgrave MacMillan, 2013), 175–178.

25. European Neighborhood and Partnership Instrument, "Azerbaijan: Country Strategy Paper, 2007–2013," 2006, 7, http://eeas.europa.eu/enp/pdf/pdf/country/enpi_csp_azerbaijan_en.pdf

26. Such a study would be published in 2010 by two Azerbaijani scholars, Nazim Muzaffarli and Eldar Ismailov, *Basic Principles for the Rehabilitation of Azerbaijan's Post-Conflict Territories* (Luleå: CA & C Press, 2010).

27. Tabib Huseynov, "The EU and Azerbaijan: Destination Unclear," 78.

28. Cf. the Partnership and Cooperation Agreement with Armenia, http://eur-lex.europa.eu/resource.html?uri=cellar:cfa0c50d-97c4-444d-84d3-7fd45943cf14.0020.02/DOC_1&format=PDF; the Partnership and Cooperation Agreement with Azerbaijan, http://eeas.europa.eu/delegations/azerbaijan/documents/eu_azerbaijan/eu-az_pca_full_text.pdf

29. See the Partnership and Cooperation Agreement with Moldova from 1994, http://trade.ec.europa.eu/doclib/docs/2007/august/tradoc_135737.pdf; and that with Georgia from 1996 at http://eeas.europa.eu/delegations/georgia/documents/eu_georgia/eu_georgia_pca_en.pdf

30. See EU/Moldova Action Plan, 3, http://eeas.europa.eu/enp/pdf/
pdf/action_plans/moldova_enp_ap_final_en.pdf
31. See discussion in Martin Malek, "The European Union and the 'Frozen
Conflicts' in the South Caucasus," *Diplomatiya Alemi*, no. 18–19 (2008):
72–80, http://mfa.gov.az/files/file/Diplomatiya_Alemi_18-19.pdf
32. EU/Georgia Action Plan, 10, http://eeas.europa.eu/enp/pdf/pdf/
action_plans/georgia_enp_ap_final_en.pdf
33. EU/Moldova Action Plan, 11. http://eeas.europa.eu/enp/pdf/pdf/
action_plans/moldova_enp_ap_final_en.pdf
34. See, for example, European Commission Staff Working Paper,
March 2005, SEC(2005)286, 11, http://www.refworld.org/docid/
42c3ba094.html
35. "EU guarantees inviolability of Ukraine, Georgia and Moldova," *mol-
dova.org*, September 3, 2008 http://www.moldova.org/eu-guarantees-
inviolability-of-ukraine-georgia-and-moldova-147252-eng/; see also
discussion in Amanda Paul, "Where is EU Support for Azerbaijan?,"
Today's Zaman, September 17, 2008, http://www.todayszaman.com/
columnists_where-is-eu-support-for-azerbaijan_153308.html; and in
Huseynov, "The EU and Azerbaijan: Destination Unclear," 76–77.
36. Paruyr Hovhannisyan, "Evolution of the EU Position vis-à-vis the
Nagorno-Karabakh Conflict," in *Europe's Next Avoidable War*, eds.
Kambeck and Ghazaryan, 170.
37. Organization for Security and Cooperation in Europe, "EU Statement
on 'Presidential elections' in Abkhazia, Georgia, 12 December 2009,"
December 17, 2009, http://www.osce.org/pc/41106?download=true
38. Organization for Security and Cooperation in Europe, "EU Presidency
Declaration on 'Parliamentary Elections' in South Ossetia," June 2,
2009, http://eu-un.europa.eu/articles/en/article_8767_en.htm
39. See, for example, 1239th Council of Europe Committee of Ministers
Deputies Meeting, November 4, 2015
    "EU Statement on the Secretary General's 12th Consolidated
Report on the Conflict in Georgia," http://eeas.europa.eu/delega-
tions/council_europe/documents/20151105_01_en.pdf;   "EU
Statement on the Geneva International Discussions," December 18,
2014, http://www.osce.org/pc/134256?download=true;
    and "Statement by High Representative/Vice-President Federica
Mogherini on the announced signature of a 'Treaty on Alliance and
Integration' between the Russian Federation and Georgia's breakaway
region of South Ossetia," March 17, 2015, http://eeas.europa.eu/
statements-eeas/2015/150317_04_en.htm
40. Council of the European Union, "Declaration by the Presidency on
behalf of the European Union on the 'referendum' in the Transnistrian
region of the Republic of Moldova," September 22, 2006, http://for-
min.finland.fi/public/default.aspx?contentid=80832&contentlan=2&
culture=en-US

41. Organization for Security and cooperation in Europe,"Annex to the OSCE Lisbon document 1996 on Armenia-Azerbaijan conflict," December 3, 1996, http://www.osce.org/mc/39539

42. Ibid. The Armenian delegation had its own statement appended to the document, which in two points stated the following: "The statement does not reflect either the spirit or the letter of the Minsk Group's mandate as established by the Budapest Summit 1994, which proposed negotiations with a view to reaching a political agreement. The problem of status has been a subject of discussion in direct negotiations which have yet to be concluded. The statement predetermines the status of Nagorno-Karabakh, contradicting the decision of the OSCE Ministerial Council of 1992, which referred this issue to the competence of the OSCE Minsk Conference, to be convened after the conclusion of a political agreement."

43. "Declaration by the Presidency on behalf of the European Union on forthcoming 'Presidential Elections' in Nagorno-Karabakh," August 2, 2002, http://europa.eu/rapid/press-release_PESC-02-105_en.pdf

44. "Statement by High Representative Catherine Ashton on Nagorno-Karabakh," May 21, 2010, http://www.consilium.europa.eu/uedocs/cmsUpload/114603.pdf

45. Verelq, "EU does not recognize Karabakh and supports territorial integrity of Azerbaijan, Donald Tusk says," July 25, 2015, http://www.verelq.am/en/node/2762

46. "EU Supports Azerbaijan's Territorial Integrity – Latvian Foreign Ministry," *Trend News Agency*, February 13, 2015, http://en.trend.az/azerbaijan/karabakh/2364132.html. Also Azertac, "Latvia supports resolution of Nagorno-Karabakh conflict within Azerbaijan's territorial integrity," July 4, 2015, http://azertag.az/en/xeber/_039Latvia_supports_resolution_of_Nagorno_Karabakh_conflict_within_Azerbaijan_039s_territorial_integrity_039-869098

47. Ralph Wilde, "Kosovo-Independence, Recognition and International Law," in *Kosovo: International Law and Recognition*, Chatham House International Law Discussion Group, April 22, 2008, https://www.chathamhouse.org/sites/files/chathamhouse/public/Research/International%20Law/il220408.pdf

48. Security Council, "Report of the Special Envoy of the Secretary-General on Kosovo's future status," *UN Report* No. 168, Marsh 26, 2007, www.un.org/en/ga/search/view_doc.asp?symbol=S/2007/168

49. European Union and European Nations Report, "EU Council Conclusions on Kosovo," February 18, 2008, http://euun.europa.eu/articles/en/article_7720_en.htm

50. See, for example, European Commission, "Kosovo," http://ec.europa.eu/enlargement/countries/detailed-country-information/kosovo/

51. German Federal Ministry of Foreign Affairs, "Rede von Frank-Walter Aussenminister Steinmeier bei der 69. Generalversammlung der Vereinten Nationen" [Speech of Foreign Minister Frank-Walter Steinmeier at the 69th General Assembly of the United Nations], September 27, 2014, http://www.auswaertiges-amt.de/DE/Infoservice/Presse/Reden/2014/140927_69_Generalversammlung_VN.html

52. Council of the European Union, "Council Conclusions on Ukraine," March 3, 2014, https://www.consilium.europa.eu/uedocs/cms_data/docs/pressdata/EN/foraff/141291.pdf

53. European Union External Action Service, "EU engagement in Ukraine since the Maidan protests," http://eeas.europa.eu/ukraine/about/maidan_protests_en.htm

54. Amanda Paul, "Where is EU Support for Azerbaijan?," *Cihan News Agency,* April 16, 2008, https://www.cihan.com.tr/en/cms-copied-news-on-26-10-514079.htm

CHAPTER 9

Moving Beyond Deadlock in the Peace Talks

Nina Caspersen

"There is a possibility of a Karabakh settlement in the course of this year," the US Co-chair of the Minsk Group declared optimistically in 2005.[1] Four years later, the Russian Co-chair was again hopeful that a meeting between the Presidents of Armenia and Azerbaijan "could lead to a breakthrough."[2] But while the international mediators tasked with finding a solution to the Armenian–Azerbaijani conflict over Nagorno-Karabakh frequently announce that a breakthrough is likely, such optimistic statements have so far amounted to nothing. The leaders of Armenia and Azerbaijan have met numerous times to try to hammer out a compromise solution that they can both accept, and that they can sell to their publics at home. Under the auspices of the Organization for Security and Co-operation in Europe's (OSCE) Minsk Group, the mediators have changed their strategy over time. They have adopted more or less directive approaches, put forward both package deals and phased solutions, and presented a series of different proposals that have each been trying, in more or less creative ways, to square the circle of territorial integrity and self-determination. Notwithstanding, the talks have repeatedly ended in deadlock.

Why have more than two decades of negotiations failed to produce a breakthrough? This chapter examines the evolution of the peace process since the signing of the ceasefire agreement in 1994 and the various proposals that have been on the table. It finds that the main obstacle to peace is a lack of political will on the part of the local actors, which is compounded by two factors: first, the "constructive ambiguity" of the proposed interim agreement, and second, the format of the Minsk Process, in particular its narrow and secretive nature and lack of international commitment. The chapter subsequently discusses

N. Caspersen (✉)
York, UK

© The Author(s) 2017   173
S.E. Cornell (ed.), *The International Politics of the Armenian-
Azerbaijani Conflict*, DOI 10.1057/978-1-137-60006-6_9

three complementary strategies for reducing insecurities and fears and moving the process forward. These include a revised proposal, a broader, more open process with increased international involvement, and envisioning a greater role for the European Union (EU).

THE MINSK GROUP

International efforts to find a solution to the conflict are led by the Minsk Group and its three Co-chairs. The Minsk Group is only linked to the Belarusian capital insofar as it owes its name to a peace conference that was supposed to have taken place in Minsk in 1992. While this first meeting was called off due to an upsurge in fighting, the name stuck. A formal chairmanship of the group was established in 1995,[3] with Russia and Sweden as the initial Co-chairs. The present system, with three Co-chairs representing Russia, France and the USA, was created in 1997. The history of the Minsk Group is unusual and a lack of clarity surrounding its precise role persists. As Thomas de Waal aptly puts it, "the Minsk Process consists of a conference which was only occasionally convened, a group which never meet as a group and a co-chairmanship functioning under a barely known mandate, all named after a city where the mediators have never met."[4] The Minsk Group was created during the war with the initial goal of ensuring a ceasefire, but the process has remained largely unchanged. de Waal[5] therefore questions if this process is geared to finding a lasting solution; indeed, the Karabakh peace process is routinely criticized for being too narrow and too secretive.[6] In fact, more cynical observers have argued that the Minsk Process has become an excuse for inaction on the part of the co-chairs and the international community writ large, who can point to an ongoing process, which nevertheless continuously fails to deliver.[7]

EVOLUTION OF THE PEACE PROCESS

The bloody war between Azerbaijani and Armenian forces over the territory of Nagorno-Karabakh came to an end with the signing of the Bishkek Protocol in May 1994. This ceasefire agreement, which had been brokered by Russia, calls upon the conflict parties to sign, as soon as possible, an agreement which includes a mechanism for the "withdrawal of troops from occupied territories" and the "return of refugees."[8] The agreement does not mention the status of the contested territory, but there was nevertheless hope that progress on a compromise settlement could be achieved before the ceasefire broke down.[9] The ceasefire did not break down and remains in place to this day despite frequent exchanges of fire across the front line. Yet a peace agreement never materialized. Both sides had an interest in a ceasefire: the Azerbaijani Army was in disarray and the Armenian forces were overextended[10]; and the economies and social infrastructure of both countries had been virtually destroyed by the war.[11] However, the peace process quickly came to a halt, with neither side showing much interest in reaching a compromise. It seemed that the conflict was simply not ripe for resolution. As P. Terrence Hopmann and I. William Zartman[12] have argued, it is a case of a "soft, stable, self-serving stalemate," not a mutually hurting one.[13] This is not to say that the conflict and the peace process are static. The mediation strategy has changed over time: the Co-chairs have been more or less directive and have alternated between package and step-by-step approaches. The proposals on the table have also evolved: from an initial emphasis on territorial integrity to attempts to blur or postpone issues of sovereignty. And on a couple of occasions, the process has hung on the verge of forward movement.[14]

Changing Mediation Strategies

The Minsk Process was slow to get off the ground, especially due to rivalry within the group, which persisted even after the formal chairmanship was established.[15] In fact, then Armenian President Levon Ter-Petrosyan argues that the OSCE only began to take the peace process seriously in 1996, "before that, it was simply a bluff, there was absolutely no peace process … They competed among themselves more than they thought about the Karabakh issue." One of the problems appeared to be that the Western countries were simply not very interested in the Nagorno-Karabakh conflict.[16] Nevertheless, the USA and France were added to the Minsk Group, and this ushered in a new push for a settlement. In 1997, two peace proposals were presented: first a package deal, then a phased approach. This new, more assertive strategy nevertheless failed to bear fruit, and actually resulted in a more hard-line Armenian leadership.

The leaders of Nagorno-Karabakh insisted on a comprehensive agreement that included a final settlement on the status of Nagorno-Karabakh, in the form of independence. The position could be summed up as "territories for status" in the sense that Armenian withdrawal from the districts surrounding Nagorno-Karabakh would only happen in return for the entity's *de jure* separation from Azerbaijan.[17] A package deal was therefore needed. The Armenian President was more flexible on this issue, but it soon became clear that his room for maneuver was limited. Azerbaijan, on the other hand, insisted that Armenian withdrawal from the occupied districts was a precondition for any discussions on Karabakh's future status[18] and therefore favored a phased, or a step-by-step, solution.

The first proposal put forward by the Minsk co-chairs in 1997 was a package deal that would formally preserve Azerbaijan's territorial integrity but would give Nagorno-Karabakh the widest possible autonomy, including its own "national guard"; effectively creating a state-within-a-state. Azerbaijan considered this "an acceptable starting point" but wavered; Armenia accepted it with "serious reservations" as a basis for further talks, but it was in any case flatly rejected by the Karabakhi leadership.[19] The mediators then put forward a step-by-step approach, which postponed the questions of Karabakh's status and of the strategic Lachin corridor that links Armenia and Karabakh. This proposal was again rejected by the Karabakh Armenians, but pragmatic considerations led the Armenian President, Levon Ter-Petrosyan, to accept the proposal, although again with "serious reservations."[20] Ter-Petrosyan was under pressure due to the catastrophic economic situation in Armenia, aware that time was not in Armenia's favor,[21] and desperately wanted to end the country's international isolation.[22] He argued that a settlement on Karabakh and the opening of borders with Turkey were vital for Armenia's prosperity: otherwise, "Armenia cannot return to normality."[23] Moreover, he assessed that due to the international support for Azerbaijan's territorial integrity, postponing the issue of Karabakh's final status was the best that could be hoped for.[24] By December 1997, both Yerevan and Baku were reportedly ready to sign the plan,[25] but the problem was that Ter-Petrosyan did not enjoy the political leeway to agree to such a compromise. His support base had been steadily weakening and he had come to rely on the support of the Karabakhi leadership and of the "power ministries," which insisted on a package deal. Ter-Petrosyan's opponents accused him of "national betrayal" and forced him to resign.[26] His replacement, Armenian Prime Minister Robert Kocharyan, was the former president of Nagorno-Karabakh and adopted a much more hard-line position: independence for Nagorno-Karabakh was non-negotiable and had to be guaranteed in any agreement. Therefore, "nothing is agreed at all unless everything is agreed."[27]

Following this setback, the Co-chairs put forward one more proposal, the so-called "common state" proposal in 1998, which rapidly faltered. They then changed their strategy: instead of using shuttle diplomacy and presenting the parties with new proposals, they took a step back and began facilitating direct meetings between the Presidents of Azerbaijan and Armenia.[28] These meetings were, as previous meetings, held under a tight cloak of secrecy,[29] but the mediators' approach seems to have been less directive, with the emphasis instead being on trying to find common ground, exploring alternative ways of achieving a compromise. This strategy reportedly came close to success in 1999 when the two presidents discussed a controversial "land swap" deal.

The presidents met regularly, on their own initiative,[30] and appear to have revised the so-called "Goble Plan" which proposed a territorial exchange to solve the conflict: in return for Armenian control of Nagorno-Karabakh as well as the Lachin corridor, Azerbaijan would obtain a land corridor across southern Armenia, connecting Azerbaijan with the enclave of Nakhichevan. Azerbaijan's President, Heydar Aliyev, hailed from Nakhichevan so had a personal interest in this solution, which would also provide mainland Azerbaijan with a direct link to Turkey, and an agreement appears to have been within reach.[31] Nevertheless, both leaders faced a domestic backlash. The proposed deal was not made public at the time, but it caused divisions within the elite. In Azerbaijan, it was interpreted as a surrender of Karabakh and three of Aliyev's top advisers resigned, apparently in protest over this plan.[32] Aliyev was reportedly shaken, but did not abandon the plan.[33] However, instability in Armenia made a compromise impossible. Giving up the Meghri region was highly controversial in Armenia as it would result in the loss of Armenia's border with Iran. Kocharyan therefore needed the support of the powerful new Prime Minister, Vazgen Sargsyan, for such a move to be possible. But on October 27, 1999, gunmen entered the Armenian Parliament and shot dead eight people, including Sargsyan and the parliament speaker, Karen Demirchyan. The motives behind the attack, and indeed who was behind it, remain controversial, but the shootings devastated the Armenian political landscape.[34]

After the parliament shooting, Kocharyan backtracked on a deal, citing the fragile security situation in Armenia.[35] High-profile talks were attempted again in 2001, in Key West, and the deal on the table was reportedly still some form of territorial swap.[36] But reports of possible compromises resulted in strong domestic criticism, and no agreement resulted.[37] Upon his return to Baku, Aliyev rejected any compromises on Karabakh's status.[38] Instead, he offered a restoration of economic links, in exchange for Armenian withdrawal from four out of seven southern occupied districts. Aliyev saw this as a significant concession, but it was rejected out of hand by Kocharyan, who continued to insist on a package solution which included Karabakh's status. A pause in the talks resulted which was prolonged by Aliyev's ill health and the process of succession in Azerbaijan. In 2003, Heydar Aliyev was replaced by his son Ilham Aliyev, who was disillusioned with the negotiations and adopted a more hardline position on Karabakh. He denounced the Key West talks, insisted on the inviolability of Azerbaijan's territorial integrity, and threatened to use force to reintegrate Karabakh.[39]

In order to re-start the talks, the Minsk Co-chairs began in 2004 to organize talks between the two foreign ministers of Armenia and Azerbaijan.[40] The movement away from the highly pressurized, and ultimately fruitless, talks between the two presidents was supposed to build trust and confidence between the two sides and a better environment for future presidential talks.[41] This resulted in the so-called Prague process. In 2005, the mediators presented a first draft of a set of BASIC PRINCIPLES that were intended to provide a framework for a comprehensive settlement. The Minsk Co-chairs had thereby returned to a more directive strategy.[42]

A lot of optimism surrounded the 2006 talks in Rambouillet, but progress again failed to materialize and the Minsk Co-chairs shortly thereafter issued a statement expressing their regret that the process "has not moved forward in recent weeks despite ample opportunity to do so."[43] The Co-chairs also took the unprecedented step of partially revealing the principles that were being proposed. The intention was to pressure the parties to agree to the principles and launch a public debate about them.[44] The mediators felt a sense of urgency as elections were due in both countries in 2007 and 2008, and they feared that domestic politics would soon make a compromise impossible.[45] The year 2006 came and went and the approach of elections did, as expected, lead to a slowing down of the talks. In 2007, the Minsk Co-chairs formally presented the "BASIC PRINCIPLES for the Peaceful Settlement of the Nagorno-Karabakh Conflict" which now constituted an official proposal.[46]

The principles seek to satisfy both parties by combining a package deal and a step-by-step approach. The agreement is to be implemented in stages, but it includes mechanisms for deciding on the final status of Nagorno-Karabakh: a popular vote is to be held after an interim period. Both presidents have accepted the principle, but only as a basis for further discussion, and these discussions have now been ongoing for a decade with little discernible progress. The principles have been revised over time, but without any fundamental changes. They include the following:

- Return of the territories surrounding Nagorno-Karabakh to Azerbaijani control;
- An interim status for Nagorno-Karabakh providing guarantees for security and self-governance;
- A corridor linking Armenia to Nagorno-Karabakh;
- Future determination of the final legal status of Nagorno-Karabakh through a legally binding expression of will;
- The right of all internally displaced persons (IDPs) and refugees to return to their former places of residence; and
- International security guarantees that would include a peacekeeping operation.[47]

As will be shown below, the devil is very much in the detail, and significant disagreement remains regarding the interpretation of each principle and their sequencing.

Whereas the proposal put forward by the Minsk Co-chairs has changed little since 2005, the international context has. The war in Georgia in 2008 in particular saw an increase in international efforts. It showed how "frozen conflicts" could experience a dangerous thaw. The rhetoric on both sides of the conflict hardened, with Azerbaijan frequently threatening to solve the conflict through military means, and an increase in shootings across the front line added to the growing sense of uncertainty and instability.[48] The USA appeared to take a greater interest in the conflict, with high-level visits to Armenia and Azerbaijan by the Secretary of State, but it was Russia that came to take a leading role. The Kremlin was keen to demonstrate that it could play a positive role in peace efforts in the region. The conflict has now again moved down on the international agenda, and Moscow clearly plays the dominant role in the Minsk Process, as evidenced by Putin's 2014 hosting of a meeting between the Armenian and the Azerbaijani Presidents in Sochi.[49]

The Minsk Process is characterized by two constant features: a striking lack of openness and a lack of inclusivity. These are confidential, elite-level talks taken to the extreme.[50] Nevertheless, some changes can be observed: the mediators have, as noted above, adopted more or less directive strategies, and they have also tried to engineer increasingly creative proposals, in an attempt to find a middle-way between Azerbaijan's insistence on its territorial integrity and Armenian insistence on independence for Karabakh. Zartman[51] once argued that the way around stark invisibility in peace talks "has been a challenge to which creativity has responded positively," but Hopmann and Zartman also contend that this is difficult or indeed impossible when it involves the issue of sovereignty: solutions necessarily fall on one side or the other of the "crest of sovereignty"; that "there is no in between."[52] Sovereignty is commonly perceived as non-divisible and creative solutions will rarely be acceptable to the conflict parties.

Changing Proposals: The Difficulty of Finding a Middle-Way

At the OSCE Lisbon Summit in 1996, the Chairman-in-Office put forward three principles that were supposed to serve as a framework for a solution to the conflict: first, Azerbaijan's territorial integrity; second, the highest degree of self-rule for Nagorno-Karabakh within Azerbaijan; and third, guaranteed security for Nagorno-Karabakh and its population and ensured compliance with the settlement.[53] Armenia vetoed these principles, as they ruled out Nagorno-Karabakh's independence from the outset, but they were supported by all other OSCE member states. This demonstrates that the international preference, at this point, was clearly for a solution that maintained the existing borders. Territorial integrity was maintained in the 1997 package proposal, but it did try to blur the issue of sovereignty. The proposal offered Nagorno-Karabakh extensive autonomy, including its own armed forces, thereby essentially creating a state-within-a-state. It moreover included a highly creative solution regarding the strategic Lachin corridor: Azerbaijan would lease it to the OSCE, which in turn would lease it to Nagorno-Karabakh.[54] Azerbaijan's territorial integrity was therefore maintained on paper only, but it was still not enough for the Karabakh leaders, and Baku also wavered.

The mediators' subsequent proposal to postpone the issue of status, however, was not acceptable to the Karabakh leaders, nor to significant forces in Yerevan: the fear was that the issue of status would then never be negotiated, and that Azerbaijani forces would launch a military offensive once Armenian forces had withdrawn from the occupied districts. There were simply not enough guarantees against a forceful reintegration.[55]

A new attempt to blur the issue of sovereignty was the "common state" proposal, also known as the Primakov Plan, from 1998 which proposed "non-hierarchical" relations between Azerbaijan and Nagorno-Karabakh. This fell short of Karabakh's demand for *de jure* recognition as an independent state, but would otherwise have institutionalized the status quo. But the proposal was strongly rejected by Azerbaijan as "defeatist." Aliyev argued that it implied that "Karabakh is an independent state...and grants it, equal with Azerbaijan, the status of the subject of the common state."[56]

Finding a way to square the circle of independence and territorial integrity was therefore anything but easy. An alternative approach, explored by the two presidents in 1999, was instead to offer compensation[57]: territories could be swapped. However, the domestic backlash demonstrated how controversial such exchanges would be: territory may be divisible but it holds immense symbolic value, it has implications for security, and, of course, it is also concerns people's homes. It is therefore not simply about the number of square kilometers controlled and it is hard to imagine what would constitute a "fair swap." The events surrounding the talks also illustrated that Armenia is no less sensitive than Azerbaijan to its territorial integrity.

When the process was restarted in 2004, the negotiations therefore returned to ways of blurring or postponing the issue of Nagorno-Karabakh's status. The BASIC PRINCIPLES outlined above try to square the circle of territorial integrity and independence by proposing an interim agreement. Status is not finally decided but it is also not simply postponed: a mechanism is to be included for determining the status of Nagorno-Karabakh at the end of the interim period. The interim period, however, will give Azerbaijan a chance to demonstrate the benefits of a joint state, and the final status is therefore not meant to be a foregone conclusion. This proposal resembles solutions reached in the conflicts in Sudan and Papua New Guinea/Bougainville where independence referenda followed, or will follow, interim periods of self-governance. What is novel about this framework is that it recognizes Nagorno-Karabakh as a self-determination unit, which has the right to independence, even if the implementation of this right is frozen for the time being.[58] At least, this is the Armenian reading of the principles.

Indeed, the problem is that the two sides interpret the principles very differently. Azerbaijan is still refusing to countenance any vote that could lead to independence for Nagorno-Karabakh, insisting that Azerbaijani IDPs must also be allowed to vote, and arguing that the whole country must have a say if the referendum includes the option of independence.[59] The Armenian side insists that the vote must be in Nagorno-Karabakh only and it must be an independence referendum. Their position on IDPs is more unclear; they argue that they will accept the right to return, but only once the issue of status is resolved.[60] Their main concern relates to the sequencing of the different phases and the worry that the security of Nagorno-Karabakh will not be protected in the interim period. They are concerned that if the withdrawal of troops happens before the vote on Karabakh's status, then the latter will never materialize, or will be manipulated by the Azerbaijani government.

Despite the gradual evolution of the process and the use of more creative proposals that attempt to blur or postpone the issue of Nagorno-Karabakh's status, a compromise agreement does not seem closer today than it did 20 years ago; if anything, the two sides seem further apart. What then are the main obstacles to a settlement?

Main Obstacles to a Political Settlement

As examined here in turn, the main obstacles to peace are three-fold: a lack of political will, the proposal itself, and the Minsk Process. These would be challenging enough on their own, but they interact in a way that exacerbates underlying insecurities and fears.

Lack of Political Will

The key problem when it comes to reaching an agreement is as simple as it is fundamental: the two presidents lack the political will, or indeed ability, to accept what will invariably be a difficult compromise. They do not face significant pressure, externally or internally, to reach a deal and both sides remain hopeful that time is on their side; that they can achieve their maximalist objectives if they just wait long enough. The Karabakhi leaders, along with their supporters in Armenia, hope that time will create irreversible facts on the ground: it will normalize the status quo and make international recognition of Nagorno-Karabakh's de facto independence more likely. In the meantime, they are working on making the status quo more attractive, which they argue is preferable to an uncertain agreement.[61] The Azerbaijani government, on the other hand, hopes that time and the international isolation of Nagorno-Karabakh will gradually weaken the entity. Combined with Azerbaijan's much-increased military spending, this is intended to weaken the resolve of the Armenian side, thereby making the reintegration of the territory more likely—through negotiations or perhaps through military means.[62]

There is therefore no sense of urgency surrounding the peace talks, and the international pressure exerted on the two presidents has been very limited. Continuing negotiations, even if fruitless, appear to be enough to satisfy the involved third parties.[63] The presidents have in fact made clever use of the ongoing peace process as a means to avoid criticism of flawed elections. They can argue that such pressure would weaken their position and hence make it impossible for them to agree to a peace settlement.[64] Internally, the unresolved conflict is also used to legitimize the two regimes, by "constructing the representations of danger and insecurities."[65] Any opposition movement or competing representation can be destroyed by depicting it as "a threat to national security."[66] In the case of Azerbaijan, both Aliyevs have invoked the need for stability to justify repressive measures, arguing that Azerbaijan's defeat in Karabakh had been due to the domestic turmoil that characterized the pre-war and wartime periods.[67] The status quo therefore in many ways benefits the local leaders.[68]

In the long term, however, this may change: Azerbaijan's continued lack of control over a significant part of its territory is a serious problem for a state without a well-established identity. This is compounded by the inability of an estimated 800,000 IDPs to return to their homes in the Armenian-controlled territories.[69] On the Armenian side, we may see a discrepancy between the incentives facing Nagorno-Karabakh and Armenia proper. Although of immense symbolic importance, the issue of status is not the existential issue in Armenia that it is in Karabakh.[70] Moreover, the effects of Turkey's and Azerbaijan's embargo on Armenia continue to hamper the country's economic development. The World Bank estimates that the opening of borders would double Armenia's exports and increase its GDP by an estimated 30 percent.[71] However, the President of Armenia is himself from Karabakh, and is therefore able to insist that he represents Karabakh's interests as well as Armenia's, and there is no currently no (open) rift on the Armenian side.

Even assuming a genuine will to compromise, the two leaders are however significantly constrained. The domestic backlashes experienced by the Armenian leaders in 1997 and 1999 have already been covered above and power is, despite democratic setbacks, still fiercely contested. The Armenian Parliament rejected the proposals that Kocharyan brought back for consultations following the 2001 Key West talks,[72] and the "Karabakh card" has been routinely used by the opposition to denounce the ruling regime.[73] Azerbaijan President Ilham Aliyev is usually seen as a stronger leader than Armenia's Serzh Sargsyan. Svante Cornell[74] has therefore argued that he would be able to better carry a settlement. However, his father's attempts to negotiate an agreement illustrate that even an authoritarian leader is likely to be constrained. The 1999 talks led, as mentioned above, to resignations from Heydar Aliyev's inner circles, and there were also large demonstrations against the rumored "land swap."[75] Heydar Aliyev was also unable to secure support from within his own ranks for the Key West talks.[76] The hardening of rhetoric since Ilham Aliyev came to power may be primarily meant for an internal audience,[77] but it similarly constrains his ability to agree to a settlement especially if it means compromising on Azerbaijan's territorial integrity.[78]

If the problem was simply one of lack of political will, then there would not be much the mediators could do. They would simply have to wait for a more opportune moment and then present the parties with a way out. However, the lack of political will and ability to compromise is reinforced by certain features of the peace process and the proposal put forward.

The Proposal: Destructive Ambiguity?

The interim agreement contained in the BASIC PRINCIPLES demonstrates the expanded "tool box" available to conflict mediators since the end of the Cold War. It escapes what Marc Weller[79] has termed the self-determination trap and is an example of greater creativity when it comes to solving a separatist dispute than what we have traditionally seen. The problem is that an interim agreement also creates a high-level of uncertainty: what will the final status be, and can the other side be expected to honor their commitment? Interim agreements are commonly used when no other solutions are possible, especially when the separatist forces have already achieved de facto independence and are refusing to budge on the issue of independence, but the parent state is equally vehement about not being willing to compromise on its territorial integrity. The benefit of an interim agreement is that it allows for a compromise settlement, despite a lack of agreement on the key underlying issue. The hope is that the interim agreement will allow for trust to be rebuilt and that the issue of status will overtime become less explosive.

But even though such interim agreements are typically all-else-fails solutions, certain preconditions must be met. First, both sides should be willing to give unity a chance. For example, in the case of Sudan, the agreement explicitly requires the two sides to "to make the unity of the Sudan an attractive option especially to the people of South Sudan."[80] Following the insistence of the Sudanese government, the South Sudan leaders also agreed to an extended interim period.[81] Second, and relatedly, there must be some uncertainty regarding the outcome of the final vote. Again, in the case of Sudan, the leader of the Southern People's Liberation Army/Movement (SPLM/A), John Garang, had visions of a New Sudan[82] and he, along with other SPLM leaders, had political ambitions in the North as well.[83] Following the death of Garang, the separatist faction of the SPLM became more dominant and the Sudanese government increasingly came to realize that an independent South Sudan would result.[84] However, this was some time after the agreement was reached. Similarly, in the case of Bougainville, the Papua New Guinea government is convinced that the common state can be maintained if (extensive) autonomy is given a chance.[85] If it is completely certain from the outset that independence will be favored, then the interim period achieves nothing. The parties might as well agree on the final status immediately, even if implementation is delayed.

These preconditions are not met in the case of Nagorno-Karabakh. The Karabakh leaders have no interest in unity and the Azerbaijani government has, despite its insistence on reintegration of the entity, made no effort to try to reach out to the Karabakh Armenians and build trust. The proposed principles also only emphasize separation, not any form of co-existence. If a referendum is held, then the result would therefore be entirely predictable and merely depend on where it is held and who is allowed to vote. If a referendum is held in Karabakh only, which is the common practice in interim agreements,[86] then the result would be a resounding Yes to independence—even if Azerbaijani IDPs returned and were able to vote. This is why Azerbaijan is adamant that a popular "expression of will," under these circumstances, must not include the option of full independence. If the referendum is held in Azerbaijan as a whole, then the No would be similarly resounding. If the vote were to be held in the areas currently controlled by the Armenian forces, that is, Karabakh and the surrounding districts, then the result would depend on whether IDPs were able to return; if they were, then it would again be a No. The questions of "who would vote, on what and when" have therefore become crucial stumbling blocks in the negotiations.[87]

Instead of constructive ambiguity, it could also be argued that the current proposal suffers from "destructive ambiguity." It is not clear if the principles are supposed to lead to independence or not. And this depends on the details of the agreement, in particular surrounding the future vote, and whether the parties will honor their commitment. It does not depend on whether autonomy can be made attractive during the interim period. The Azerbaijani side fears that the ambiguity of the principles means that they would eventually have to comply with a decision against their will: the independence of Nagorno-Karabakh.[88] The Armenian side, on the other hand, fears that a promised referendum will never be held or that the process will be manipulated; that they will be cheated if they agree to withdraw their troops. The agreement is supposed to provide international guarantees against such "cheating," in the form of an international peacekeeping force. However, the Armenian side maintains that they would not trust such a force to protect Nagorno-Karabakh. They point to the Serb statelet in wartime Croatia which was forcefully reintegrated, despite the presence of UN forces who were supposed to uphold the ceasefire.[89] As Tabib Huseynov[90] has argued, in the absence of an agreement on the outcome, technical procedures become crucial, which helps explain why negotiations over a framework agreement have been ongoing for more than a decade. The proposal therefore adds to existing insecurities and fears, and this is further exacerbated by the characteristics of the peace process.

The Minsk Process: Too Secretive, Narrow and Disengaged

The arguments against the Minsk Process are fairly well rehearsed: the process is too narrow, it is too secretive, and there is a lack of international will to apply the pressure and supply the resources needed to get an agreement. What makes these features particularly unfortunate is that they add to the problems identified above.

Too Secretive

Peace processes are usually characterized by a degree of secrecy which is seen as necessary for the parties to reach difficult compromises. Publicity too early in the process could lead to a domestic backlash and make it too difficult for the parties to reach an agreement; it would make it harder to try out ideas and explore possible trade-offs. However, this is taken to extremes in this case. Very unusually, the process has no spokesman and virtually no public profile.[91] Any progress in the negotiations therefore remains confidential and the public has no knowledge of what is being discussed, apart from when the broad principles were released in 2006 or when the leaders have decided to leak proposals.

The problem is that the lack of publicity encourages rumors and conspiracy theories. This is particularly problematic when the leaders are discussing such an ambiguous proposal. Every time the presidents meet the rumor mill goes into overdrive: "Armenian forces will be withdrawn, leaving us defenseless"; "the rights of IDPs will be sacrificed"; "Karabakh has been lost"—or more generally, "our leaders are selling us out," "they are betraying our nationalist interest." Such speculations are clearly not conducive to peace. However, the presidents are not blameless. They prefer a confidential process, which means that there is no pressure on them, and they make no attempt to prepare their publics for the painful concessions that will invariably be part of a compromise agreement.

Too Narrow

Most peace processes are elite-led: they bring together the political and military leaders and only broaden the process once an agreement has been reached. But this is again taken to extremes by the Karabakh peace process. The talks only involve the two presidents and, on occasion, their foreign ministers. There is no mechanism for involving civil society or any other groupings, even if the Co-chairs do on occasion meet with them,[92] and no attempt to transform attitudes or prepare the ground for reconciliation.[93] Such a narrow format would perhaps be understandable if there was a great deal of urgency and an agreement had to be reached quickly in order to stop the fighting. But a ceasefire agreement has largely held for over 20 years, and although the number of deaths on the Line of Contact has increased steadily in recent years, a new full-scale war does not appear imminent.

The talks do not even include representatives from the Nagorno-Karabakh authorities, as Azerbaijan refuses to negotiate with them directly, even though the Minsk Co-chairs and the Armenian negotiators do have regular contacts with the Karabakh leaders. Representatives of the Karabakh Azerbaijanis are also not included.

The two presidents again have an interest in such a narrow process; the two (semi-)authoritarian regimes are suspicious of civil society activists and they want to be in charge of every detail of the discussion.[94] They have therefore obstructed efforts to increase the involvement of civil society in the peace process.[95]

The narrow process makes the lack of openness even more acute, as the complete lack of involvement of civil society means that there is no attempt to build trust and confidence before an agreement is reached. This lack of trust makes it even less likely that an interim agreement with its built-in uncertainties will prove acceptable. The two sides either have to trust each other, or they have to have faith in the ability of third parties to guarantee a deal. This brings us to the third problem: the lack of international commitment.

Insufficient International Engagement

Despite the involvement of great powers, who could have the means to pressure the conflict parties or, conversely, offer them advantages if they agree to a compromise settlement, such incentives are not used explicitly in the process. "What goes on in the negotiations does not affect the multi-million dollar cooperation and aid programs the U.S., Russia and EU have with Armenia and Azerbaijan."[96] Moreover, the Co-chairs are even careful not to publicly criticize one side. They instead reprimand "the sides" in general.[97] If the presidents reject a proposal, the mediators simply go back to the drawing board. The local leaders are not assigned any responsibility for failed talks and bear no costs.[98]

This lack of pressure is a problem since the local leaders, as argued above, do not feel a sense of urgency to agree to a settlement, and other incentives are consequently needed.

The lack of international willingness to become deeply engaged is particularly problematic when negotiating an interim agreement. The Minsk Group has not been preparing for the post-settlement phase, for example by designing the peacekeeping force that is meant to form a cornerstone of a settlement.[99] But such preparations are crucial for an interim agreement to succeed; it matters for its sustainability *and* it is necessary in order to get the parties to agree to a settlement in the first place. The commitment has to be credible. The security guarantees have to be robust and there has to be commitment to make the interim phase workable.

ALTERNATIVE STRATEGIES

Given the distance between the two sides on the issue of status, and the lack of incentives for either side to compromise, it is hard to get away from the need for some kind of interim agreement. However, are there ways in which to improve the proposal, and can the process be designed in a way that would make compromise more likely?

Revised Proposal

One problem with interim agreements is that they offer little incentive for separatist leaders to implement the agreement: they have their sights set on the independence referendum and have little incentive to make co-existence work.[100] The central government will consequently be reluctant to accept such a proposal. One way to reduce the risk of non-cooperation in the interim period would be to make the referendum conditional: it will only be held if certain conditions are met, such as the return of IDPs and minority rights. In the case of Bougainville, for example, the independence referendum is conditional on the achievement of certain standards of governance.[101] Such conditions, however, come with the risk of manipulation by the central government, which will have an interest in non-implementation, and international oversight is therefore crucial.

Another possibility that would promote co-existence would be to insist on a double majority or a super-majority in the referendum, which would necessitate that at least a proportion of returning IDPs supported independence.[102] However, such a requirement would presently result in deadlock and would have to be combined with a prolonged interim period. This would allow the gradual development of confidence, perhaps over one or two generations, and would consequently make unity a more realistic outcome. The length of the proposed interim period is not publicly known. Ten to fifteen years is a common speculation but Azerbaijani analysts have suggested that this is too short and that there should ideally not be a time limit.[103] The problem with a prolonged or indeed indefinite interim period is that this would only heighten Armenian suspicions that an independence referendum would never be held; that Azerbaijan will renege on its promises once Armenian forces have been withdrawn. This risk could also, to some extent, be addressed through conditionality, for example by specifying that if Azerbaijan fails to implement the agreement, then Nagorno-Karabakh would immediately be recognized by the international community. As with the other strategies, this requires a robust international commitment to the peace process, which has so far been lacking. It also requires greater openness and a more inclusive process.

Revised Process

The Minsk Co-chairs are sometimes criticized for being partisan, for having a vested interest in the Karabakh conflict. But the peace process may actually need third parties that have a strategic interest and therefore are willing to make the necessary commitment, not just to the current talks but also to the post-settlement phase. Planning for the future is always important for peace agreements, but even more so when the issue is interim agreements, as the interim period will determine the final outcome. International guarantees must therefore be believable and the planning for this should be an integral part of the ongoing talks.

There also appears to be a need for increased international pressure on the local leaders. International Crisis Group quotes a retired US official who argues that "there has to be a historical compromise but it's not going to happen without some incentives and some pressure from the mediators."[104] Although the mediators could clearly put more pressure on the leaders, and be more honest about the difficulties they are facing,[105] there is a limit to what international pressure can do. As Andrzej Kasprzyk, the Personal Representative for the OSCE Chairman-in-Office for Nagorno-Karabakh, has argued, the solution has to be acceptable to the parties: enforcing a solution would both be extremely costly and risky for the international community.[106] Another problem is a lack of agreement between the three Co-chairs. Pressure will only work if Russia, the USA and France agree, for example, to withhold investment unless an agreement is forthcoming. In the present international climate, that seems highly unlikely. Otherwise, the mediators are left with the options of public shaming in case of non-cooperation or the promise of various carrots that can make a settlement appear more attractive. This will not fundamentally alter the incentives facing the parties, but it will add to their overall calculations.

The Co-chairs could also put pressure on the local parties to broaden the process and open it up, and circumvent them if need be. A more open and inclusive process is by no means a panacea. There is no "silent majority" for peace in Armenia, Azerbaijan and Karabakh that just needs to be given a chance to have its voices heard. Decades of propaganda have effectively ensured that this is not the case. However, the broadening of the process is necessary in order to create such a peace constituency. The inclusion of civil society would also provide a mechanism for including the Karabakhis, both Armenians and Azerbaijanis, in the process.[107] If the peace process is not made more inclusive, it will be extremely risky for the leaders to agree to a compromise and the danger of an interim agreement simply resulting in renewed instability would be considerable.

There are therefore possibilities for a revised international strategy. However, who should be in charge of this process? Should it be left to the Minsk Group and the three Co-chairs, or is it time for a change of cast?

A Greater Role for the EU

One actor's absence from the peace process is striking: the EU. The Minsk Process, in its current format, leaves little room for the EU and this is in many ways a missed opportunity. Like the OSCE, the EU primarily relies on "soft power" in its foreign policy, but the EU has the economic power and the lure of closer integration which the OSCE lacks. The USA and Russia can, of course, also make use of such economic incentives, but the EU is, perhaps, less likely to be accused of harboring ulterior motives, and can therefore act as a counterweight to the competing great powers. The EU's soft power could moreover also play an important role in planning for the post-settlement, interim, phase and in creating an environment more conducive to peace.

The EU has generally refrained from linking its soft power directly to conflict resolution,[108] and has denied that it is increasing its involvement in the Karabakh conflict. The EU Special Representative for the South Caucasus has stated that "we support [the Minsk Group's] work and do not want to create problems with the OSCE, especially since we all want the same thing."[109] However, the EU could work in parallel with the OSCE through its European Neighborhood Policy (ENP), whose objective is to reinforce "stability and contribute to conflict resolution," or it could indeed replace France as Co-chair of the Minsk Group, thereby giving it a direct role in the peace process.[110] The EU's Commissioner for the ENP and Enlargement, Johannes Hahn, recently stated that new methods are needed to solve the Karabakh conflict and announced that the EU would focus on promoting cross-border cooperation between Armenia and Azerbaijan.[111] Greater involvement of the EU, combined with some (or all) of the other changes mentioned above, is perhaps what is needed to invigorate the stalled peace process.

CONCLUSION

Without the necessary political will, there will be no negotiated solution to the Nagorno-Karabakh conflict. However, this chapter has argued that the Minsk Process, in its current form, and the principles that the mediators have put forward exacerbate existing insecurities and fears, and thereby make it less likely that the leaders will be willing and able to compromise. A level of ambiguity is unavoidable in peace processes and can even be constructive, but it can also fuel suspicions and mistrust, especially in the framework of an interim agreement and when part of a process that is characterized by an extreme lack of publicity. This does not mean that the Minsk Process or the proposal must be fundamentally altered, which would be time-consuming, costly, and would add further uncertainty. But rather those smaller changes could reinvigorate the process: namely, greater openness and inclusivity, a proposal that more fully considers what will happen in the interim period, and greater international commitment including a more prominent role for the EU.

NOTES

1. International Crisis Group, "Nagorno Karabakh: A Plan for Peace," *Europe Report* No. 167, 2005, http://www.crisisgroup.org/en/regions/europe/south-caucasus/azerbaijan/167-nagorno-karabakh-a-plan-for-peace.aspx

2. Liz Fuller, "Minsk Group Co-Chairs Hopeful of Karabakh 'Breakthrough,'" *Radio Free Europe/Radio Liberty*, July 10, 2009, http://www.rferl.org/content/Minsk_Group_CoChairs_Hopeful_Of_Karabakh_Breakthrough_/1774141.html

3. Thomas de Waal, "Remaking the Nagorno-Karabakh Peace Process," *Survival* 52, no. 4 (2010): 161; Thomas de Waal, *Black Garden: Armenia and Azerbaijan through Peace and War* (New York: New York University Press, 2003), 229.

4. De Waal, "Remaking the Nagorno-Karabakh Peace Process": 162.

5. Ibid.

6. See for example, Anna Zamejc, "Seeking Peace: What Needs to be Done for the Nagorno-Karabakh Conflict," *Caucasus Edition*, July 15,2013,http://caucasusedition.net/analysis/seeking-peace-what-needs-to-be-done-for-the-nagorno-karabakh-conflict/; Irina Ghaplanyan, "Empowering and Engaging Civil Society in Conflict Resolution: The Case of Nagorno Karabakh," *International Negotiation* 15, (2010): 81–106.

7. Svante E. Cornell and S. Frederick Starr, *Caucasus: A Challenge for Europe* (Uppsala and Washington, D.C.: Central-Asia Caucasus Institute & Silk Road Studies Program, 2006).

8. The Bishkek Protocol, May 5, 1994. See UN Peacemaker, UN Department of Political Affairs, http://peacemaker.un.org/sites/peacemaker.un.org/files/ArmeniaAzerbaijan_BishkekProtocol1994.pdf

9. Nicolas Tavitian, "An Irresistible Force Meets an Immovable Object: The Minsk Group negotiations on the status of Nagorno Karabakh," Woodrow Wilson School of Public and International Affairs Case Study 1/00, 2000, 4.

10. Ibid.

11. Moorad Mooradian and Daniel Druckman, "Hurting Stalemate or Mediation? The Conflict over Nagorno-Karabakh, 1990-95," *Journal of Peace Research* 36, no. 6 (1999): 173.

12. P. Terrence Hopmann and I. William Zartman, "Overcoming the Nagorno-Karabakh Stalemate," *International Negotiation* 15, no. 1 (2010): 2.

13. See also Mooradian and Druckman, "Hurting Stalemate or Mediation?"

14. Hopmann and Zartman, "Overcoming the Nagorno-Karabakh Stalemate."

15. De Waal, "Remaking the Nagorno-Karabakh Peace Process": 161.

16. De Waal, *Black Garden*, 228–9.

17. Gerard J. Libaridian, "The Elusive 'Right Formula' and the 'Right Time': A Historical Analysis of the Official Peace Process," in *The Limits of Leadership, Elites and Societies in the Nagorny Karabakh Peace Process*, ed. Laurence Broers (London: Conciliation Resources, 2005), 36, http://www.c-r.org/downloads/17_Nagorny_Karabakh.pdf

18. Tavitian, "An Irresistible Force Meets an Immovable Object," 5.

19. Libaridian, "The elusive 'right formula' and the 'right time'" and Tofik Zulfuqarov, "Obstacles to Resolution: An Azerbaijani Perspective," in *The Limits of Leadership, Elites and Societies in the Nagorny Karabakh Peace Process*.

20. Libaridian, "The elusive 'right Rformula' and the 'right time,'" 37.

21. The President's thoughts were developed in an article, Levon Ter-Petrosyan, "Paterazm te Khaghaghutyun, Larjanalu Pahe" [War or Peace? Time for Thoughtfulness], *Hayastani Hanrapetutyun*, November 2, 1997; see discussion in Arus Hatutyunyan, *Contesting National Identities in an Ethnically Homogeneous State: The Case of Armenian Democratization*, Ph.D. Dissertation, Western Michigan University, 2009, 171–177. (http://scholarworks.wmich.edu/cgi/viewcontent.cgi?article=1669&context=dissertations)

22. Nina Caspersen, "Between Puppets and Independent Actors: Kin-state involvement in the Conflicts in Bosnia, Croatia and Nagorno Karabakh," *Ethnopolitics* 7, no. 4 (2008).

23. Behlül Özkan, "Who Gains from the 'No War No Peace' Situation? A Critical Analysis of the Nagorno-Karabakh Conflict," *Geopolitics* 13, no. 3 (2008): 586.

24. Tavitian, "An Irresistible Force Meets an Immovable Object"; Özkan, "Who Gains from the 'No War No Peace' Situation?": 585.

25. Tim Potier, *Conflict in Nagorno-Karabakh, Abkhazia and South Ossetia* (The Hague: Kluwer Law International, 2000), 96.

26. Caspersen, "Between Puppets and Independent Actors," and Özkan, "Who Gains from the 'No War No Peace' Situation?": 586.

27. Özkan, "Who Gains from the 'No War No Peace' Situation?": 583.

28. Libaridian, "The elusive 'right formula' and the 'right time,'" and Esmira Jafarova, "OSCE Mediation of Nagorno Karabakh Conflict," *The Washington Review of Turkish and Eurasian Affairs* (2014).
29. De Waal, "Remaking the Nagorno-Karabakh Peace Process."
30. Taleh Ziyadov, "Nagorno Karabakh Negotiations: Through the Prism of a Multi-Issue Bargaining Model," *International Negotiation* 15, no. 1 (2010): 117.
31. Ibid.
32. De Waal, *Black Garden*, 264.
33. Ziyadov, "Nagorno Karabakh Negotiations": 117.
34. De Waal, *Black Garden*, 265.
35. Ziyadov, "Nagorno Karabakh Negotiations": 119.
36. International Crisis Group, "Nagorno Karabakh," 14.
37. Tabib Huseynov, "Mountainous Karabakh: New Paradigms for Peace and Development in the 21st Century," *International Negotiation* 15, no. 1 (2010): 15.
38. Ziyadov, "Nagorno Karabakh Negotiations": 119, and International Crisis Group, "Nagorno Karabakh," 14.
39. Svante E. Cornell, *Azerbaijan Since Independence* (Armonk: M.E. Sharpe, 2011), 148. Ziyadov, "Nagorno Karabakh Negotiations": 119.
40. Ibid.
41. Jafarova, "OSCE Mediation of Nagorno Karabakh Conflict."
42. Huseynov, "Mountainous Karabakh": 16.
43. Julie Corwin, "US: Minsk Group Fails to Produce Results on Nagorno Karabakh," *Radio Free Europe/Radio Liberty*, March 9, 2006, http://www.rferl.org/content/article/1066548.html
44. Huseynov, "Mountainous Karabakh": 16.
45. Corwin, "US: Minsk Group Fails to Produce Results on Nagorno Karabakh."
46. Huseynov, "Mountainous Karabakh": 16.
47. This is the version made public by the Co-chairs in 2009, http://www.osce.org/mg/51152
48. Nina Caspersen, "Mounting Tensions over Nagorno Karabakh," *CACI Analyst*, August 7, 2010, http://old.cacianalyst.org/?q=node/5363
49. "Putin Hosts Azeri, Armenian Leaders for Karabakh Talks," *Radio Free Europe/Radio Liberty*, August 10, 2014, http://www.rferl.org/content/putin-sochi-karabakh-sarkisian-aliyev/26523298.html
50. De Waal, "Remaking the Nagorno-Karabakh Peace Process."
51. I. William Zartman, "Sources and Settlements of Ethnic Conflicts," in *Facing Ethnic Conflicts: Towards a New Realism*, ed. Andreas Wimmer (Oxford: Rowman & Littlefield, 2004), 153.
52. Hopmann and Zartman, "Overcoming the Nagorno-Karabakh Stalemate": 3.

53. See the Lisbon Summit Declaration, Annex 1: http://www.osce.org/mc/39539?download=true

54. Tavitian, "An Irresistible Force Meets an Immovable Object," 15.

55. Boris Navasardian, "A Battlefield of Confrontation or a Common Problem?" in *The Karabakh Conflict: To Understand Each Other*, eds. E. Poghosbekian and A. Simonian (Yerevan: Yerevan Press Club, 2006), 111.

56. Huseynov, "Mountainous Karabakh": 15.

57. Hopmann and Zartman, "Overcoming the Nagorno-Karabakh Stalemate."

58. For more on interim agreements see Marc Weller, "Self-Governance in Interim Settlements: the case of Sudan," in *Autonomy, Self-Governance and Conflict Resolution*, eds. M. Weller and S. Wolff, (London: Routledge, 2005).

59. See for example, "Azerbaijani Presidential Administration: Recognition of illegal 1991 'referendum' in Nagorno-Karabakh is impossible," *Trend News Agency*, January 27, 2011, http://en.trend.az/azerbaijan/karabakh/1818873.html

60. Author's interview with David Babayan, advisor to the NKR president, Stepanakert, October 28, 2008. The recent ECHR ruling that the rights of Azeri IDPs have been violated by their inability to return has made this position even more problematic for the Armenian side. See http://www.asil.org/blogs/european-court-human-rights-rules-rights-refugees-displaced-nagorno-karabakh-conflict-june-16

61. Nina Caspersen, "The Pursuit of International Recognition after Kosovo," *Global Governance* 21, no. 3 (2015).

62. See, for example, De Waal, "Remaking the Nagorno-Karabakh Peace Process": 160, and Özkan, "Who Gains from the 'No War No Peace' Situation?": 583.

63. Özkan, "Who Gains from the 'No War No Peace' Situation?"

64. Nina Caspersen, "Regimes and Peace Processes: Democratic (non) development in Armenia and Azerbaijan and its impact on the Nagorno-Karabakh peace process," *Communist and Post-Communist Studies* 45 (2012).

65. Özkan, "Who Gains from the 'No War No Peace' Situation?": 574.

66. Ibid.

67. Rasim Musabekov, "You will not be better off if your neighbour is in trouble," in *The Karabakh Conflict: To Understand Each Other*; see also Nina Caspersen, "Regimes and Peace Processes."

68. Charles King, "The Benefits of Ethnic War: Understanding Eurasia's Unrecognized States," *World Politics* 53, no. 4 (2001).

69. See, for example, Hopmann and Zartman, "Overcoming the Nagorno-Karabakh Stalemate."

70. Caspersen, "Between Puppets and Independent Actors."

71. Özkan, "Who Gains from the 'No War No Peace' Situation?"

72. De Waal, *Black Garden,* 267.
73. Hratch Tchilingirian, "New structures, old foundations: state capacities for peace," in *The Limits of Leadership.*
74. Cornell, *Azerbaijan Since Independence,* 153.
75. Ibid., 145–146.
76. Musabekov, "You will not be better off if your neighbour is in trouble."
77. Author's interview with Fariz Ismailzade, political analyst (Baku, June 11, 2009).
78. Musabekov, "You will not be better off if your neighbour is in trouble"; see also Nina Caspersen, "Regimes and Peace Processes."
79. Marc Weller, *Escaping the Self-Determination Trap* (Leiden: Martinus Nijhoff Publishers, 2008).
80. Weller, "Self-Governance in Interim Settlements," 166.
81. Ibid.
82. Johan Brosché, "CPA: New Sudan, Old Sudan or Two Sudans?" in *Post-Conflict Peace-Building in the Horn of Africa,* ed. U. J. Dahre (Lund: Department of Social Anthropology and Department of Political Science, Lund University, 2008), 247.
83. Weller, "Self-Governance in Interim Settlements," 176.
84. Brosché, "CPA: New Sudan, Old Sudan or Two Sudans?" 238–39.
85. Weller, "Self-Governance in Interim Settlements," 161.
86. Since the territories have been recognized as units of self-determination (see Weller, "Self-Governance in Interim Settlements").
87. Huseynov, "Mountainous Karabakh": 16.
88. Ibid.: 19.
89. Author's interviews in Nagorno-Karabakh, September–October 2008.
90. Huseynov, "Mountainous Karabakh": 20.
91. De Waal, "Remaking the Nagorno-Karabakh Peace Process": 163.
92. Ibid.
93. Aytan Gahramanova, "Paradigms of Political Mythologies and Perspectives of Reconciliation in the Case of the Nagorno-Karabakh Conflict," *International Negotiation* 15, no. 1 (2010).
94. De Waal, "Remaking the Nagorno-Karabakh Peace Process."
95. Zamejc, "Seeking Peace: What Needs to be Done for the Nagorno-Karabakh Conflict."
96. International Crisis Group, "Nagorno Karabakh," 8.
97. Ibid.
98. See also De Waal, "Remaking the Nagorno-Karabakh Peace Process."
99. Ibid.
100. Nina Caspersen, *Peace Agreements: Finding Solutions to Intra-State Conflicts* (Cambridge: Polity Press, 2016).
101. Bougainville Peace Agreement, 2001.
102. See Huseynov, "Mountainous Karabakh."

103. Author's interview with Eldar Namazov, political analyst, Baku, June 16, 2009; see also Musabekov, "You will not be better off if your neighbour is in trouble."

104. International Crisis Group, "Nagorno Karabakh," 8.

105. De Waal, "Remaking the Nagorno-Karabakh Peace Process."

106. Andrzej Kasprzyk, "How should the OSCE deal with the Nagorno Karabakh Conflict," *Helsinki Monitor* 14, no.1 (2003).

107. De Waal, "Remaking the Nagorno-Karabakh Peace Process."

108. International Crisis Group, "Conflict Resolution in the South Caucasus: The EU's role," *Europe Report* No. 173, 2006, http://www.crisisgroup.org/en/regions/europe/south-caucasus/173-conflict-resolution-in-the-south-caucasus-the-eu-role.aspx

109. Paul Rimple, "What is the EU's Game in the Caucasus Separatist Territories?," *EurasiaNet.org*, February 26, 2015, http://www.eurasianet.org/node/72301

110. This was mooted when Peter Semneby was the EU Special Representative for the South Caucasus, but no longer seems to be on the agenda.

111. Jamila Aliyeva, "Armenia, Azerbaijan must use new methods to solve conflict," *Trend News Agency,* May 21, 2015, http://en.trend.az/azerbaijan/karabakh/2397231.html

CHAPTER 10

Reversing Escalation: The Local and International Politics of the Conflict

Svante E. Cornell

In April 2016, for the third year in a row, news channels carried reports of the gravest violations of the cease-fire between Armenia and Azerbaijan since 1994. Taken together, the incidents of fighting since 2014 indicate that the military situation in the conflict has entered an entirely new stage, bearing little resemblance to the limited shelling that characterized the first 20 years of the cease-fire regime. One reason for this escalation is, no doubt, intrinsic to the two protagonists. Yet it is equally clear that the changing international politics of the conflict are an important factor explaining these developments. Although the conflict has so obviously entered a path of escalation that could trigger a major war, Western states and organizations have shown remarkably little interest, let alone provided a coherent policy response. Other more acute crises have monopolized attention; and the complex dynamics of the conflict, and indeed of its escalation, remain poorly understood. This chapter aspires to build on the contributions to this volume to explain the dynamics of escalation of the conflict, which in turn could lead to a discussion of the potential steps that could help prevent a new war—and perhaps put the conflict on a path to resolution.

A Shifting Balance of Power: Local Drivers of Escalation

Since 2008, the conflict has been on an almost linear path of escalation. The first serious clash took place near the region of Mardakert/Ter-Ter in March 2008—an area on the northeastern part of the frontline.[1] As would be the case

S.E. Cornell (✉)
Nacka, Sweden

© The Author(s) 2017
S.E. Cornell (ed.), *The International Politics of the Armenian-Azerbaijani Conflict*, DOI 10.1057/978-1-137-60006-6_10

in forthcoming years, both sides blamed each other for starting the violence, and not surprisingly, published widely diverging estimates of casualties. In this instance, Yerevan blamed Baku for taking advantage of its internal troubles over a contested presidential election, while Baku blamed Yerevan for seeking to divert the public's attention from them. The number of servicemen killed were in the single digits on both sides: nevertheless, these skirmishes were the most deadly since 1994.[2] Mardakert/Ter-Ter was again at the center of skirmishes that killed up to five servicemen in June 2010,[3] and a similar number in September that year, bringing the number of dead in to the double digits. During 2011, the death toll receded somewhat, although several smaller clashes took place throughout the year. Violence flared up again in June 2012, and the death toll topped 30 servicemen. This time, the most serious fighting took place not along the cease-fire line, but near the Azerbaijani town of Tovuz, along the international border between Armenia and Azerbaijan.[4]

The situation worsened in 2014. Over a dozen servicemen were killed in the first half of the year, and major fighting erupted on July 30, which escalated rapidly after Armenia mounted an offensive on three fronts, (Qazakh, Mardakert/Ter-Ter and Agdam) including over the international border.[5] In November that year, Azerbaijani forces shot down an Armenian helicopter along the cease-fire line.[6] The number of casualties rose past 60 for the year. The next year saw sporadic bouts of fighting during the entire year, including the winter months. While no one clash compared to the August 2014 fighting, the death toll nevertheless climbed to over 80 people.

In early April 2016, major fighting erupted in both the northeastern and southeastern sections of the frontline. The fighting, which subsided on April 5, has come to be referred to as the "four day war." Both parties claim the other started the shelling, but both the magnitude of the fighting and the implications exceeded all previous skirmishes. The Azerbaijani side initiated a major offensive, which for the first time managed to recapture some of the territories occupied by Armenia in 1993–94. While an Armenian counter-offensive managed to restore control over some of the lands, the fighting nevertheless left Azerbaijani in control of at least one strategic height and several villages once populated by Azerbaijanis. The fighting included the deployment of heavy weaponry, including attack drones; accordingly, the number of casualties jumped remarkably. The number of servicemen killed likely exceeded 200, though there are no reliable sources on either side.

Many reasons both intrinsic to the region as well as external combine to explain the conflict's escalation. Indeed, as will be seen, there is enough in the relationship between Armenia and Azerbaijan to explain the return of large-scale violence. But to that, there is an eerie tendency of significant violence to occur in connection to major external events, suggesting a geopolitical context to this escalation.

Within the region, two major developments have occurred hand in hand: the buildup and reform of Azerbaijan's defense sector, and the alteration of Armenia's military doctrine. Azerbaijan's defense sector had long been plagued by serious problems of management and corruption. The Soviet-style Minister of Defense, Safar Abiyev, remained in his post from 1995 to 2013. But in 2013, he was replaced by the 54-year old Zakir Hasanov, who had commanded the special forces of the Ministry of Interior, and made a name as a strong leader with integrity and absolute loyalty to President Aliyev. While the Azerbaijani defense sector is opaque, it is clear that Hasanov has sought address the corruption and mismanagement in the defense sector. With Turkish and Israeli help, he appears to have turned the Azerbaijani armed forces into a far more disciplined force with a developing *esprit de corps*—the lack of which was a major cause of defeat in 1993–94. Earlier, problems of discipline including hazing and poor equipment, food and conditions led young Azerbaijanis to desperately seek to avoid military service. But Hasanov's reforms appear to be affecting perceptions in society, and increasingly, military service is coming to be seen as something honorable or even desirable. The procurement of advanced weaponry, including Israeli-made drones, has also created a tactical superiority over the Armenian forces, which lack equipment to match that which Azerbaijani now possesses.

This was coupled with growing military rhetoric from the Azerbaijani side. President Aliyev's comments in April 2011 indicate the evolving position of Azerbaijan:

> We are living in state of war. Our territories are under the occupation. And every moment we must be ready to liberate our lands and restore territorial integrity of our country. We are trying to settle the conflict by diplomatic means. But at the same time our military potential has a positive influence on peace talks. We are all witnesses of it.[7]

In June 2015, Defense Minister Hasanov stated that the "country's leadership in the first place aims to liberate our occupied territories by further strengthening the combat capabilities of the Armed Forces."[8] On several occasions, he has announced the military's readiness to "liberate the occupied territories."[9] It became increasingly clear that the Azerbaijani leadership was no longer ready to accept the continuation of the status quo, and that it would use its military buildup to put pressure on both Armenia and the international community to instill urgency in the negotiations. It appears to be no coincidence that the conflict escalated most significantly after 2014—a year that marked 20 years since the cease-fire had been reached, and thus formed an important psychological milestone.

The evolution of Azerbaijani policy, and the growing imbalance in terms of resources and armament, gradually led Armenia to adapt its military doctrine accordingly. Aside from its reliance on the alliance with Moscow, Yerevan had relied on a doctrine of "static defense," based on the conviction that the inhospitable and mountainous terrain provided the Armenian side with a considerable superiority. Foreign observers largely agreed, and military observers contended that a numerical superiority of ten to one would be required for

Azerbaijan to retake the occupied territories.[10] Yet such assessments may have ignored the importance of technological advances, which may reduce traditional assumptions regarding the importance of terrain. Already in May 2013, the Karabakh-born Armenian defense minister, Seyran Ohanyan, stated that "the doctrine of using our armed forces for the country's defense envisages numerous measures that can be not only defensive but also preemptive."[11] President Sargsyan made the point even more bluntly in early 2015.[12] By February 2016, Armenia's deputy defense minister announced that Armenia would abandon the "static defense" doctrine and instead gradually turn "to the 'deterrence system.'"[13] By "deterrence," the Armenian leadership made it clear that it could react pre-emptively to signs of Azerbaijani attacks—presumably, by using positions on strategic heights to target military and civilian infrastructure in Azerbaijan.

In turn, it appears this led Azerbaijani defense planners to respond by crafting plans to capture those strategic heights in the vicinity of Azerbaijani civilian settlements and infrastructure. Certainly, this is the logic behind the Azerbaijani military operations in April 2016. And in hindsight, it is likely no coincidence that much of the violence in recent years has taken place in the Mardakert/Ter-Ter area—the closest that the cease-fire line gets to Azerbaijan's oil and gas export infrastructure. In sum, the logic of escalation appears to have generated a vicious cycle leading the two sides toward growing confrontation.

GROWING GEOPOLITICAL VOLATILITY: REGIONAL DRIVERS OF ESCALATION

Aside from these dynamics intrinsic to the two parties, the escalation has also taken place in tandem with a gradually worsening geopolitical environment. This is no accident, as the increasing volatility of the entire region—defined broadly as Eastern Europe and the northern edge of the Middle East—has exacerbated these intrinsic dynamics. Within this context, there are general and indirect effects on the conflict, as well as evidence of more direct manipulation.

The deterioration of the security situation surrounding the Caucasus is discussed in detail in this volume's first chapter. Yet to summarize, the greater volatility of the region was triggered in principle by events from 2008 onward. In retrospect, the recognition of Kosovo's independence triggered a domino effect. All assurances that Kosovo constituted a "unique" case aside, it appeared to strengthen Armenia's position in support of the connection between self-determination and secession, while undermining the respect for the territorial integrity of states cherished by Azerbaijan. It was also one of several triggering factors behind the Russian invasion of Georgia, a war that lowered the threshold of the use of force in the post-Soviet space as a whole. Initially, the war appeared a significant blow to the Azerbaijani side's efforts to alter the status quo in its favor. Indeed, because the West failed to prevent (or meaningfully address) a brazen territorial grab on its closest ally in the region, it indicated that Russia's allies in the region—like Armenia—were in a stronger position than those choosing a Western orientation—like Azerbaijan. Since Moscow also recognized the independence of Georgia's two secessionist regions, it appeared initially to boost Armenia's regional position and secure its position on the ground.

But subsequent events had contrary implications. In particular, the Obama administration's perceived disengagement from the region through the "reset" policy reduced the restraining influence of the West on both of the conflict's protagonists, as well as on Moscow. And the prioritization of the Turkish–Armenian normalization process drove home to Azerbaijan the dangers of allowing the conflict to remain unresolved. Indeed, even though Baku succeeded in halting the process and inducing Turkey to return to its traditional position of support for Azerbaijan, the episode was seen in Baku as a close call. It showed that Baku's policy since 1994—seeking to pressure Armenia to a negotiated solution over the long term—was fraught with danger, as Baku could no longer rely on the forces through which it exerted pressure on Yerevan. Moreover, both events in Georgia and in the Middle East, such as the war in Lebanon in 2006, drove home the lesson that escalation was a risky way, but the only way, to achieve meaningful international attention and intervention. Thus, the cumulative effect of developments in 2008–09 was to lead the conflict toward escalation. Subsequent events in the Middle East, particularly the evolution of the Syrian conflict into a Russian–Turkish proxy war, also had the effect of exacerbating the volatility of the region.

Meanwhile, the growing confrontation between Russia and the West, apparent since the mid-2000s, had important but confusing implications. On the one hand, it risked turning the conflict into another geopolitical battlefield: Russia asserted greater influence over Armenia, while the geopolitical importance of the South Caucasus as a corridor linking the West to Central Asia continued to grow. But the mixing of foreign and domestic politics had a somewhat different effect: Western disengagement from security and energy affairs meant the weakening of two legs in the figurative tripod that Western policy consisted of—leaving promotion of democracy and human rights, by default, as the most visible concern of the West. This further exacerbated the gulf between Azerbaijan and the West. And as Pavel Baev's chapter in this volume shows, Armenia fit neatly into Moscow's *foreign* policy agenda, but not in its *domestic* regime agenda: the paramount importance of rolling back the wave of "color revolutions." In this regard, Azerbaijan came to be seen in a more positive light as a reliable bulwark against revolutions, while Moscow saw itself forced to intervene abruptly to halt Armenia's flirtation with a European Union (EU) Association Agreement. The conflict in Ukraine, moreover, confused matters further: Russia's annexation of Crimea buoyed Armenian hopes, while it constituted a further dangerous precedent for Azerbaijan. Yet the strong Western reaction to Russia's violation of Ukraine's sovereignty, in contrast to the lukewarm concern for Azerbaijan's territorial integrity, initially made Azerbaijani

leaders furious. Only with time did Western leaders gradually work to establish some consistency in their policies, something which favored Azerbaijan's
stance.

THE RUSSIA FACTOR: DIRECT OR INDIRECT MANIPULATION?

Few of the dynamics of this conflict are more contentious than the role of
Russia. Officially, Moscow is one of the mediators in the conflict and in recent
years has been the most active one. But throughout the span of this conflict, it
has acted far from being an honest broker. Few observers dispute that Moscow
alternated in supporting both sides of the conflict from 1988 to 1994 to serve
its own purposes; but opinions diverge on Moscow's stance today. Is Moscow
directly manipulating the conflict, is it merely content with observing a status
quo that it finds favorable, or does it, in fact, fear a process of escalation that it
does not control, which could lead it to cooperate with its Western partners to
achieve a resolution?

The latter argument is occasionally advanced whenever the conflict flares
up.[14] But it does not hold water: if the Kremlin did not see any benefit in
the escalation of conflict, then it would not be the primary force fueling the
arms race between the two parties. Armenia has relied on transfers of Russian
weapons since the mid-1990s, when a Russian parliamentary investigation discovered covert arms shipments valued at $1 billion to Armenia.[15] Similarly, in
2008, Russia transferred $800 million worth of arms to Armenia.[16] Yet when
Azerbaijan's military buildup began, Moscow was the primary provider of
weapons to Azerbaijan as well—providing a full 85 percent of Azerbaijan's
arms purchases.[17] Those figures appear to under-report the total Azerbaijani
arms purchases, however, and it is likely that they underestimate the amount
of Israeli weapons purchased by Baku.[18] In any case, despite Armenia's alliance
with Russia, Moscow has sold advanced weapons systems to Azerbaijan that
Armenia does not appear to possess. That may change, as Moscow in February
2016 loaned Yerevan another $200 million with which to purchase advanced
weaponry. In its official rhetoric, Moscow makes the somewhat lurid claim that
its arms sales serve to ensure "parity" between the two parties.[19] While this
policy has generated visible anger in Armenia, pro-Russian commentators have
sought to mollify this anger by arguing that Russian arms sales to Baku actually
serve Armenia's interests, since Moscow has a restraining effect on Baku that
other arms suppliers would not.[20] In reality, given its regional clout, Moscow
could conceivably have refrained from supplying arms to both parties, and
exerted pressure on others to follow suit—just like it blackmailed Israel to cease
supplying weapons to Georgia after the 2008 war.[21]

In reality, Moscow's has sought to combine the roles of peace broker, arms
provider to both, as well as "ally" with one (Armenia) and "strategic partner" with the other (Azerbaijan) belligerent, a combination that speaks for
itself. From the outset of the conflict, there is little to counter the argument
that Moscow has seen the conflict as a tool to maximize its influence over the

South Caucasus as a whole. In fact, there is considerable evidence to argue that Moscow sees the maintenance of the conflict as the fundamental element allowing it to prevent the loss of its dominant position in the region. Indeed, the conflict makes the South Caucasus decidedly less attractive to both the EU and North Atlantic Treaty Organization (NATO), and hampers the building of east–west corridors of energy and trade. It also ensures Armenia's security dependence on Russia, and it was the very factor that allowed Moscow to halt Armenia's Association Agreement with the EU in 2013. Conversely, it is the maintenance of the conflict that attaches a cost to Azerbaijan for its pro-Western foreign policy—while the prospect of a Russian-sponsored resolution provides a carrot, frequently spelled out aloud, for joining Russian-led integration mechanisms. Even if Baku has failed to take the bait, the conflict perpetuates Moscow's influence in the country—indeed, the arms sales are one of the main remaining Russian levers on Azerbaijan. By contrast, a resolution of the conflict would free Armenia from a dependence on Russia that it increasingly resents; lead to an opening of its border with Turkey; and perhaps, over time, generate momentum for the integration of a more harmonious South Caucasus into European and Euro-Atlantic institutions.

In the final analysis, Moscow's general position toward the conflict and its resolution is clear: its preference is the continuation of the status quo. This does not necessarily mean that Moscow is opposed to a resolution—but it would support it only as long as the modicum of a solution cement, rather than erodes, Moscow's domination of the South Caucasus. In practice, this would likely mean a significant Russian military presence on the ground, as well as the integration of Azerbaijan into Russian-led institutions such as the Collective Security Treaty Organization and the Eurasian Economic Union. In the absence of such a prospect, the status quo is preferable. As for the escalation of the conflict, it provides Moscow with the opportunity to solidify its position with both parties—as long as that escalation does not spiral out of control, or lead to a major Western intervention that threatens Moscow's position. But there is little in the experience from Georgia or Ukraine that suggests any chance of such an intervention materializing.

On this basis, the real question is whether Moscow's manipulation of the escalation of the conflict is indirect, in the manner suggested above, or direct, as in explicitly triggering instances of military escalation. An overview of the Kremlin's policies across the post-Soviet space makes it unlikely that Moscow would lack the capability of doing so, should it so desire. Indeed, the Kremlin has deployed a bewildering array of instruments of statecraft in neighboring states and beyond, ranging from information and economic warfare to subversion, co-optation of elites, espionage, support for opposition forces, sabotage, terrorism and overt warfare. The manipulation of unresolved conflicts has taken center-stage in Moscow's initiatives in Georgia, Moldova and most recently Ukraine—that is, every former state west of the Caspian that has rejected membership in Russian-led security institutions.[22] That being the case, the burden of proof would seem to be on whoever argues that the Nagorno-Karabakh conflict differs from this pattern. In practice, hard evidence of a Russian hand in the escalation is, naturally, hard to come by; but circumstantial evidence abounds. This includes not only the realm of anecdotes of Russian behavior told by Armenian and Azerbaijani officials but also the mounting number of coincidences, whereby violations of the cease-fire takes place in tandem with important international visits.

Thus, the fighting of summer 2010 took place just after Russian President Dmitry Medvedev hosted a trilateral meeting with Presidents Sargsyan and Aliyev,[23] and immediately before US Secretary of State Hillary Clinton's July 1–5 visit to the two countries, a rare occurrence.[24] Only three months later, the skirmishes of early September occurred the day before President Medvedev visited Baku.[25] Again in 2012, the upsurge in fighting took place immediately before Clinton's next visit to the region.[26] This does not in and by itself prove that Moscow instigated the violence: conceivably, either of the parties could have an interest in raising attention to the urgency of the conflict. Given the situation on the ground, fingers most often are pointed at Azerbaijan, simply because it is Baku that is the power seeking to alter the status quo, and which is most intent on bringing international attention to the conflict. This interpretation does have validity, certainly for many of the smaller skirmishes of 2010–13, but the timing of the fighting in both 2014 and 2016 does not support this interpretation.

The fighting of July–August 2014 took place only shortly after the Russian invasion of eastern Ukraine, at a time when the mood in Azerbaijan was one of forbearance—put otherwise, when Azerbaijan adopted a policy of non-alignment, eschewing outwardly pro-Western moves while seeking to stay off the Russian radar screen.[27] But it occurred after the US government announced a new policy statement on the conflict, indicating interest in stepping up the US effort in the Minsk Group.[28] This was to materialize at the NATO summit in Wales in September, where US Secretary of State John Kerry planned to convene a top-level meeting between Presidents Aliyev and Sargsyan to discuss the conflict. More to the point, the fighting began while the Azerbaijani president and defense minister were both abroad;[29] and immediately after President Putin invited both presidents to a trilateral summit on the conflict outside of the framework of the Organization for Security and Co-operation in Europe (OSCE) Minsk Group. President Sargsyan had accepted the invitation; President Aliyev had not.[30] Because Washington failed to respond in a substantial manner, the outcome of the fighting was to consolidate Moscow's control over the peace process, and to undermine the Minsk Group. While numerous skirmishes had taken place for two months, the serious outbreak of violence in late July resulted from a major Armenian offensive,[31] which given the level of Russian influence over the Armenian armed forces, would be unlikely to happen without coordination with Moscow.[32]

In April 2016, the fighting erupted while both Presidents Aliyev and Sargsyan were in Washington, attending a Nuclear Security Summit that Mr. Putin boycotted—indeed, the day after Vice President Joe Biden sought to reinvigorate the peace process through meetings with both presidents. Pointedly, the visit was Mr. Aliyev's first visit to Washington in ten years, and the culmination of a process of restoration of bilateral ties with Washington that had been ongoing since the fall of 2015. Aside from his meeting with Biden, Aliyev met repeatedly with Secretary Kerry, and both US and Azerbaijani officials considered the visit a major success. Clearly, this event was a blow to Moscow's decade-long effort to bring Baku into the Russian orbit with a delicate mix of carrots and sticks. The Azerbaijani territorial gains that resulted from the four-day war led most analysts to argue that the cease-fire violation was planned by the Azerbaijani side. Yet this omits the fact that Baku had jumped at the opportunity to rebuild its relations with Washington, and not least to build a personal rapport and confidence between Aliyev and the US leadership. It would make no sense to immediately squander that accomplishment with a provocation in Karabakh, and the Armenian side was clearly unprepared for the fighting that ensued.

As former US Minsk Group co-chair Matthew Bryza put it, "the presidents of Armenia and Azerbaijan had little interest in these unprecedented military clashes occurring just as they were trying to persuade the White House to engage in the Nagorno-Karabakh peace process."[33] As Bryza argued, it had long been feared that the proverbial "outside actor" might "prod a local military commander to reignite the conflict"—and the lack of a rapid US response led both Armenia and Azerbaijan "left with the impression that Russia alone calls the shots in the South Caucasus." In sum, there is considerable evidence to suggest Moscow's manipulation of the conflict is not only indirect and geopolitical but also very concrete and hands-on.

IMPLICATIONS FOR WESTERN POLICY

In 2016, Western policy-makers confront a situation not unlike the one in Georgia in 2007: in Georgia's Relationship with Russia—and by proxy with the breakaway territories of Abkhazia and South Ossetia—there was a gradual and visible escalation toward war. But in part because of a failure of imagination, few Western leaders saw the potential of escalation, and the actions they took in 2008 to halt the process were too little, too late. Less than six years later, they were again taken by surprise as new unresolved conflicts were created in Crimea and the Donbass. Given the gradual and highly visible escalation of the conflict between Armenia and Azerbaijan, a war should not come as a surprise, and Western leaders have no excuses for inaction. It has become an increasingly accepted notion that the conflict will erupt again if nothing is done to change its path to one of de-escalation and resolution. Yet the lessons of Georgia and Ukraine do not appear to have been learnt. The "four-day war" in 2016 did not result in a visible international reaction. In fact, the US government failed to issue a statement on the events for two weeks, although it did, belatedly, take the welcome initiative in mid-May to organize a summit in Vienna under the auspices of the OSCE to address the conflict. Yet at the time of writing, it was by no means clear that this international reaction would be substantive and sustained.

In this regard, the analysis provided in this book leads to several implications for Western policy.

A first conclusion, implicit in the very title of this volume, is that the conflict cannot be understood in isolation—that the international politics of the conflict are key both to its escalation as well as to its management and possible resolution. In practice, this means that Western diplomats and policy-makers must understand that this conflict exists at several different levels. As such, to understand the dynamics of the conflict, it is necessary to study not only the local dynamics on the ground, or the dynamics within and between the chief protagonists, but also the regional geopolitical environment that strongly influences the situation.

In other words, the escalation of the Nagorno-Karabakh conflict is a result not *only* of developments in Armenia and Azerbaijan, or in their bilateral relationship—though these are undoubtedly key drivers. It is *also* a result of the increasingly volatile security situation not only in the South Caucasus but also across Eastern Europe and the Middle East—ranging from the Baltic Sea across the Black and Caspian seas to the Mediterranean. In the first place, this means the dubious role of Russia in the conflict; but it also includes the volatility produced by policies and actions undertaken by Turkey and Iran, as well as those most often *not* undertaken by Europe and the USA.

As a result, a reversal of the escalation of the Armenia–Azerbaijan conflict will not result simply from the negotiation process between the two parties; but will be a function of the improvement of the regional security situation as a whole. The implication is that a greater involvement of Western powers in the Minsk Group process will not, in and of itself, contribute to pacifying the conflict—unless that is part and parcel of a broader policy toward region, which reverses the Western, and primarily American, disengagement from its security affairs. In other words, a greater Western involvement in the Minsk Group is necessary, but not sufficient, for ameliorating the conflict: it needs to be coupled with greater involvement across the board in the security, political and economic affairs of the South Caucasus. In effect, halting the escalation to war of the Nagorno-Karabakh conflict requires stabilizing the South Caucasus, something that in turn calls for a revised and upgraded Western strategy toward the region.

The key elements of such a strategy have been elaborated elsewhere.[34] But several key elements pertinent to the Armenia–Azerbaijan conflict should be noted. First, the relative failure of Western policy in the region derives in great part from the inability of the US government and European institutions to coordinate their policies and priorities among themselves—that is, both *within* the US government and Europe, as well as *between* the USA and EU. In the face of rising challenges to the region's security, only improved coordination among government institutions and on a Transatlantic level is likely to provide enough gravitas to counter the forces of destabilization.

More specifically, there must be a united Western approach to how to handle Moscow's policies in the South Caucasus, and specifically in the Nagorno-Karabakh conflict. At present, Western powers are pursuing a policy of "compartmentalizing" their relations with Russia. In Ukraine, there has been Western unity in opposing Russian objectives, including a sanctions regime. In Syria, Western powers sought to cooperate with Russia, only to witness a Russian military intervention targeted at Western-supported groups, rather than at the common enemy, the Islamic State. In Georgia and Moldova, Western policy is focused on the implementation of Association Agreements with the EU and on the consolidation of democracy; but there is little attention to security concerns arising from Russian aggressive policies in the unresolved conflicts. Finally, in Nagorno-Karabakh, the West is pursuing cooperation with Russia, in spite of plentiful evidence (detailed above) of the fundamental divergence between Russian and Western interests. Clearly, an increased Western focus on this conflict will need to include holding Russia accountable for its actions. Western leaders have yet to forcefully call out the contradiction in Moscow's policy of fueling the arms race between Armenia and Azerbaijan, while also seeking to portray itself as an honest broker between them. Both in rhetoric and in concrete terms, there are steps the Western powers can take to counter this Russian approach, while also increasing intelligence capabilities to detect more direct efforts of Russian manipulation of this and other conflicts.

The Minsk Group has been the subject of considerable criticism, most of which is warranted. Over the past 20-odd years, it has failed to achieve concrete progress toward a resolution of the conflict. Its co-chairs have occasionally showed a surprising degree of passivity, while at other times intervening more forcefully to achieve results. It is clear that the process suffers from serious flaws, as Nina Caspersen describes in her contribution to this volume; should one create a conflict resolution mechanism from scratch today, it would be unlikely to take the shape of the Minsk Group. The issue of the Group's composition is the most thorny. First of all, the role of Russia as a mediator does not reflect the reality of Russia's behavior in the conflict. But removing Russia from the Minsk Group would hardly improve matters, because it would do nothing to address Moscow's ability to manipulate and destabilize the conflict, while reducing avenues for the West to counter such meddling. Indeed, the very reason that Russia was brought in as a co-chair of the Minsk Group was to include Moscow in the process, in a situation where it was pursuing a rival mediation effort that undermined the Minsk Group. It should be noted that Moscow has lately seemed to return to a tendency to undermine the Minsk Group by unilateral action, most notably with Putin's 2014 summit in Sochi. This has been possible only because of Western neglect of the conflict, and a seeming reluctance to challenge Moscow's lead in the process. Clearly, the only solution is for Western powers to match Russia's level of involvement in the Minsk Group Process and call out any efforts to undermine it.

A second issue is the role of France in the process. If the process had been created today, it is more than likely that the EU rather than France would have occupied the third co-chair position—indeed, the EU has a seat at the table in all other unresolved conflicts in Eurasia. As a result, the argument has often been advanced (and recommended by the European Parliament[35]) that France should be replaced by the EU in the Minsk Group—something that forced the Minsk Group in 2015 to make the somewhat pitiful argument that "attempts to change the format or create parallel mechanisms can disrupt the negotiation process and impede progress towards a settlement."[36] While such a move would make a lot of sense, it is unlikely to happen. France's resistance surely renders the issue moot within the EU. That could potentially be overcome by a solution that maintained the French co-chairmanship under an EU flag, headquartered at the Quai D'Orsay and supported by EU institutions; but in any case, both Russia and Armenia oppose the idea. But this does not mean the EU cannot take a more substantial role. Conceivably, the EU could create, under the auspices of the EU Special Representative for the South Caucasus, a support group for the French Co-chairmanship that provides institutional liaison with relevant EU bodies.

Such a mechanism would allow the EU to take a direct role in important issues regarding the peace process. One of the most thorny substantial issues is that of post-settlement security. Russia has always sought to insert Russian peacekeeping forces into the conflict zone, something both Baku and Yerevan have opposed. But since no other credible provider of security is on the horizon, the issue hovers over the peace process and sustains the insecurity that is a chief reason for the lack of a solution. In this context, an EU "support group" could draw from its considerable experience from the Balkans, as well as from the EU Monitoring Mission in Georgia, to begin planning the security of a post-settlement situation. Similarly, the rehabilitation of the conflict zone— including the occupied territories, Nagorno-Karabakh itself, and adjoining lands in Armenia as well as Azerbaijan—is an important task whose planning and sequencing is complex and costly. Two Azerbaijani experts have written an extensive study of the challenges involved, but international organizations have yet to study the matter.[37] In the current international environment, the EU would be best placed not only to plan such a program but also eventually to implement it if and when a political solution is reached. Moreover, the very existence of serious post-conflict planning would itself increase the prospects of a solution. After the violence in April 2016, the possibility of an Armenian withdrawal from one or several occupied territories was floated in negotiations, but the absence of a concrete plan for what would happen the day after a political deal to that effect would be reached surely impedes the prospects of a deal.

Aside from its composition, the Minsk Group has a further flaw that could more easily be remedied: the level of its negotiators. When Jan Eliasson was appointed Chairman of the Minsk Group in 1993, he had considerable experience of international mediation and politics. Before taking the post, he had been part of the Swedish mediation effort in the Iran–Iraq war, and later served as the UN Secretary-General's personal representative to that conflict; he had also served as Undersecretary General of the UN. He went on to become Swedish Minister of Foreign Affairs and Deputy Secretary General of the UN. His successor, Heikki Talvitie, had been Finnish Ambassador to Moscow and went on to become the first EU Special Representative to the South Caucasus. Comparing these resumes with most co-chairs of the Minsk Group in the past decade, the contrast is glaring. While these are all competent diplomats, it is patently clear that the position as co-chair is not a task that Parsi and Washington assign to distinguished statesmen with substantial clout or extensive experience of conflict resolution. In fact, none of the later co-chairs have *subsequently* held high-level positions. In other words, while the geopolitical importance of the conflict and its surroundings has continuously grown, the diplomatic level of its mediators has declined. This is quite telling, and has concrete implications: it means that the US and French governments can only accord intermittent high-level attention to the conflict, and that aside from times of considerable violence or high-level summits, the activities of the Minsk Group are outside the radar of the political leadership.

Clearly, therefore, a priority of the first order is for the French and American governments to increase the level of the Minsk Group, and appoint experienced and seasoned diplomats to the Minsk Group, as the USA has done concerning Israel–Palestine or Northern Ireland. While this will not guarantee success, it will go a long way toward turning the moribund Minsk Group into a more active institution, in which the Western representatives can measure up with the level of Russian involvement in the conflict, very often in the shape of Foreign Minister Lavrov's personal role.

CONCLUSIONS

The Armenian–Azerbaijani conflict over Nagorno-Karabakh has gone on for far too long. The irony is that the conflict is in fact solvable—and that there is a relative consensus on the modalities of its resolution. While the remaining bones of contention should not be underestimated—especially the issue of Nagorno-Karabakh's status—the building blocks of a solution are well known. The process would begin with the Armenian withdrawal from at least five of the seven Azerbaijani occupied territories, in return for which the economic linkages between the two countries are opened. An international police force is deployed to the conflict zone, while a reconstruction package is launched. In turn, the Turkish–Armenian border is opened, and over time, arrangements are made for the liberation of the Kelbajar region, and for the safeguarding of the Lachin corridor forming the lifeline between Armenia and Nagorno-Karabakh. The question of the status of Nagorno-Karabakh is postponed, while international security guarantees are created in the interim period. Undoubtedly, the devil will be in the detail, but the point is that the conflict is not impossible to resolve. What is required is for the regional as well as international "stars" to align in such a matter that they encourage the conflict's resolution, rather than its escalation.

In the current international environment, the escalation of the conflict forms part and parcel of the major geopolitical developments affecting the South Caucasus in the past decade: the reassertion of Russian power, combined with the gradual disengagement of the West, particularly the USA. If the current trend toward escalation is to be reversed, the main missing ingredient is not just political will in Yerevan and Baku but a reversal of the Western disengagement from the South Caucasus. It is often said that the mediators "cannot want peace more than the parties." But in fact, that is precisely what is needed. If they do not, the "four-day war" of April 2016 will appear a minor skirmish compared to what is sure to follow.

NOTES

1. Mardakert is the Armenian name of the area; Ter-Ter the Azerbaijani. Only 15 percent of the official Azerbaijani province of Ter-Ter is under Azerbaijani control, the remaining 85 percent forming part of the Mardakert region of the self-proclaimed Nagorno-Karabakh republic.
2. "Karabakh Casualty Toll Disputed," *BBC News*, March 5, 2008, http://news.bbc.co.uk/2/hi/europe/7278871.stm
3. Suren Musayelyan, "Four Armenian soldiers killed in Karabakh clash; Yerevan condemns Azeri 'provocation,'" *Armenianow.com*, June 19, 2010, https://www.armenianow.com/karabakh/23755/azerbaijan_attack_karabakh_armenia
4. Alexander Jackson, "Fighting Escalates between Armenia and Azerbaijan" *Caspian Intelligence*, June 5, 2012. http://caspianintelligence.blogspot.se/2012/06/fighting-escalates-between-armenia-and.html
5. "Qazax, Ağdam və Tərtərdə şiddətli atışma", *Milli.az*, August 3, 2014. http://news.milli.az/karabah/285926.html
6. "Azerbaijan Downs Armenian Helicopter," *BBC News*, November 12, 2014, http://www.bbc.com/news/world-europe-30025296
7. "President Ilham Aliyev: 'We must be ready to liberate our lands and restore territorial integrity of our country,'" *Azertag*, April 23, 2011, http://azertag.az/en/xeber/605509
8. "Zakir Hasanov: Armenia realized that Azerbaijan is now real military power," *News.az*, June 1, 2015, http://news.az/articles/politics/98405
9. "Zakir Hasanov: Azerbaijani army is ready to liberate the occupied territories," *Vestnik Kavkaza*, October 16, 2015, http://vestnikkavkaza.net/news/Zakir-Hasanov-Azerbaijani-army-is-ready-to-liberate-the-occupied-territories.html
10. Conversations with NATO military experts, Washington D.C., 2015.
11. Sargis Hautyunyan, "Armenian 'Pre-Emptive Strike' in Karabakh not Ruled Out," *Azatutyun.am*, May 9, 2013, http://www.azatutyun.am/content/article/24981715.html

12. "Armenia Reserves Right to Preemptive Strikes, Says Sarkisian," *Asbarez*, January 26, 2015, http://asbarez.com/131121/

13. "Armenia to Switch to Karabakh 'Deterrence' Strategy," *RFE/RL*, February 19, 2016, http://www.rferl.org/content/armenian-karabakh-strategy-change-azerbaijan/27562092.html

14. Vladimir Mikhev, "Why the Armenia-Azerbaijan Conflict is a No-Win Situation for Moscow," *Russia Beyond the Headlines*, April 4, 2016, http://rbth.com/international/troika/2016/04/04/why-the-armenia-azerbaijan-conflict-is-a-no-win-situation-for-moscow_581805; Arzu Geybullayeva, "De Waal: Kremlin 'Not Primary Actor' Behind Nagorno-Karabakh Conflict," *RFE/RL*, April 4, 2016, http://www.rferl.org/content/russia-armenia-azerbaijan-nagorno-karabakh-de-waal-kremlin-not-primary-actor/27654309.html

15. "Armenia Armed by Russia for battles with Azerbaijan," *Washington Times*, April 10, 1997, http://www.lchr.org/a/15/rn/arms1.htm

16. Fariz Ismailzade, "Russian Arms to Armenia Could Change Azerbaijan's Foreign Policy Orientation," *Central Asia-Caucasus Analyst*, January 28, 2009, http://old.cacianalyst.org/?q=node/5021

17. Joshua Kucera, "Report: Azerbaijan Gets 85 Percent Of Its Weapons From Russia," *Eurasianet*, March 17, 2015, http://www.eurasianet.org/node/72581

18. The data is based on the Stockholm International Peace Research Institute's statistics and provide a total of $2.6 billion in purchases from 2008 through 2015 (see: http://armstrade.sipri.org/armstrade/page/toplist.php). However, media sources and Azerbaijani officials regularly report the size of the Russia–Azerbaijan arms trade to be $4 billion. ("Azeri-Russian Arms Trade $4 Billion Amid Tension With Armenia," *Bloomberg*, August 13, 2013, http://www.bloomberg.com/news/articles/2013-08-13/azeri-russian-arms-trade-4-billion-amid-tension-with-armenia). In addition, Azerbaijan has procured at least $ 1.6 billion in weaponry from Israel. ("Israel Signs $1.6 Billion Arms Deal With Azerbaijan," *Ha'aretz*, February 26, 2012, http://www.haaretz.com/israel-news/israel-signs-1-6-billion-arms-deal-with-azerbaijan-1.414916). Azerbaijan has also procured arms from Turkey.

19. John C.K. Daly, "Russia Proclaims 'Parity' in Arms Sales to Armenia and Azerbaijan," *Eurasia Daily Monitor*, vol. 13 no. 71, April 12, 2016.

20. Marko Marjanovic, "Armenians are Wrong to Complain: Russia-Azerbaijan Arms Trade is to Armenia's Advantage," *Russia Insider*, April 17, 2016, http://russia-insider.com/en/politics/armenians-are-wrong-complain-moscow-arming-azerbaijan-really-their-advantage/ri13929

21. "Israel Tells Businessmen to Stop Visiting Georgia," *Ha'aretz*, September 10, 2008, http://www.haaretz.com/israel-tells-businessmen-to-stop-visiting-georgia-1.253537

22. S. Frederick Starr and Svante E. Cornell, "Tactics and Instruments in Putin's Grand Strategy," in S. Frederick Starr and Svante E. Cornell, *Putin's Grand Strategy: The Eurasian Union and Its Discontents* (Washington and Stockholm: Central Asia-Caucasus Institute & Silk Road Studies Program, 2014), 59–81, http://www.silkroadstudies. org/resources/1409GrandStrategy.pdf

23. "Trilateral Meeting of S. Sargsyan, D. Medvedev and I. Aliyev Held in Saint Petersburg," *Armenpress*, June 18, 2010, https://armenpress. am/eng/news/608124/trilateral-meeting-of-s-sargsyan-d-medvedev-and-i-aliyev-held-in-saint-petersburg.html

24. "Hillary Clinton to Visit Volatile South Caucasus Region," *Reuters*, June 25, 2010, http://www.reuters.com/article/us-usa-caucasus-idUSTRE65O5JZ20100625

25. "Medvedev Heads to Baku Amid Growing Tensions in South Caucasus," *RFE/RL*, September 2, 2010, http://www.rferl.org/content/Russian_President_To_Azerbaijan_Amid_Karabakh_Tensions/2146006.html

26. "Serious Escalation In Armenia-Azerbaijan Violence Greets Clinton," *Eurasianet*, June 5, 2012, http://www.eurasianet.org/node/65501

27. See discussion in Svante E. Cornell, "Azerbaijan: Going It Alone", in Starr and Cornell, eds., *Putin's Grand Strategy*, 146–155, http://www.silkroadstudies.org/resources/pdf/publications/12-1409GrandStrategy-Azerbaijan.pdf

28. "Ambassador James Warlick: Nagorno-Karabakh: The Keys to a Settlement," U.S. Department of State, May 7, 2014, http://armenia. usembassy.gov/news050714.html

29. Thomas de Waal, "Karabakh's Guns of August," *Carnegie.ru*, August 5, 2014, http://carnegieendowment.org/2014/08/05/karabakh-s-guns-of-august

30. "Azerbaijan, Armenia Accuse Each Other Of Escalating Tensions," *RFE/RL*, August 4, 2014, http://www.rferl.org/content/armenia-nagorno-karabakh-azerbaijan-soldiers-killed-tense-blaming/25480582.html

31. As de Waal puts it, "this latest violence may have been the result of a big Armenian operation or counter-operation that came after numerous smaller Azerbaijani attacks." de Waal, "Karabakh's Guns of August."

32. See the analysis of Brenda Shaffer in "Russia's Next Land Grab," *New York Times*, September 9, 2014, http://www.nytimes.com/2014/09/10/opinion/russias-next-land-grab.html

33. Matthew Bryza, "Putin Fills Another Leadership Void in Nagorno-Karabakh," *Washington Post*, April 11, 2016, https://www.washingtonpost.com/opinions/nagorno-karabakh-conflict-is-too-dangerous-to-ignore/2016/04/11/1e32fc44-ff23-11e5-9d36-33d198ea26c5_story.html

34. Such a strategy is proposed in Svante E. Cornell, S. Frederick Starr, and Mamuka Tsereteli, *A Western Strategy for the South Caucasus* (Washington & Stockholm: Central Asia-Caucasus Institute & Silk Road Studies Program, Silk Road Paper, February 2015), http://www.silkroadstudies.org/publications/silkroad-papers-and-monographs/item/13075

35. "Will France be replaced with EU in the OSCE MG?," *Times.am*, March 23, 2012, http://www.times.am/?l=en&p=6053

36. OSCE, "Press Release by the Co-Chairs of the OSCE Minsk Group," November 12, 2015, http://www.osce.org/mg/199471

37. Nazim Muzaffarli and Eldar Ismailov, *Basic Principles for the Rehabilitation of Azerbaijan's Post-Conflict Territories* (Stockholm: C&C Press, 2010).

BIBLIOGRAPHY

BOOKS AND PAPERS

Altstadt, Audrey. 1992. *The Azerbaijani Turks: Power and Identity Under Russian Rule.* Stanford: Hoover Institution Press.

Assenova, Margarita, and Zaur Shiriyev. 2015. *Azerbaijan and the New Energy Geopolitics of Southeastern Europe.* Washington, DC: Jamestown Foundation.

Blank, Stephen (ed.). 2012. *Perspectives on Russian Foreign Policy.* Carlisle Barracks: Strategic Studies Institute/U.S. Army War College.

Blank, Stephen. 2013. *Azerbaijan's Security and U.S. Interests: Time for a Reassessment.* Washington, DC/Stockholm: Central Asia-Caucasus Institute/Silk Road Studies Program.

Broers, Laurence (ed.). 2005. *The Limits of Leadership: Elites and Societies in the Nagorny Karabakh Peace Process.* London: Conciliation Resources.

Brzezinski, Zbigniew. 1998. *The Grand Chessboard: American Primacy and Its Geostrategic Imperatives.* New York: Basic Books.

Caspersen, Nina. 2016. *Peace Agreements: Finding Solutions to Intra-state Conflicts.* Cambridge: Polity Press.

Coppieters, Bruno, and Robert Legvold (eds.). 2005. *Statehood and Security: Georgia After the Rose Revolution.* Cambridge/London: MIT Press.

Cornell, Svante E. 1999. *The Nagorno-Karabakh Conflict.* Uppsala: Department of East European Studies, Report No. 46. http://expert-translations.ro/uploads/Nagorno%20Karabah.pdf.

Cornell, Svante E. 2001. *Small Nations and Great Powers.* London/New York: Routledge Curzon.

Cornell, Svante E. 2011. *Azerbaijan Since Independence.* Armonk: M.E. Sharpe.

Cornell, Svante E., S. Frederick Starr, and Mamuka Tsereteli. 2015. *A Western Strategy for the South Caucasus.* Washington, DC/Stockholm: Central Asia-Caucasus Institute/Silk Road Studies Program.

Croissant, Michael P. 1998. *The Armenia-Azerbaijan Conflict: Causes and Implications.* Westport: Praeger.

© The Author(s) 2017
S.E. Cornell (ed.), *The International Politics of the Armenian-Azerbaijani Conflict*, DOI 10.1057/978-1-137-60006-6

de Waal, Thomas. 2013. *The Black Garden: Armenia and Azerbaijan Through Peace and War*. New York/London: New York University Press.

Dov, Lynch (ed.). 2003. *The South Caucasus: A Challenge for the EU*. Paris: European Union Institute for Security Studies/Chaillot Papers 65.

Ergün, Ayça, and Hamlet Isaxanli (eds.). 2013. *Security and Cross-Border Cooperation in the EU, Black Sea Region and the Southern Caucasus*. Amsterdam: IOS Press.

Giles, Keir, Philip Hanson, Roderic Lyne, James Nixey, James Sherr, and Andrew Wood (eds.). 2015. *The Russian Challenge*. London: Chatham House Report.

Goltz, Thomas. 1999. *Azerbaijan Diary*. London: Routledge.

Human Rights Watch. 1992. *Bloodshed in the Caucasus – Escalation of the Conflict in Nagorno-Karabakh*. September, 1992. https://www.hrw.org/report/1992/09/01/bloodshed-caucasus/escalation-armed-conflict-nagorno-karabakh.

Human Rights Watch. 1993. *The Former Soviet Union – Human Rights Developments*. 1993. https://www.hrw.org/reports/1993/WR93/Hsw-07.htm.

Human Rights Watch. 1994. *Azerbaijan: Seven years of conflict in Nagorno-Karabakh*. December, 1994. https://www.hrw.org/sites/default/files/reports/AZER%20Conflict%20in%20N-K%20Dec94.pdf.

International Crisis Group. 2005a. *Nagorno Karabakh: A Plan for Peace*, Europe Report No. 167, 11 Oct, 2005.

International Crisis Group. 2005b. *Nagorno-Karabakh: Viewing the Conflict from the Ground*. Europe Report No. 166, 14 May 2005.

International Crisis Group. 2006. *Conflict Resolution in the South Caucasus: The EU's Role*, Europe Report No. 173, 20 Mar 2006.

Kambeck, Michael, and Sargis Ghazaryan (eds.). 2013. *Europe's Next Avoidable War*. Basingstoke: Palgrave Macmillan.

Kruger, Heiko. 2010. *The Nagorno-Karabakh Conflict: A Legal Analysis*. Berlin/Heidelberg: Springer.

Libaridian, Gerard J. 2007. *Modern Armenia: People, Nation, State*. New Brunswick: Transaction.

Mkrtchyan, Tigran, Huseynov Tabib, and Gogolashvili Kakha (eds.). 2009. *The European Union and the South Caucasus*. Gütersloh: Bertelsmann Stiftung.

Muzaffarli, Nazim, and Eldar Ismailov. 2010. *Basic Principles for the Rehabilitation of Azerbaijan's Post-Conflict Territories*. Stockholm: CC Press.

Nichol, Jim. *Armenia, Azerbaijan, and Georgia: Political Developments and Implications for U.S. Interests*. Congressional Research Service, 2 Apr 2014. https://www.fas.org/sgp/crs/row/RL33453.pdf.

Oliphant, J.C. 1992. *Nationalities Problems in the Former Soviet Union*. Sandhurst: Soviet Studies Research Centre/Royal Military Academy.

Poghosbekian, Elina, and Anna Simonian (eds.). 2006. *The Karabakh Conflict: To Understand Each Other*. Yerevan: Yerevan Press Club.

Popescu, Nicu. 2011. *EU Foreign Policy and Post-Soviet Conflicts: Stealth Intervention*. London: Routledge.

Potier, Tim. 2000. *Conflict in Nagorno-Karabakh, Abkhazia and South Ossetia*. The Hague: Kluwer Law International.

Shaffer, Brenda. 2002. *Borders and Brethren: Iran and the Challenge of Azerbaijani Identity*. Cambridge: MIT Press.

Sherr, James. 2013. *Hard Diplomacy and Soft Coercion: Russia's Influence Abroad*. London: Chatham House.

Sherr, James. 2015. *The New East–west Discord: Russian Objectives, Western Interests*. The Hague: Netherlands Institute of International Relations/Clingendael Report.

South, Caucasus. 2011. *20 Years of Independence*. Berlin: Friedrich Ebert Stiftung.

Starr, S. Frederick, and Svante Cornell (eds.). 2014. *Putin's Grand Strategy: The Eurasian Union and Its Discontents*. Washington, DC/Stockholm: Central Asia-Caucasus Institute/Silk Road Studies Program.

Starr, S. Frederick, Svante E. Cornell, and Norling Nicklas. 2015. *The EU, Central Asia, and the Development of Continental Transport and Trade*. Washington, DC/ Stockholm: Central Asia-Caucasus Institute/Silk Road Studies Program.

Weller, Marc. 2008. *Escaping the Self-Determination Trap*. Leiden: Martinus Nijhoff Publishers.

Weller, Marc, and Stefan Wolff (eds.). 2005. *Autonomy, Self-Governance and Conflict Resolution*. London: Routledge.

Welt, Cory, and Alexander Schmemann (eds.). 2010. *After the Color Revolutions, Political Change and Democracy Promotion in Eurasia*. Washington, DC: PONARS Eurasia.

Wimmer, Andreas (ed.). 2004. *Facing Ethnic Conflicts: Towards a New Realism*. Oxford: Rowman & Littlefield.

Zürcher, Christoph. 2007. *The Post-Soviet Wars: Rebellion, Ethnic Conflict and Nationhood in the Caucasus*. New York/London: New York University Press.

Journal Articles

Aydın, Mustafa. 2004. Foucalt's Pendulum: Turkey in Central Asia and the Caucasus. *Turkish Studies* 5(2): 1–22.

Baev, Pavel, and Indra Øverland. 2010. The South Stream versus Nabucco pipeline race. *International Affairs* 65(5): 1075–1090.

Blank, Stephen. 1995. Russia and Europe in the Caucasus. *European Security* 4(4): 622–645.

Blank, Stephen. 2013. "AWOL: US Policy in Central Asia," *Central Asia-Caucasus Analyst*, 30 Oct 2013. http://www.cacianalyst.org/publications/analytical-articles/item/12848-awol-us-policy-in-central-asia.html.

Blank, Stephen. 2014. "Washington Misses the Point on Nagorno-Karabakh," *Central Asia-Caucasus Analyst*, 18 June 2014. http://www.cacianalyst.org/publications/ analytical-articles/item/12998-washington-misses-the-point-on-nagorno-karabakh.html.

Blank, Stephen. 2015. US policy, Azerbaijan, and the Nagorno Karabakh Conflict. *Mediterranean Quarterly* 26(2): 99–114.

Bölükbasi, Süha. 1997. Ankara's Baku-Centered Transcaucasia Policy: Has It Failed? *Middle East Journal* 50(1): 80–94.

Broers, Laurence. 2015. From 'Frozen Conflict' to Enduring Rivalry: Reassessing the Nagorny Karabakh Conflict. *Nationalities Papers* 43(4): 556–576.

Caspersen, Nina. 2008. Between Puppets and Independent Actors: Kin-state involvement in the Conflicts in Bosnia, Croatia and Nagorno Karabakh. *Ethnopolitics* 7(4): 357–372.

Caspersen, Nina. 2012. Regimes and Peace Processes: Democratic (non)development in Armenia and Azerbaijan and Its Impact on the Nagorno-Karabakh Peace Process. *Communist and Post-Communist Studies* 45: 131–139.

Caspersen, Nina. 2015. The Pursuit of International Recognition after Kosovo. *Global Governance* 21(3): 393–412.

de Waal, Thomas. 2010. Remaking the Nagorno-Karabakh Peace Process. *Survival* 52(4): 159–176.

de Waal, Thomas. 2015. "The Karabakh truce under threat," *Carnegie Moscow Center: Eurasia Outlook*, 12 Feb 2015. http://carnegie.ru/eurasiaoutlook/?fa=59049.

Frolov, Andrei. 2014. "Military build-up in the South Caucasus: An arms race?" *Russian International Affairs Council*, 10 Jul 2014. http://russiancouncil.ru/inner/?id_4=4026#_ftnref9.

Gahramanova, Aytan. 2010. Paradigms of Political Mythologies and Perspectives of Reconciliation in the Case of the Nagorno-Karabakh Conflict. *International Negotiation* 15(1): 133–152.

Ghaplanyan, Irina. 2010. Empowering and Engaging Civil Society in Conflict Resolution: The Case of Nagorno Karabakh. *International Negotiation* 15: 81–106.

Grigoryan, Armen. 2015a. "Turkey-Armenia relations and Turkey's elections," *Central Asia-Caucasus Analyst*, 27 May 2015. http://www.cacianalyst.org/publications/analytical-articles/item/13225-turkey-armenia-relations-after-turkey%E2%80%99s-elections.html.

Grigoryan, Armen. 2015b. "Armenia and the Iran Deal," *Central Asia-Caucasus Analyst*, 31 Aug 2015. http://www.cacianalyst.org/publications/analytical-articles/item/13263-armenia-and-the-iran-deal.html.

Hopmann, P.T., and I.W. Zartman. 2010. Overcoming the Nagorno-Karabakh Stalemate. *International Negotiation* 15(1): 1–6.

Huseynov, Tabib. 2010. Mountainous Karabakh: New Paradigms for Peace and Development in the 21st Century. *International Negotiation* 15(1): 7–31.

Kasprzyk, Andrzej. 2003. How should the OSCE deal with the Nagorno Karabakh conflict. *Helsinki Monitor* 14(1): 1–6.

King, Charles. 2001. The Benefits of Ethnic War: Understanding Eurasia's Unrecognized States. *World Politics* 53(4): 524–552.

Mearsheimer, John. 2014. America Unhinged. *The National Interest* 129: 9–30.

Mooradian, Moorad, and Daniel Druckman. 1999. Hurting Stalemate or Mediation? The Conflict over Nagorno-Karabakh, 1990–95. *Journal of Peace Research* 36(6): 709–727.

Muradyan, Vahagn. 2010. "Armenia and Georgia in the Context of Turkish-Armenian Rapprochement," *Central Asia-Caucasus Analyst*, 17 Mar 2010. http://old.cacianalyst.org/?q=node/5287/print.

Özkan, Behlül. 2008. Who Gains from the 'No War No Peace' Situation? A critical analysis of the Nagorno-Karabakh Conflict. *Geopolitics* 13(3): 572–599.

Pokalova, Elena. 2015. Conflict resolution in frozen conflicts: Timing in Nagorno Karabakh. *Journal of Balkan and Near East Studies* 17(1): 68–85.

Tavitian, Nicolas. 2000. "An Irresistible Force Meets an Immovable Object: The Minsk Group negotiations on the status of Nagorno Karabakh," *Woodrow Wilson School of Public and International Affairs*, Case Study 1/00.

Whitman, Richard, and Stefan Wolff. 2010. The EU as Conflict Manager? The Case of Georgia and Its Implications. *International Affairs* 86(1): 87–107.

Zarifian, Julien. 2015. U.S. foreign policy in the 1990s and 2000s, and the case of the South Caucasus (Armenia, Azerbaijan, Georgia). *European Journal of American Studies*. 10.

Ziyadov, Taleh. 2010. Nagorno Karabakh Negotiations: Through the Prism of a Multi-Issue Bargaining Model. *International Negotiation* 15(1): 107–131.

DOCUMENTS

Council of Europe Parliamentary Assembly Resolution 1416. *The conflict over the Nagorno-Karabakh region dealt with by the OSCE Minsk Conference*, 25 Jan 2005.

European Commission for democracy through law (venice commission) opinion no. 516/2009. *Opinion on the Law on Occupied Territories of Georgia*, CDL-AD(2009)015, Adopted at its 17th Plenary Session, 12–14 Mar 2009. http://www.venice.coe.int/webforms/documents/default.aspx?pdffile=CDL-AD(2009)015-e,

European Union External Action. 2016a. "Partnership and Cooperation Agreement between the European Communities and their member states, of the one part, and the Republic of Azerbaijan, of the other part." Accessed on 21 Feb 2016. http://eeas.europa.eu/delegations/azerbaijan/documents/eu_azerbaijan/eu-az_pca_full_text.pdf.

European Union External Action. 2016b. "EU/Georgia Action Plan." Accessed on 21 Feb 2016. http://eeas.europa.eu/enp/pdf/pdf/action_plans/moldova_enp_ap_final_en.pdf.

European Union External Action. 2016c. "EU/Moldova Action Plan." Accessed on 21 Feb 2016. http://eeas.europa.eu/enp/pdf/pdf/action_plans/moldova_enp_ap_final_en.pdf.

League of Nations. 1920. *Admission of Azerbaijan to the league of nation: Memorandum of the secretary-general*, 20/48/108, November, 1920.

Organization for Security and Co-operation in Europe. 1996. Lisbon Document 1996. Lisbon Summit, 2–3 Dec 1996.

The Bishkek Protocol, 1994. Bishkek. Available at: http://peacemaker.un.org/sites/peacemaker.un.org/files/ArmeniaAzerbaijan_BishkekProtocol1994.pdf.

United Nations general assembly resolution 62/243. *The situation in the occupied territories of Azerbaijan*. 62nd session, 14 Mar 2008. http://www.un.org/en/ga/search/view_doc.asp?symbol=A/RES/62/243.

United Nations High Commissioner for Refugees. *Azerbaijan: Analysis of gaps in the protection of Internally Displaced People (IDPs)*. October, 2009. http://www.unhcr.org/4bd7edbd9.html.

United Nations Security Council Resolution 853. S/RES/853 (1993), 3259th Meeting, 29 Jul 1993.

United Nations Security Council Resolution 884. S/RES/884 (1993), 3313th Meeting, 12 Nov 1993.

INDEX

© The Author(s) 2017   219
S.E. Cornell (ed.), *The International Politics of the Armenian-
Azerbaijani Conflict*, DOI 10.1057/978-1-137-60006-6

CPSIA information can be obtained
at www.ICGtesting.com
Printed in the USA
BVOW06s0824210317

479046BV00006B/34/P